Public Libraries
and Social Justice

JOHN PATEMAN
Information for Social Change, UK

JOHN VINCENT
The Network, UK

ASHGATE

Published by
Ashgate Publishing Limited
Wey Court East
Union Road
Farnham
Surrey, GU9 7PT
England

Ashgate Publishing Company
Suite 420
101 Cherry Street
Burlington
VT 05401-4405
USA

www.ashgate.com

British Library Cataloguing in Publication Data
Pateman, John, 1956-
  Public libraries and social justice.
  1. Public libraries--Aims and objectives--Great Britain.
  2. Libraries and people with social disabilities--Great
  Britain. 3. Libraries and minorities--Great Britain.
  I. Title II. Vincent, John, 1948-
  027.4'41-dc22

Library of Congress Cataloging-in-Publication Data
Pateman, John, 1956-
  Public libraries and social justice / by John Pateman and John Vincent.
    p. cm.
  Includes bibliographical references and index.
  ISBN 978-0-7546-7714-7 -- ISBN 978-0-7546-9432-8 (ebook)
1. Libraries and society--Great Britain. 2. Libraries and people with social disabilities-
-Great Britain. 3. Libraries and the poor--Great Britain. 4. Public libraries--Aims and
objectives--Great Britain. 5. Marginality, Social--Great Britain. I. Vincent, John, 1948- II.
Title.
  Z716.4.P38 2010
  027.60941--dc22

ISBN 9780754677147 (hbk)
ISBN 9780754694328 (ebk)

Mixed Sources
Product group from well-managed
forests and other controlled sources
www.fsc.org Cert no. SA-COC-1565
FSC © 1996 Forest Stewardship Council

Print
MPC

Contents

List of Figures and Tables

Figures

Tables

List of Abbreviations

BME	black and minority ethnic
CAA	Comprehensive Area Assessment
CAP	Community Access Point
CILIP	Chartered Institute of Library and Information Professionals
CIPFA	Chartered Institute of Public Finance and Accountancy
CISSY	Campaign for Impeding Sex Stereotyping in the Young
CPA	Comprehensive Performance Assessment
DCMS	Department for Culture, Media and Sport
EHRC	Equalities and Human Rights Commission
EU	European Union
IDeA	Improvement and Development Agency
ILEA	Inner London Education Authority
IPPR	Institute for Public Policy Research
JRF	Joseph Rowntree Foundation
LCLA	Libraries Change Lives Award
LGA	Local Government Association
LGBT	lesbian, gay, bisexual and transgender
LINks	Local Involvement Networks
LSP	Local Strategic Partnership
MLA	Museums, Libraries and Archives Council
NDC	New Deal for Communities
NEF	New Economic Foundation
NIACE	National Institute of Adult Continuing Education
NYR	National Year of Reading
PHF	Paul Hamlyn Foundation
RFID	Radio Frequency Identification
SCL	Society of Chief Librarians
WHO	World Health Organization

Acknowledgements

We would like to thank particularly the CILIP Information Team; Laura Swaffield (CILIP); Devon Library Service; London School of Economics and Political Science Library; Maria Cotera and Matthew Reynolds (University College Library); and the Working Together project and Kenneth Williment for giving us permission to quote freely from his article.

Chapter 1

Introduction

While carrying out the literature search for *British Librarianship and Information Work 1991–2000* (Bowman 2006) and *2001–2005* (Bowman 2007), it became clear that little had been written about public libraries and social exclusion. There were a number of articles but no monographs.

As a new term begins with a coalition government, it is timely to look back and examine what New Labour achieved in one of their key social policy areas, social exclusion. It is also important to examine the professional response to the social exclusion agenda and its impact on traditional professional values such as 'fairness' and 'neutrality'.

Much attention has been paid to two of the main themes underpinning *Framework for the Future* (DCMS 2003), the government's strategic blueprint for public library development:

- Books and reading have been the subject of significant pilots, programmes, funding streams, professional events and discussion.
- ICT has also enjoyed significant investment via the People's Network and, more recently, RFID (self-issue).

But the third main *Framework* theme – social exclusion – has been relatively neglected. There have been some inspiring local projects but no binding, robust and sustained strategic impetus. It is still widely claimed that public libraries are 'open to all' but much of the evidence suggests otherwise. Instead of coming from within the profession, the driving force for social exclusion initiatives has come from elsewhere – for example, from the seminal *Open to All?* research (Muddiman et al. 2000a, 2000b and 2000c) and the network of practitioners which it created (see, for example, The Network 2008).

While much of the library profession remains in denial about social exclusion, the need to tackle this agenda becomes ever more urgent as the gap between rich and poor continues to widen and the very survival of public libraries is open to debate. If public libraries are to develop and grow in the future and become relevant to the majority of their local communities, then they need to abandon outmoded concepts of excellence and fully grasp the equity agenda.

This book examines the historical background to social exclusion and the strategic context in terms of government and professional policy. It investigates definitions of social exclusion and suggests an appropriate service response. Most importantly, it proposes a manifesto for change and ways in which public libraries can be transformed into needs-based services.

One of the themes which runs through this book is that of 'boom and bust', which is very topical in the current economic climate. We want to understand why there have been waves of progressive librarianship which have not been sustainable. For example, the boom of community librarianship in the 1970s was followed by the bust of Thatcherite library policies in the 1980s. Since 1997, we have seen a boom of activity around libraries and social exclusion, but this looks likely to be followed by the bust of a coalition government. Like Gordon Brown and Alistair Darling, we want to understand how this cycle of boom and bust works and attempt to break it, if possible.

The problem with the boom and bust of progressive librarianship is that the booms are never very high or long-lasting; while the busts are very low, and go on for years, with 1979–97 being the most recent and painful example. One reason for this is that lip-service is paid to equity when it is expedient to do so, and then it is dropped when it is no longer necessary. Equity is not embedded in our professional culture and sometimes excellence and professional standards are used as an excuse or smokescreen for not pursuing social justice objectives and outcomes.

Another theme which runs through this book is that of co-production, which we define as 'handing over the keys of the public library to the local community'. It is sometimes said that public libraries should return to their historical roots of helping the 'deserving poor'. We would argue that you should go even further back in history to the time when local communities ran their own libraries. Some communities continued to do this right up until the Public Libraries Act was passed in 1964. In these communities all aspects of library provision, including staffing and stock selection, were managed by local people.

At some point, public libraries were hijacked by the middle classes who came to dominate both the running and the use of library services. Public libraries need to be given back to local communities by actively engaging them in the planning, design, delivery and assessment of library services. To date, this has been mostly in the form of using volunteers, but this approach is much too limited. Volunteers tend often to be middle class and part of the problem rather than the solution. Also, volunteers have no power, which remains in the hands of middle-class professionals. For equity to assert itself over excellence this power has to be shifted from librarians to the community.

This should not mean that cash-strapped local authorities simply dump the libraries they cannot afford to run on the local community. Instead the transfer of power should be in keeping with the principles of co-production. Good examples of co-production are patients' self-help groups and time banks, where members swap free services that can range from babysitting to legal advice. The word was coined in the 1970s and the application to public libraries is obvious. A central concept is 'the core economy' – the vast fund of goodwill and bright ideas at grassroots level, which in reality is what keeps services, families and communities going (see, for example, Cahn 2007).

Co-production is supported by a wide range of organisations, including UNISON, the Cabinet Office, the New Economic Foundation (NEF) and Compass.

As Lucie Stephens from the NEF explained 'Co-production is not more passive choice. Co-production is action taken. We need to re-focus on the relationships between individual people at the frontline, working as facilitators to release huge assets in the community – skills, talents, networks, social capital, reciprocity. One-way transactions create dependency' (Swaffield 2008).[1] In other words, library users must not be treated as mere consumers of 'choices' provided from above by library professionals. Instead, power and resources must be shared with local communities.

UNISON point out the need 'for people to have meaningful control over their lives and the services they receive' (UNISON 2009, 13), and Compass believe that it is the 'alliance between public servants and members of the public that will provide the strongest and most durable basis for effective, responsive and popular public services' (Gannon and Lawson 2008, 26).

The NEF are clear that local communities must be encouraged to 'use the human skills and experience they have to help deliver public ... services' (Stephens et al. 2008, 10) and 'broadening and deepening public services so that they are no longer the preserve of professionals or commissioners, but a shared responsibility ... This is a challenge to the way professionals are expected to work' (Stephens et al. 2008, 10–11). 'By shifting professional practice in this way, the basic objective shifts as well. Delivering public services ceases to be merely about tackling symptoms and immediate needs. It depends on reaching out into the surrounding neighbourhood to build the social networks that can tackle the underlying causes and increase the capacity of the core economy' (Stephens et al. 2008, 14).

Since 1979, the UK has become one of the most unequal countries in the world: the rich have become richer and the poor have become poorer. This process started under Thatcher's Conservative government and continued under New Labour, led by both Blair and Brown. In addition to the UK becoming more unequal and the gap between rich and poor getting wider, social mobility has also stalled and gone into reverse. People born in the late 1950s have a greater chance of becoming socially mobile than those born since the late 1970s.

These backward trends are evidenced in the latest update of the UK government strategy indicators (Department for Environment, Food and Rural Affairs 2009). The first thing to note is that in terms of social justice, the indicator is 'to be developed':

- The Government Equalities Office and the Equalities and Human Rights Commission are jointly developing a framework for the measurement of inequality. This will aim to measure outcomes, discrimination and the degree of choice and control people have in achieving specific aspects of life.

1 Lucie Stephens was speaking at the joint launch of the NEF (Gannon and Lawson 2008) and the UNISON reports (UNISON 2009).

Table 1.1　　Proxy measures of inequality

Performance indicator	Proxy measure
Infant mortality	There were 3.3 more infant deaths per 1,000 live births for those in semi-routine occupations than for those who were higher managerial.
Life expectancy	Life expectancy in deprived areas was 2.0 fewer years for men, and 1.6 fewer years for women.
Mortality rates	103 people per 100,000 died from circulatory diseases in deprived areas compared to the average of 79; and 133 compared with 115 people per 100,000 died from cancer.
Smoking	Smoking is more common in lower socio-economic groups – 25 per cent of routine and manual workers compared with 21 per cent of the total population
Diet	20 per cent of men and 25 per cent of women on the lowest incomes consumed five or more portions of fruit and vegetables per day, compared to 34 per cent and 36 per cent of men and women in the highest income group.
Environmental equality	Around 0.3 per cent of people in the least deprived areas experience four or more environmental conditions that are 'least favourable', compared with 20 per cent of people living in the most deprived areas.
Housing conditions	1.1m dwellings, 29 per cent of those in the social sector, are below the Decent Homes Standard. 1.2m vulnerable households, 39 per cent of those living in private sector properties, were in dwellings that are below the Decent Homes Standard.
Influencing local or national decisions	Between 2001 and 2009 the per cent of people who felt they could influence decisions affecting their local area fell from 43 per cent to 39 per cent .
Overall life satisfaction	63 per cent of social group E (casual labourers, state pensioners and the unemployed) were broadly satisfied with their lives compared to 79 per cent of those in social group AB (doctors, solicitors, accountants, teachers, nurses, police officers). The per cent of social group E rating themselves as extremely dissatisfied with their lives was about four times higher than for other groups.
Positive and negative feelings	The proportion of social group E experiencing positive feelings (58 per cent) was much lower than the average, and the proportion of social group AB (76 per cent) was much higher than the average. The per cent of people in social group E regularly experiencing negative feelings was much higher than average.
Child wellbeing	Fewer children who receive free school meals rated their local area as very or fairly good as a place to live and fewer rated themselves as healthy or physically active. Children who receive free school meals were more likely to say they had been bullied on most days.
Mental health	There is a correlation between above average positive mental health and household incomes of more than £36,400. There is a correlation between below average positive mental health and household incomes of less than £5,200.

- Indicators are being developed across 10 dimensions and for all the equality strands of gender, disability, ethnicity, religion and belief, age and sexual orientation. (Department for Environment, Food and Rural Affairs 2009, 102)

However, in the absence of these social justice indicators, there are a number of proxy indicators which can be used to measure how unequal, unfair and less cohesive the UK has become (see Table 1.1, drawn from the Department for Environment, Food and Rural Affairs 2009).

Some of these figures are a national disgrace, given that the UK is one of the richest countries in the world.

A recent job advert by Oxfam for a Policy and Communications Manager was headlined 'Poverty in the UK? That's rich' and went on to say:

> The UK is the world's sixth richest country. And yet one in five people live in poverty. The kind of poverty that means their children go to school hungry, and that they can't afford to heat their homes. At Oxfam, we know people don't choose to be poor. The fact is they find themselves in circumstances that leave them trapped. In this role, you'll overturn misconceptions and you'll transform policies. You'll make sure that UK poverty is firmly on the agenda. It means striking a balance between pressurising the government for change and winning the hearts and minds of the public. If you're an expert influencer and policy analyst, are confident in speaking out for change, and are tenacious and resilient, visit our website. (guardian.co.uk 2009)

We have quoted this advert at some length because it is a good template for the type of skills which library workers will need in the future if they are to identify, prioritise and meet community needs. These workers will need to be able to overturn misconceptions about socially excluded communities, and they will have to mainstream these communities within library strategies and policies. These workers will have to make sure that social exclusion is firmly on the agenda of the library service and the local authority. They will need to pressure their managers and Elected Members for change, and, at the same time, win the hearts and minds of front-line staff and local communities. They will need to have strong influencing skills and be passionate and committed advocates for socially excluded people. This will require tenacity, resilience and courage. But, as this book aims to show, UK public libraries have a proud, if somewhat patchy, history of tackling social exclusion, and the library workers of tomorrow can stand on the shoulders of those who have blazed a path in the past and those who continue to hold a beacon for social justice today.

An Historical Overview

Even in 2009, some people behave as though social exclusion is an entirely new policy concept – and, in addition, others seem to cling to the belief that social policy has nothing to do with public libraries!

Chapter 2 looks briefly at the recent history of social policy in the UK, and then fits tackling social exclusion into this framework.

It also reassesses public library responses to this agenda from the 1850s onwards. It is clear that many Victorian libraries did engage with working people, but, at the same time, 'inclusion in the Victorian public library was ... to be largely on the terms of the includers' (Muddiman 1999a, 18).

The chapter follows the development of approaches to people outside library buildings, especially during the period from 1950–70, and the growing realisation that much more would need to be done to reach, for example, black and minority ethnic communities:

> The research [by Claire Lambert in 1969] showed that some public libraries were developing a level of book provision (for example particularly in Birmingham, Wolverhampton, Rochdale, Newcastle and Glasgow); some had started to develop links with local communities (working with volunteers for example); and some were using imaginative promotional methods, for example 'At Dewsbury the librarian has used the local Pakistani cinema to advertise the Urdu collection' (Lambert 1969, 47).
>
> However: 'Some librarians offered little information or few comments, and when this was the case in library authorities with large immigrant communities, it can be indicative only of an almost total lack of communication between the librarians and the immigrants themselves' (Lambert 1969, 42). (Vincent 2009c, 138)

We follow this assessment through to the current day. As John Vincent highlights:

> There have been immense changes in the past 40 years, not only in UK society generally, but also in public libraries' provision for BME communities specifically. Many public libraries have built strong links with their local communities, creating (often iconic) places where people come together; they also recognize the importance of diversity, and are looking beyond the notion that people are simply one-dimensional (for example Black) to seeing people as belonging to many communities. Yet, at the same time, some of the problems that Claire Lambert identified are still with us – the desire for someone else to solve issues for us, the lack of real communication with parts of our communities. Finally, this brief analysis of events over the past 40 years has also highlighted a major failing by public libraries and public library agencies so far – the lack of engagement in wider public policy. There has been a number

of opportunities when libraries could have engaged – for example around citizenship, race relations, migration, diversity – showing how they contribute to these wider agendas, even taking a bold stand to start debate (on how to break down the 'mono-cultural' approach to communities noted above, for example), and working with partners to demonstrate their value to society, yet examples where this has happened are few and far between. (Vincent 2009c, 144)

We chart the rise and fall of community librarianship, beset as it was by a combination of 'managerialism, consumerism and other ideologies of the market' (Black and Muddiman 1997, 112–13), highlighting some of the immense gains that were made during this relatively short boom period.

We also use stock selection as an indicator of the ways in which attitudes to library materials have changed (again setting this in its wider context – of the 'political correctness' debate and the introduction of Clause 28 to the statute book).

What is Social Exclusion?

What is social exclusion, and where has it come from? Chapter 3 outlines some of the debates around what exactly to call this area of social policy work. Had the UK embarked on this work now, it might well have drawn on the experience in Scotland and elsewhere, and called it 'social justice'; however, the UK government decided that its preferred term was 'social exclusion'. Whilst some people appear to think that 'social exclusion' as a term has had its day, it is also clear that, at an international level, it is still very much the key term: the EU has declared 2010 as the European Year for Combating Poverty and Social Exclusion (Department for Work and Pensions 2009a).

We chart the development of social exclusion policy from the establishing of the Social Exclusion Unit to the (current) Social Exclusion Task Force, taking on board the growth in awareness of just what is involved – moving from relatively simplistic definitions to those currently in use, which reflect the complexity of tackling exclusion:

> a shorthand term for what can happen when people or areas suffer from a combination of linked problems such as unemployment, poor skills, low incomes, poor housing, high crime, bad health and family breakdown. (Social Exclusion Unit 2001, 10)

> Social exclusion is a short-hand term for what can happen when people or areas have a combination of problems, such as unemployment, discrimination, poor skills, low incomes, poor housing, high crime and family breakdown. These problems are linked and mutually reinforcing. Social exclusion is an extreme consequence of what happens when people do not get a fair deal throughout their

lives and find themselves in difficult situations. This pattern of disadvantage can be transmitted from one generation to the next. (Social Exclusion Task Force 2009)

This chapter also draws on recent work by the Joseph Rowntree Foundation (Hills et al. 2009a) and by Derek Birrell (Birrell 2009) to evaluate just what progress has been made across the UK in tackling social exclusion; this can neatly be summarised as:

> The UK's experience in the 1980s and 1990s showed that the laissez-faire strategy of hoping that rapid growth in living standards at the top would 'trickle down' to those at the bottom did not work. The last decade has shown that a more interventionist strategy of 'pump up' is hard. The period since 1997 shows that gains are possible, but they require continuous effort to be sustained. (Hills et al. 2009b, 359)

Strategic Context

Public libraries exist within a strategic context which is wider than library services and local government. This strategic context encompasses issues such as community empowerment, equality and diversity, equity and excellence, identity and social class. Public libraries need to understand and respond positively to these agendas if they are to provide relevant and modern library services and meet the needs of their local communities.

Communities in Control: Real People, Real Power (Communities and Local Government 2009) is:

> an agenda for empowerment that reaches right across the board, from supporting people who want to take an active role in their communities to giving them better access to information and the chance to get more involved in key local public services. These themes lie at the heart of our public service reform agenda – the transfer of power both to front-line professionals and to users, who we want to be able to play a far greater role in shaping the services they use. (Brown 2009b, 1)

A Fairer Future: the Equality Bill and Other Action to Make Equality a Reality (Government Equalities Office 2009) will place a new Equality Duty on local authorities who will need to think about the needs of everyone who uses their services or works for them. Councils will also need to consider what action they can take to reduce the socio-economic inequalities people face. This means that social class will become another key strand of the equality agenda, along with age, race, gender, sexuality, disability and faith.

Equity and Excellence in the Public Library: Why Ignorance is Not Our Heritage (Usherwood 2007) argues that excellence should not be compromised in the pursuit of equity. We believe that adherence to high professional standards (which is our definition of excellence) did not prevent the cycle of boom and bust referred to above, and may even have contributed to it. Equity (which we define as social justice) on the other hand offers a better chance of breaking the cycle, or at least of future-proofing the service when the going gets tough. Excellence, in the form of outdated professional practices, attitudes and behaviour has contributed to the steady decline in the use of public libraries, and a new approach based on equity is needed to halt and reverse this decline. Being excellent for a dwindling number of traditional library users will not safeguard our future. Instead, libraries need to develop new audiences, widen access and participation, and become more relevant and, dare we say it, more popular, by which we mean more relevant to the lives of local communities. Populism does not have to be the enemy of excellence; but excellence can be the enemy of equity. High professional standards can be received and perceived as cultural elitism.

Identity in the 21st Century: New Trends in Changing Times (Wetherell 2009) is the first systematic investigation into subjective attitudes to class in the UK, and how they have changed over five decades. The balance between the working and middle classes has not varied significantly over this period, which suggests that, despite all the social progress made since the 1960s, the class system has remained relatively static. Indeed, other evidence suggests that social mobility has declined and so the working and middle class proportions are likely to stay around the 60/40 level for some time. This has huge significance for social policy and the planning of public services. Public libraries should be increasing their efforts to engage with the working class who still make up two-thirds of the population.

Who Cares About the White Working Class? (Sveinsson 2009a) explored issues of race, class and identity and concluded:

> What we learn here is that life chances for today's children are overwhelmingly linked to parental income, occupations and educational qualifications – in other words, class. The poor white working class share many more problems with the poor from ethnic communities than some of them recognize. All the most disadvantaged groups must be helped to improve their joint lot. Competition between them, real or imagined, is just a distraction. (Gavron 2009, 2)

Sources of Resentment, and Perceptions of Ethnic Minorities Among Poor White People in England (Garner et al. 2009) stressed the importance of engaging with white working-class communities who feel deserted and let down by national and local government: 'We identified some key recurrent emotional themes: resentment; betrayal; abandonment; loss; defensiveness; nostalgia; unfairness and disempowerment. Local and central government are identified as doing the abandoning and betraying, while the communities experience loss and disempowerment' (Garner et al. 2009, 8).

Such engagement is even more necessary at a time of economic recession and the rise of the British National Party who seek to exacerbate community tensions to advance their electoral fortunes. The white working class do not use public libraries anywhere near as much as the middle classes. Library workers need to engage with the white working class and ensure that their voice is heard in the planning, design, delivery and assessment of library services.

Tackling Social Exclusion

Chapter 5 looks at the policy and service developments since 1997. It follows the progress of the raft of policies, including Annual Library Plans; *Libraries for All* (DCMS 1999a); *Public Libraries, Ethnic Diversity and Citizenship* (Roach and Morrison 1998); and *Open to All?* (Muddiman et al. 2000a, 2000b and 2000c). It also looks briefly at some of the initiatives that came out of *Open to All?*, including the Quality Leaders Project and The Network.

We identify key spurs to the development of work to tackle social exclusion:

- Tackling social exclusion had become a UK government and local government priority, emphasised, for example, by *Framework for the Future* (DCMS 2003) and the Shared Priorities between central and local government (Local Government Association 2002).
- Organisations such as the MLA emphasised the need to tackle social exclusion.
- External funding became available, assisting in the development of these services.
- There was a considerable emphasis on training and staff development in order to gain the necessary skills to build inclusive services.
- Library staff who were committed to tackling social exclusion saw an opportunity to develop community-based service provision.

Within this context, we then highlight some major areas of good practice, amongst other things, the Libraries Change Lives Award, the National Year of Reading, and external funding.

Yet this chapter also questions why the impact of many of these major initiatives has been relatively limited, and begins to challenge some of the bases on which public library services are provided – projects, non-mainstreamed, marginal services, for example. It looks critically at the role played by the Department for Culture, Media and Sport (DCMS) and the Museums, Libraries and Archives Council (MLA), and at the continuing lack of evidence of impact by public libraries, especially in relation to government and other agenda.

Finally, we assess the progress that has been made by public libraries since 1997, and go on to outline key areas for inclusion in our final chapter.

Developing a Needs-Based Library Service

In 2003 NIACE (the National Institute of Adult Continuing Education) published *Developing a Needs Based Library Service* (Pateman 2003) in their 'Lifelines in adult learning' series. It is interesting to note that this book was commissioned by the adult learning sector rather than the public library sector. Put quite simply, a needs-based library service is based on that good Marxist principle of 'from each according to their ability, and to each according to their needs'. In practical terms this means developing a library service that has the strategies, structures, systems and culture which enable it to identify, prioritise and meet community needs. In order to identify these needs, all sections of the local community have to be actively engaged in the planning, design, delivery and assessment of library services.

Issues of equity tend to exist at the margins of professional practice and are rarely mainstreamed. The starting point for developing a needs-based library service would be a vision and strategy which has equity as its core value. This strategy should itself be developed by using an inclusive approach which engages all key stakeholders in the process. A typical community is made up of 21 per cent active library users, 27 per cent passive/lapsed users and 52 per cent non-users. Traditionally most effort is put into engaging active users, some effort is put into engaging passive or lapsed users and little or no effort is put into engaging non-users, yet they are the majority of our communities.

Once an equity-based strategy has been developed, the staffing and service structures need to be aligned with this strategy to ensure that they are fit for purpose and able to deliver the new strategic objectives. Staffing structures need to be made flatter, less hierarchical and less professionalised. Professional skills sets need to be replaced with more people- and community-focused skills.

The service structure also needs to be aligned with the equity-based strategy, and this means putting library services where people can access them easily and conveniently. The age of the stand-alone library is over, and it is now necessary to co-locate public libraries with other services and adopt a multi-use and one-stop-shop approach. There is much to be learnt from bookshops and other retail operations in terms of creating a quality library experience. In doing this the transactional/customer-based approach of the high street should not be adopted, because one of the public library service's greatest strengths is that it is both democratic and accountable.

Similarly, systems and procedures need to be aligned with the equity-based strategy, and this will require the ditching of many professional practices which do not meet community needs but which provide safe and secure comfort zones for library staff. Many of these procedures are barriers to access, and, in our view, every public library service should scrap the following processes tomorrow: the requirement to show proof of address and identity before joining a library; fines and charges; overdue notices; fixed issue periods for everybody; limits to the number of books which can be borrowed; plus looking again at staff's attachment to library counters and desks!

Finally, the organisational culture needs to be aligned with the equity-based strategy. Culture has been defined as 'the way we do things around here' and it is manifested in the attitude, behaviour and values of library staff. An equity-based strategy requires an inclusive culture and culture change can be accelerated by service planning, performance management and workforce development. But ultimately, as Tom Peters once said, 'if you cannot change people, then you have to change the people'.

Community engagement is central to a needs-based library service, and the question of who in the community is heard and who, more importantly, is not heard, was explored in the Joseph Rowntree Foundation (JRF) research on community engagement and community cohesion (Blake et al. 2008). This research found that population fluidity and super diversity pose additional challenges for community engagement in local government: 'Newer arrivals were identified as being those least likely to have their voices heard effectively. These groups include migrant workers from the accession states, as well as refuges and asylum seekers, with varying aspirations and needs' (Blake et al. 2008, ix). The research identified some 'ways in which local structures of governance were reaching out to enable diverse voices to be heard effectively' (Blake et al. 2008, ix). 'While these examples provide illustrations of promising practices, however, these in turn depend upon the development and implementation of community development strategies as centrally important for local governance strategies more generally' (Blake et al. 2008, ix). In other words, reaching out to communities is good practice, but community development is even better.

Community engagement has featured strongly in all three of the recent national library reviews by UNISON (Davies 2008); the Department of Culture, Media and Sport (DCMS 2008b); and the All-Party Parliamentary Group on Libraries, Literacy and Information Management (Brown 2009c).

The UNISON report *Taking Stock: the Future of Our Public Library Service* recommended the empowerment of staff and communities to shape services together:

> Libraries rest on a bed of goodwill from local communities. They are valued and trusted. But much more could be done to involve both the staff and the local communities in the shaping of the service. This should involve current users, the Friends of the Library, supporters groups, but should also develop means of reaching out to those who currently do not use the library as well. New and imaginative methods should be deployed rather than relying on the blunt tools of market exit. (Davies 2008, 5)

The protracted DCMS Library Modernisation Review set out to 'explore and make recommendations on innovative models of service delivery that integrate libraries with other local services; that make libraries increasingly responsive to the needs of their communities and that involve users in their design' (DCMS 2008b).

The All-Party Parliamentary Group Inquiry into the Governance and Leadership of the Public Library Service in England considered:

> Should local communities have a greater say in decisions about the public library service? For many commentators, the concept of a library at the very heart of a community is a powerful vision. Is this local focus reflected appropriately in local governance and consultation arrangements? Are there other mechanisms for engaging local people in service planning and delivery? (All-Party Parliamentary Group on Libraries, Literacy and Information Management 2009, 6)

Where Next?

Chapter 7 aims to highlight some examples of best practice and research from the UK and abroad, which can be used to create a framework for developing inclusive and needs-based library services.

It begins by highlighting the three major themes running through this book, and then draws these together to begin to chart a roadmap for how public library services could be developed.

These themes are:

- the need to put social justice at the heart of what public libraries are about;
- the vital need for leadership and direction for services; and, as a result,
- the development of proper needs-based library services.

We argue that, without social justice at its heart, the public library service could end up meaning 'nothing to nobody'! We also reaffirm that social justice work is not some new, radical approach, but one that has been recognised and cited as key to public libraries' role and survival over many years, most recently by 'library leaders' in their papers for *Empower, Inform, Enrich* (DCMS 2009b).

We then go on to re-state the critical importance of effective leadership and direction, at three levels:

- pan-UK, national
- regional
- local

Finally, in this section, we stress that local leadership is vital. Whatever governance model is in operation, it is critical that local people feel real ownership of their local services, and that 'library leaders' hear and listen to what they say.

Within this framework, we also identify the following as key issues:

- working in partnership with the local community, other local agencies, the Third Sector, commercial organisations, etc.;
- ensuring that, to keep social justice work at the core, there is sustained, mixed funding;
- co-production of services;
- co-location of our services with other relevant providers;
- providing different kinds of service to meet local needs …
- … delivered by different kinds of library staff;
- breaking the sad image that many people have of libraries – and their staff!
- the urgent need to move away from thinking 'library-centrically' and looking at how we can work with other agencies to help them hit their targets;
- exploring how we can stop being so risk-averse (successful work with communities in the way we have described does involve taking risks).

When public libraries put social justice at their core and have effective leadership in place, then this will lead, we argue, to the development of proper needs-based services.

We draw on three case study models to identify key themes and an agenda for action:

The Working Together Project in Canada sent Community Development Librarians into urban neighbourhoods in Vancouver, Regina, Toronto and Halifax and worked with diverse communities that are traditionally considered marginalised or socially excluded. These communities included people new to Canada, such as immigrants and refugees, people of aboriginal descent, people living in poverty, people recovering from or living with mental illness, people recently released from federal institutions, young people at risk, and many more.

A community development based approach was taken by librarians working with communities in this project. This approach moved community-based library work beyond discussions amongst library staff on how best to meet community needs, to being based upon the lived experiences of socially excluded community members and the librarians who engaged them as equal members of the community. The life experiences of community members drove the project, not library-based beliefs held by librarians or internally generated professional literature. The project found that the traditional approach commonly used by librarians to generate library services inadequately addressed the needs of socially excluded community members.

The Right 'Man' for the Job? The Role of Empathy in Community Librarianship was a research project carried out by Kerry Wilson and Briony Birdi at the University of Sheffield. Like many other very important pieces of research, this report was launched in a blaze of publicity, articles were written in the professional press, but it has now disappeared without trace. No doubt it is collecting dust on the shelves of many librarians who themselves are not the 'right man for the job'.

Every Chief Librarian in the country should read this report and implement its recommendations immediately. But it does not make for comfortable reading. It points out that library staff are strikingly homogenous in terms of gender, age, ethnicity and social class and yet the communities they serve are increasingly diverse. The older, female, white, middle-class librarian is a reality and not a stereotype. To compound this there is a strain between the traditional skill set of the librarian and the more generic skills which are required to meet community needs. To quote the research, this mismatch in skills has 'raised some debate over the role and value of accredited library qualifications and professional status for library staff working in community based and social inclusion roles ... a library qualification is not a prerequisite for effective community based library services'.

Social exclusion has become a common expression and concept since it was first introduced from France by New Labour in 1997. The term is used widely in the media and there have been a raft of reports written about the subject, most notably *Open to All? Public Libraries and Social Exclusion* which was published in 2000. Yet when Wilson and Birdi carried out their research in 2006, over 50 per cent of library staff claimed to be only partly aware of national social exclusion policy and debate, and the qualitative data suggests that awareness is considerably lower than this. Lack of appropriate training is partly to blame for this and another factor is the 'tick box' approach to equality and diversity which demonstrates lip-service to these issues and engenders cynicism among staff. Social inclusion services are regarded as add-ons rather than part of the core library offer.

Capturing the Impact of Libraries was an attempt by BOP Consulting to provide evidence of the type of data and research that is effective at demonstrating the impact of libraries on their local communities. Of particular interest was how the intrinsic benefits delivered through libraries (for example, enjoyment, participation and learning) could contribute to extrinsic benefits or 'social goods' (such as improved wellbeing and greater civic participation). There are essentially two mechanisms by which this happens: the wider effects of learning, both formal and informal; and social capital formation by establishing networks and relationships, and/or facilitating links to resources.

In terms of short-term or intermediate outcomes, the contribution of libraries is strongest with regard to cognitive and non-cognitive skills development, health and wellbeing and social capital formation. The ability to evidence this contribution does, however, vary according to different sub-groups of the population. Early priorities for 'quick wins' in demonstrating libraries' impact to government stakeholders lie in the broad learning agenda and for children and young people, particularly early years activities.

The policy areas in which libraries' impact is weak are business support and economic development more generally, with the exception of adult basic skills, and environmental sustainability, where the sector is nowhere at present. Given this significant weakness in the evidence base BOP have made a number of very useful recommendations regarding ways in which the impact of libraries can be better captured and demonstrated: public libraries need to improve the comprehensiveness and consistency of basic management information on services and users; baselines of activity are particularly urgent with regard to learning activities, and for children and young people; there is very little comprehensive data on the degree to which people, particularly young people, are involved in the design, planning, delivery and evaluation of library services; libraries should be able to demonstrate a significant contribution towards wellbeing and health; baselines of library activity need to be national and they should include demographic information; there should be a biennial census of library users.

We would like to end with some dictionary definitions of 'equity' and 'excellence' because language is the basis of culture and if the professional language is changed this can help to shift the professional culture. The dominant paradigm for a long time has been excellence, which one dictionary defines as 'to be better than' and 'cleverness'. Another dictionary describes excellence as 'to be surpassingly clever or eminent' and 'superiority'. These same dictionaries define equity as 'acting fairly or justly' and 'the principle of fair-mindedness and impartial unprejudiced judgement'. In our view it is time for cleverness and superiority to be replaced by fairness and justice. The age of excellence should end and a new era of equity should begin.

Chapter 2
An Historical Overview

What social exclusion (and its related topics, such as community cohesion) actually is will be explored in Chapter 3. Here, we want to look back briefly to examine where it fits into the policy framework, and what impact this has had on libraries' work.

Where Has Social Exclusion Emerged From?

In the UK, there has been a long history of social policy development, looking at issues around class, poverty and discrimination – albeit with different names – and this section aims to draw together briefly some key points, covering broadly the same period as there have been public libraries.

In many ways, the ambivalence that we can note today about class, poverty and social issues was all too prevalent in Victorian times. For example, there was an immense growth in philanthropy:

> One survey of London estimated that in 1861 there were no fewer than 640 charitable institutions, of which nearly half had been founded in the first half of the nineteenth century and 144 in the decade from 1850. London charities had an income of £2.5 million, and ... [this] still exceeded the amount spent by Poor Law authorities in the capital. (Fraser 2003, 136)

Many of the famous charity movements also began at this time.

However, at the same time, one of the major underlying reasons for this growth in charity and concern about the poor was the fear of social revolution, especially following the shows of strength by the Chartists in 1848. As Derek Fraser described it:

> The most frequent image used was that the *bonds* of society would snap under the strain of abject misery and deprivation. In order to prevent an assault upon the whole basis of society and the division of wealth within it, men [*sic*] were prepared, almost as an insurance against social revolution, to siphon off some of their wealth for use by those in need. (Fraser 2003, 137, emphasis in original)

This bears a strong resemblance to the discussions of social capital today (see, for example, Putnam 2000).

Charity was also seen as 'a means of social control, an avenue for the inculcation of sound middle-class values' (Fraser 2003, 139).

Although there had been recognition throughout the early to mid-nineteenth century of exactly what levels of poverty some people were living in (for example, Mayhew 1851; Hill 1883; Mearns and Preston 1883), it was not until Charles Booth began his immense task of mapping the realities of poverty (Booth 1889), followed by B. Seebohm Rowntree's work in York (Rowntree 1901), that wider society saw and began to understand how at least one-third of the population lived.

There was also a growing 'state' in that healthcare, education and sanitation were all improved, and, to deal with this, local government also began to flourish.

During the period 1905–14:

> The Liberal government laid the foundations of contemporary social services. Concerns with 'national efficiency' fuelled the desire to provide an infrastructure of public services: these services were deliberately provided outside the Poor Law, to avoid the stigma associated with pauperism. (Robert Gordon University no date)

The period from 1900–48 saw a gradual shift from the Poor Law mentality towards the introduction of insurance and pensions, family allowances, and also powerful arguments for increasing the minimum wage, all culminating in the Beveridge Report (Beveridge 1942).

However, after the initial post-Second World War enthusiasm for social reform, 'fundamental flaws' – as Howard Glennerster described them (Glennerster 2004, 82) – in the Beveridge model became clear, and there has been an increasing struggle to deal with the causes and results of poverty ever since.

> Today both the drivers of poverty and the policies that might be marshalled to tackle it are more diverse, and the politics of doing so correspondingly more complicated. Wider conceptualisations of disadvantage increase the dimensions across which failure to achieve inclusion is seen as a problem. Problems have changed their shape as well – in 1899 children in large families represented a major cost in money and cause of poverty; now families are smaller but children also represent a *time* cost that leads to earnings forgone for some parents but also pressured lives for others. (Glennerster et al. 2004, 163–4)

From the 1960s onwards, the need to grapple with 'disadvantage' became increasingly urgent:

> There have been many initiatives aimed at tackling the broader problems of poor neighbourhoods from the 1960s onwards – the Urban programme, then the Urban Development Corporations and Task Forces in the 1980s, and the Single Regeneration Budget in the 1990s. All tried new approaches and all

had some successes. But none really succeeded in setting in motion a virtuous circle of regeneration, with improvements in jobs, crime, health and housing all reinforcing each other.

There are many reasons for this failure. They include the absence of effective national policies to deal with the structural causes of decline; a tendency to parachute solutions in from outside, rather than engaging local communities; and too much emphasis on physical renewal instead of better opportunities for local people. Above all, a joined up problem has never been addressed in a joined up way. (Social Exclusion Unit 1998, 9)

In addition, the liberation movements of the 1960s and 1970s gave voice to more people who, until then, had frequently been marginalised – women, lesbian, gay, bisexual and transgender people (LGBTs), disabled people, for example. They too began to challenge the way that society – and its resources – was organised.

Where Did Social Exclusion Appear From?

According to Janie Percy-Smith, the term 'social exclusion' originated in the social policy of the French governments of the 1980s 'and was used to refer to a disparate group of people living on the margins of society and, in particular, without access to the system of social insurance' (Percy-Smith 2000b, 1).

In the UK, tackling social exclusion was one of the very early policy priorities when New Labour came to power in 1997 – the cross-departmental Social Exclusion Unit was set up in 1997, although it applied to England only (for further details of how this work was taken forward in Northern Ireland, Scotland and Wales, see Chapter 3).

Although it only applies to England, the core reasons which were identified for the failure of previous attempts to tackle social exclusion can be seen as pretty universal, including:

the absence of effective national policies to deal with the structural causes of decline; a tendency to parachute solutions in from outside, rather than engaging local communities; and too much emphasis on physical renewal instead of better opportunities for local people. Above all, a joined up problem has never been addressed in a joined up way … And at the neighbourhood level, there has been no one in charge of pulling together all the things that need to go right at the same time. (Social Exclusion Unit 1998, 9)

Research at a local level in the late 1990s (London Voluntary Service Council 1998; Corrigan 1999) also added to the urgent need for all agencies to begin to address social exclusion.

How Have Public Libraries Reacted?

Again, this section aims to draw together briefly some key themes specifically related to reaching people who are socially excluded, often via extension or outreach activities – there are more detailed histories elsewhere (see, for example, Kelly 1977; Kelly and Kelly 1977; Black 1996; Black and Muddiman 1997; Muddiman 1999a, 2006).

The Early Period, 1850–1950

There is a widespread assumption that public libraries were originally established as 'working class' institutions, and it is undoubtedly true that many Victorian libraries did engage with working people:

> Large urban centres like Manchester and Leeds established 'branch' libraries in what we would now call inner city neighbourhoods where the overwhelming majority of residents were poor. (Muddiman 1999a, 17)

In addition, again as Dave Muddiman notes:

> Reading rooms, including special rooms set aside for youths and women, were also set up in Manchester and elsewhere and appear to have been very popular with working class users because of their open access and their provision of popular and topical magazines and newspapers. (Muddiman 1999a, 17)

However, it is also clear that these public libraries were uncertain about welcoming everybody, and, as Dave Muddiman concludes, 'inclusion in the Victorian public library was … to be largely on the terms of the includers' (Muddiman 1999a, 18). As the nineteenth century progressed, so librarians started to develop approaches to different clientele (for example, by establishing children's library services), and also began to declare that public libraries were universal in appeal. This theme was carried over into the first half of the twentieth century, with, for example, Lionel McColvin declaring that 'What is good for one man, one class, one age can with necessary modifications be good for another' (McColvin 1937, 4, quoted in Muddiman 1999a).

Although there were attempts to extend the public library's reach, as Martin Hewitt says, 'We still know relatively little about library outreach before 1930' (Hewitt 2006, 72). Much of the descriptions of what took place in (and out of) libraries concentrated on systems and internal management – 'pride of place went to the catalogue, the touchstone, before 1900, of librarianship' (Hewitt 2006, 72).

The main extension activity was lectures, often on aspects of the bookstock, and, later, exhibitions and the occasional club or society. According to Dave Muddiman:

Traditionalists argued against an overt societal role: in their view, the public library should remain a limited, passive, book-based service aimed at the individual reader ... Progressives, in contrast, envisaged a wider public library: in 1927 the authors of the Kenyon Report urged that libraries should become an 'engine of great potentiality for state welfare'.[1] (Muddiman 2006, 82)

Thomas Kelly too notes that 'On the subject of library extension activities there seems at this period to have been a certain ambivalence of attitude' (Kelly 1977, 249), and goes on to demonstrate this with examples from the Kenyon Report (Great Britain. Board of Education. Public Libraries Committee 1927), with its praise for libraries that were running lectures and supporting Workers' Educational Association classes, contrasting with the Adult Education report (Joint Committee of the Library Association and British Institute of Adult Education 1923) which 'devotes most of its attention to the problem of book supply to adult classes' (Kelly 1977, 249).

It seems clear that there were not huge attempts to break through barriers to library use for a large part of the population – indeed, again as Martin Hewitt neatly describes it:

Certainly, just below the surface lurked a profound unease at the demands of library outreach, nicely encapsulated by the concluding phrase of the *Library Association Record*'s grudging review of Lionel McColvin's Library extension work[2] ... 'publicity can be overdone'.[3] (Hewitt 2006, 81)

However, Lionel McColvin was clearly one of the 'progressives' – in his book (McColvin 1927), he argued the case for delivering books to those unable to reach library buildings, including people who were geographically remote, those who worked long hours and sick and disabled people (although, by 1942, he seems to have changed his opinion: 'We feel that the library should stick to its own job' (McColvin 1942, quoted in Kelly 1977, 411)).

Some librarians did support these views, and, in 1933, the Library Association Conference in Harrogate included debates about services outside the library – to hospitals, prisons and seafarers (cited in Muddiman 2006, 83). The 1930s and 1940s also saw the development of hospital services, mobile libraries (with Manchester's 'bibliobus'), a prison library service in Suffolk, the first deposit collection in a local authority residential care home, and the first comprehensive housebound delivery service.

In 1938, came two calls for the role of the public library to be widened to begin to break down barriers to take-up and use. Edward Sydney, Borough Librarian of Leyton, argued that the public library should be 'the headquarters of

---

1 Great Britain. Board of Education. Public Libraries Committee 1927, 37.
2 McColvin 1927.
3 'N' 1927.

all local cultural activities' (Sydney 1938, 476, quoted in Kelly 1977, 307); and Eric Leyland, Librarian of Walthamstow, wrote of the need to interest the two-thirds of the population who were not making use of library services, beginning by analysing the groups involved (Leyland 1938, cited in Kelly 1977, 307).

According to Thomas Kelly (1977), the war years (and immediately post-war) saw arguments raging back and forth about the role of the public library – for example, whether it should be a cultural centre or not, how far it should go beyond book-lending as a core activity, and so on – yet it also saw the growth of libraries as real cultural centres, perhaps most significantly in Swindon, led by Harold Jolliffe who was later to become the leading exponent of extension activities (Jolliffe 1962).

Public Libraries 1950–70

The 1950s saw the consolidation of many 'standard' forms of service to socially excluded people (such as mobile libraries, prisons and, later, hospital library services), and, by the 1960s, 'a majority of public library services had incorporated into their mainstream provision a series of mobile services, prison and hospital services to local institutions and a housebound reader service, usually operated in part by volunteers' (Muddiman 2006, 84).

The 1960s also saw a mushrooming in activities for children and young people, such as Lambeth's outdoor summer storytelling programme which began in a small way in the mid-1960s before becoming an established programme in 1970 (Hill 1973). Influences from abroad (especially the United States) were also being felt, for example following the availability in the UK of Eleanor F Brown's inspiring 'source book' (Brown 1971):

> no fines for overdue books, no 'hush-hush' signs anywhere in sight, wandering story tellers roaming the streets like Pied Pipers of Hamelin, leading groups of children to the friendly neighborhood library … new ideas and bustling activity going on from morning until night. Here is a library – and a staff – reaching out into the community in every conceivable manner, no longer waiting only for those who would come of their own accord, finding the real needs of the people, and satisfying those needs – with something for everyone!
>
> Did we say this *is* the new public library? Not all libraries can claim this image yet, but the new image has been created by the pioneers and it is spreading fast. This *is* the new public library in the sense that it is what the times demand, and inner-city librarians who cling to tradition, shocked by innovations, will soon find their public will pass them by … and so will their financial support. (Brown 1971, 1)

In 1969, one of the very first articles to consider public library provision for Indian and Pakistani communities in Britain was published (Lambert 1969). It reported the results of a survey sent to 50 public library authorities in 1967, which revealed both the levels of provision for these communities and the attitudes towards them.[4]

The research showed that some public libraries were developing a level of book provision (for example particularly in Birmingham, Wolverhampton, Rochdale, Newcastle and Glasgow); some had started to develop links with local communities (working with volunteers, for example); and some were using imaginative promotional methods, for example 'At Dewsbury the librarian has used the local Pakistani cinema to advertise the Urdu collection' (Lambert 1969, 47).

However:

> Some librarians offered little information or few comments, and when this was the case in library authorities with large immigrant communities, it can be indicative only of an almost total lack of communication between the librarians and the immigrants themselves. (Lambert 1969, 42)

In addition, some librarians argued that external funding was required before there can be any real improvement in provision:

> The problem of provision for immigrants was referred to the Department of Education and Science and has also been considered by the Library Advisory Council … In the meantime the initiative remains entirely with individual library authorities, and without central Government funds, it is difficult to see how a breakthrough can ever be achieved. (Lambert 1969, 47–8)

From 1970 Onwards

As we have seen more recently, the focus on libraries shifts! At the start of the 1970s, they came back into view, and this section summarises what occurred, how this led to the development of community librarianship – and what happened to that.

Challenges to the Public Library – and the Development of Community Librarianship

As A.E.D. Fleming stated in an interesting piece in the *Library Association Record*:

> As a group, librarians in British public libraries lack a vision and are unsure of their objectives and priorities … new ideas are needed urgently. (Fleming 1971, 33)

---

4   For a reassessment of Claire Lambert's research in the context of the last 40 years, see Vincent 2009c.

In 1971, the Library Association published the results of an investigation by sociologist Bryan Luckham; one of his significant comments on what he had found was:

> It seems to be an accepted fact today that those who are leaders in society ... have special claims on the service. On the other hand, the disadvantages of the less-privileged have been brought out and the question is raised whether the public library now has an obligation to discard its traditional reluctance to play a dynamic role and should go out to create a new public. (Luckham 1971, 126)

There was clearly growing criticism of 'traditional' public library provision, and a growing number of voices calling for a different kind of service, for example:

> It is long past time to take books to people, instead of waiting for people to come to books. (Adams 1973, 154)

This was followed by a piece of research carried out in the London Borough of Hillingdon, looking at what exactly makes an 'effective' library (Totterdell and Bird 1976). Interestingly, this was one of the earliest works about libraries to begin to tease out the differences between goals, inputs, outputs and needs – and also to identify that there needed to be a lot more investigation into library service users' and non-users' needs (rather than focusing on the service first):

> We would suggest that most services are largely supplier-oriented, quite unwittingly, as when planners simply do not realize how far from their public they are – or how far they are imposing themselves on their services. (Totterdell and Bird 1976, 130)

Given all of this, the Library Advisory Council of England commissioned a report on library services for 'the disadvantaged' (Department of Education and Science 1978), which, whilst tackling a broad sweep of disadvantage, also ended up being fairly weak (for example, by recommending a series of pilot programmes, rather than wholesale change).

The Library Association also commissioned a major piece of work, published in 1978 as *A Public Library Service for Ethnic Minorities in Great Britain* (Clough and Quarmby 1978). This was a 'first', in that it assessed public library provision for black and minority ethnic (BME) communities in the UK for the first time, but it too was weak (and somewhat backward-looking).

In 1981, Pat Coleman published a key report, *Whose Problem?* (Coleman 1981), which argued for a much more major overhaul of service provision, connecting public libraries more closely to the communities in which they were located. From here, both the Chartered Institute of Library and Information Professionals (CILIP) Community Services Group (CILIP 2009h) and the general 'community librarianship' movement (for more information, see Black and Muddiman 1997) were founded.

Perhaps the greatest response in the early 1980s by public libraries was to the needs of BME communities. This was partly because of an increased focus on the specific library and information needs of particular BME groups (see, for example, Gundara 1981; Wellum 1981; Alexander 1982; Simsova 1982; Simsova and Chin 1982); and there was also the development of specialist stock provision; the development of stock selection guidelines and processes (particularly in library services for children); and the production of guidelines and standards for levels of service to particular groups (Domiciliary Services Group and London Housebound Services Group 1991; Machell 1996; Collis and Boden 1997); all of which was reflected in the development of more sophisticated training programmes for library staff.

Yet, at the same time, there was also limited commitment by many public libraries to provide adequate, sustainable resources. As Alistair Black and Dave Muddiman noted:

> The predominant strategy adopted by public libraries was the appointment of an 'ethnic minority' librarian under Section 11 of the 1966 Local Government Act, which enabled part payment of salary from central government funding. Provision for black and minority ethnic communities as a result often developed as a separate entity having only a marginal impact on mainstream services, despite the many valuable and creative initiatives undertaken. (Black and Muddiman 1997, 83)

The result was a service which, in many cases, was highly focused and well used, but with separate staff who were not integrated into the mainstream. When Section 11 funding ceased, many of the posts were cut.

Sadly, this approach was reflected in other service priority areas too. For example, in the early 1980s, many local authorities (including public libraries) responded positively to the then levels of unemployment by developing focused services for unemployed people, including community information packs, improved links with other advice/information providers, and an enhanced range of relevant stock. However, many of these projects were supported only whilst external funding existed, and they disappeared as soon as the funding ceased (see, for example, Barugh and Woodhouse 1987).

Community librarianship – which, in many ways, represented the key way of meeting the needs of different disadvantaged communities – also began to wither in the later 1980s. This happened for a number of reasons, including:

- reductions in funding (especially government schemes which had supported the inner city);
- strong signals from the government that it was no longer prepared to see any expansion of public library provision via public expenditure – and

introducing the notion of 'free' applying to 'core' services only (see, for example, Office of Arts and Libraries 1988);

- changes in the political 'atmosphere', so that community-related activities became a lower priority for local authorities – included in the Conservative Party's 'back-to-basics' approach (see, for example, MacIntyre 1993);
- an increased focus on managerialism;
- increasing reluctance by some library staff to get involved in community librarianship work.

As Alistair Black and Dave Muddiman summed it up:

> Community librarianship, by the early 1980s, had become more than simply a series of initiatives and service practices. It represented a whole philosophy of public librarianship which was based on the essentially idealistic conviction that libraries could initiate and support social change and improvement in a shifting and diversifying society. It held that such improvement might be achieved through a balance of public provision, professional commitment and communal involvement. For a short time, these ideas reinvigorated the public library profession and gave public libraries a renewed sense of purpose amid the confusions and conflicts of the late seventies and early eighties. But such purpose has, our study reveals, been dissipated and fragmented. Community librarianship has been challenged by managerialism, consumerism and other ideologies of the market. It is now one of a number of approaches to public librarianship; according to many librarians it has been redefined in lesser and more conservative terms as 'marketing', 'customer focus', 'networking' or 'community care'. Library services have been rationalised, reinstitutionalised and, like a 'business', required to demonstrate a degree of utilitarian efficiency. What looms as a result is a community librarianship with little sense of its ideals and a drift towards private provision and technological extinction. (Black and Muddiman 1997, 112–13)

So, by 1997, what were public libraries doing about social exclusion? And how have they developed this area of work since? These questions will be examined in more depth in Chapter 5.

Stock Selection

One area which particularly shows how these changes affected public libraries and their users from the early 1970s onwards is the selection of library materials.

> One of the tensions in librarianship has always been between those who considered that public libraries were neutral places and that, as such, they should purchase and stock all kinds of materials, and those who thought that no agency (including public libraries) could be neutral, that libraries in modern Britain

were another product of the capitalist society within which they developed, and
that published materials were equally value-laden. (Vincent 2000, 351)

In 1971, a group of London children's librarians produced the first critical
assessment of all children's books then in print on selected countries (Hill 1971),
which had a major impact on the way that public libraries viewed both BME
communities and the library materials that they selected for them.

In addition, many public library services did not stock paperbacks (or popular
children's fiction) until into the 1970s; for example, Janet Hill was still having to
argue the case for paperbacks in 1973 (Hill 1973, 121–2).

Also during the early 1970s, a number of lobby groups and individuals started
working to challenge and develop the ways in which books for children were
produced and sold, including the Children's Rights Workshop, CISSY and Bob
Dixon (Dixon 1977a, 1977b). The Children's Rights Workshop went on to set
up the annual 'Other Award', through which it had a real influence on writing,
publishing, reviewing and bookselling – and on stock selection in libraries –
and which, during its lifetime (1974–87) moved from being a 'fringe' event to
becoming a part of the annual children's book world calendar (for a summary, see
Stones 1988).

As a result of all this activity, and encouraged by innovative approaches in a
number of education and library authorities (such as the Inner London Education
Authority), many libraries introduced stock selection policies – along with the
reviewing of books – as part of their selection process for children's books.
These policies were used to encourage the presentation of positive images (of, for
example, gender, race, sexuality, disability) and also to form the basis for rejecting
material which perpetuated stereotypes and other negative images. In addition,
some librarians worked closely with publishers, writers and booksellers to help
them produce appropriate materials to meet these growing demands.

From these beginnings in children's literature, the idea of discussing and
selecting stock for adults in a similar way also grew, and, following the lead
of a handful of pioneering library authorities, work began on developing stock
selection policies and criteria. For example, Lambeth developed stock selection
policies which looked at particular genres of fiction (Vincent 1986a).

In 1986, the picture looked quite rosy, and John Vincent commented (1986b):

> Opposition to mainstream views has strengthened; since the misdirection of
> the 'swinging sixties', women, blacks and gays have grouped together to fight
> for equality and an end to discrimination … and their arguments have begun
> to affect all areas of life, even the booktrade and libraries! An ever-increasing
> range of publications is available since the development of black, women's and
> gay publishers … and the number of writers from these communities who are
> now being published by both mainstream and small presses. This, at last, gives
> librarians the opportunity to select a wider range of stock and therefore to offset
> the traditional fiction output. (Vincent 1986b, 131)

He also commented:

> [Comments conflating stock selection and censorship] confuse the right
> to intellectual freedom with the damage that some materials do: how can
> intellectual freedom be achieved at the expense of the rights of women, blacks,
> gays, working people? It is within this framework that librarians must select
> stock, and selection cannot be made in isolation. Librarians must select material
> in relation to their communities, must have constant contact with their in-library
> users and non-users in the locality, not just with vocal minorities, but all kinds of
> people. Gone are the days when librarians can rest back in *their* libraries, waiting
> for people to come to them; active participation by librarians in the community,
> and by local people in the library has to develop. (Vincent 1986b, 132)

However, by the mid-1980s, the 'mood' had changed, and the ground that had
been gained was being lost (see, for example, Vincent 1993).

Whilst all this positive activity was taking place within the world of literature
and libraries, the world outside was moving on in different directions. Rightly or
wrongly, during the 1980s, particularly in London and other metropolitan areas,
opposition was growing to what were seen as some of the over-indulgences of
'Old Labour', and, at the same time, the government embarked on a campaign to
attack, ridicule and reduce the powers of local authorities. They were joined in
this work by some of the media, so that a campaign grew to vilify Labour councils
and their activities as 'loony lefties'. One of the tools which they employed was to
pick up the negative usage of 'political correctness' and to run a series of stories
criticising local authorities for their 'politically correct' stance.

Sadly, public libraries were an easy target, partly because they had become
high profile (particularly with some of the stories circulating about 'political
correctness' in some London boroughs and the ILEA), and partly because they
were becoming centre-stage for possible contracting-out and/or severe reductions
in resources. As a result, there was a spate of stories – true or otherwise – about
'book-banning', and, to cope with this unwelcome focus, many libraries simply
stopped their positive stock selection and equalities work.

One by-product of this concentration on children's books, 'political correctness',
and what children should (or should not) have access to was the passing into law
of 'Clause 28',[5] possibly the final blow to an already weakening position that
public libraries needed to promote positive images, certainly of LGBTs.

---

5   'Clause 28' was passed into law in 1988 (Great Britain 1988), as an amendment to
the 1986 Local Government Act Great Britain 1986, and stated that a local authority 'shall
not intentionally promote homosexuality or publish material with the intention of promoting
homosexuality' or 'promote the teaching in any maintained school of the acceptability of
homosexuality as a pretended family relationship'. It was repealed in Scotland in 2000, but
not until 2003 in the rest of the UK.

As Rosemary Stones, one of the founder members of the Children's Rights Workshop and the 'Other Award', succinctly put it, there was:

> ...a new social climate of ridicule and alienation around equalities issues which it has become socially acceptable to dismiss as 'political correctness'. (Stones 1994)

By 1995:

> There was general agreement amongst chief executives, politicians and chief librarians that some of the contentious issues of the 1980s involving, in particular, sexism and racism were not now matters of high debate in terms of library stock holdings. (Aslib 1995, 128)

In a survey of 30 UK and 30 Canadian library directors, Ann Curry (1997) uncovered some interesting attitudes:

> 'It is a dangerous political situation to say that the library promotes social change. If you say that with a hung council ... the library will get short shrift and funding reductions down the road' (UK director). (Curry 1997, 42)

> 'Sex, politics and religion are things which one keeps to oneself. I have no objection to homosexuality, provided it is kept quiet and out of sight as that sort of thing should be. I object to it being paraded' (UK director). (Curry 1997, 224)

Conclusions

By 1997, according to Alistair Black and Dave Muddiman:

> Library services have been rationalised, reinstitutionalised and, like a 'business', required to demonstrate a degree of utilitarian efficiency. What looms as a result is a community librarianship with little sense of its ideals and a drift towards private provision and technological extinction. (Black and Muddiman 1997, 113)

Yet, at the same time, there was opposition to the proposals to turn libraries into 'businesses':

> The commercial approach is not suitable for the services we offer. Commercial attitudes are based on a different kind of motivation. For the private sector the main aim is profit, not the provision of services to meet user needs, at least not those needs that are uneconomic to provide. Public services should not

be organised or assessed in a way that assumes they simply mirror the private sector. (Pateman 1996)

However, some sparks of community librarianship still glowed, and, in the following chapters, we shall explore how public libraries reacted to a major change in political context.

Chapter 3
What is Social Exclusion?

Introduction

In this chapter, we want to consider briefly current definitions of social exclusion (and the related terms, social inclusion, community cohesion and social justice), and then look at what sorts of responses are required to each. In addition, we want to examine how these relate to wider issues, such as equality and diversity.

So, Where Shall We Start?

At the time that this work began in the UK in 1997, it was called 'social inclusion' (or, more rarely, 'tackling social exclusion'). Although some people may be arguing that 'social exclusion' as a policy priority has 'had its day', interestingly, the EU has declared 2010 as the European Year for Combating Poverty and Social Exclusion (Department for Work and Pensions 2009a).

However, if the work were to be started today, we would hope that the term 'social justice' would be used instead (although, as with any political definition, this too comes with 'baggage').

Why Social Justice?

Whilst the term 'social justice' has been core to centre-left politics for some considerable time, it came to the fore in terms of current social policy as a result of the inquiry by and final report from the Commission on Social Justice (1994, 10).

In their book on social justice, the think-tank, Institute for Public Policy Research (IPPR), talked about the four principles of social justice, which they identified as being:

- Equal citizenship
- The social minimum – 'All citizens must have access to resources that adequately meet their essential needs, and allow them to lead a secure and dignified life in today's society.'
- Equality of opportunity
- Fair distribution – of 'Resources that do not form part of equal citizenship or the social minimum' (Miller 2005, 5).

In Scotland, this work has been called 'social justice' from the start:

> Delivering social justice is no short-term fix. But with a UK Government and Scottish Executive working in partnership now we have the opportunity to deliver a better future for our children, families, neighbourhoods and Scotland.
>
> Our vision of a Scotland where everyone has the opportunity to participate to the maximum of his or her potential will require sustained effort over many years. But with determination and a readiness to embrace social justice as a common, central goal of Scottish society, it can be achieved. (Scottish Executive 1999, 17)

Yet, despite this, 'social justice' was not the term chosen in England – why was this?

Perhaps part of the reason was that it was – and is – still without a universally-agreed definition, despite being used by many politicians as the headline term for this whole area of work.

Perhaps, too, there was a reluctance to embrace this term; as David Miller argues (2005, 3):

> To pursue social justice is to believe that society can be reshaped – its major social and political institutions changed – so that each person gets a fair share of the benefits … Neo-liberals reject this idea because they believe it is destructive of a free market economy.

Whatever the reason, the term 'social justice' has tended to be less used in England.

However, at the same time, there are a growing number of useful definitions which would allow us to make it clear what we mean by 'social justice'.

For example, at a first meeting of the 'Global Greens' (the global network of Green parties and political movements) held in Australia in 2001, participants committed themselves to a Global Greens Charter; this included six guiding principles:

- Ecological wisdom
- Social justice
- Participatory democracy
- Nonviolence
- Sustainability
- Respect for diversity. (Wikipedia 2009)

The Charter (Global Greens 2001) defined social justice as:

> We assert that the key to social justice is the equitable distribution of social and natural resources, both locally and globally, to meet basic human needs

unconditionally, and to ensure that all citizens have full opportunities for personal and social development.

We declare that there is no social justice without environmental justice, and no environmental justice without social justice.

This requires

- a just organization of the world and a stable world economy which will close the widening gap between rich and poor, both within and between countries; balance the flow of resources from South to North; and lift the burden of debt on poor countries which prevents their development;
- the eradication of poverty, as an ethical, social, economic, and ecological imperative;
- the elimination of illiteracy;
- a new vision of citizenship built on equal rights for all individuals regardless of gender, race, age, religion, class, ethnic or national origin, sexual orientation, disability, wealth or health. (Global Greens 2001, 3)

Closer to home, the Welsh Assembly argued:

> Social Justice is about every one of us having the chances and opportunities to make the most of our lives and use our talents to the full. (Welsh Assembly Government no date)

The Commission on Integration and Cohesion (2007) also reinvigorated the use of the term 'social justice':

> This is a question not just of social justice – with its emphasis on fairness and an inclusive share of the benefits of economic prosperity – but of making that social justice visible to all groups in the community. It is a reflection of what we have heard about the importance of transparency in local areas where allocation of resource is being questioned ... But also of the importance of a continuing commitment to tackling inequalities for all groups – the underperformance of White working class boys at school just as much as the disproportionate disadvantage faced by Muslim groups.
>
> Visible social justice should not be about the reassertion of group identities to make progress. Our principle of shared futures applies just as much here – pigeonholing can still be damaging to integration and cohesion if it means groups privileging one identity over others to access shared resource, and relying on the difference between them as a bargaining chip. (Commission on Integration and Cohesion 2007, 98)

In 2007, the MLA organised a series of workshops to look in more depth at aspects of the *Blueprint for Excellence* (Dolan 2007), and the Social Justice and Inclusion

Topical Workshop decided to use the following as a running definition, and this is the sense in which 'social justice' is employed here:

> Giving people access to the information, services and facilities that they have a right to, and making sure that they are fully aware of and know how to take up their entitlement to these services – with a particular emphasis on providing services for the most needy. (Museums, Libraries and Archives Council 2007, 9)

Interestingly, most recently, the term 'social justice' has been used as the chosen term by the Centre for Social Justice: 'The Centre for Social Justice is an independent think tank established, by Rt Hon Iain Duncan Smith MP in 2004, to seek effective solutions to the poverty that blight parts of Britain' (Centre for Social Justice 2009).

Most recently, especially in the United States, the term 'social justice' has been taken up by different political lobbies to mean two very different things – neither of which exactly coincides with the meaning used here. Firstly, opponents of President Obama's healthcare reforms are calling this political move 'social justice', by which they mean the covert introduction of socialist policies (see, for example, Boyd 2009); and, secondly, many Christian organisations have taken up the term 'social justice' to mean specific faith-based activities (for example, Clock 2009).

Social Inclusion or Social Exclusion? Or Social Cohesion?

As noted in Chapter 2, the term 'social exclusion' originated in the social policy of the French governments of the 1980s 'and was used to refer to a disparate group of people living on the margins of society and, in particular, without access to the system of social insurance' (Percy-Smith 2000b, 1). Incidentally, some writers locate the beginnings of social exclusion as a policy term even earlier, to the 1970s (see, for example, Atkinson 2000).

From the start, there has been a range of views as to what 'social exclusion' actually is, with a number of writers (e.g. Sandell 1998; Atkinson 2000) identifying a split between those who see the social exclusion model as a relational one (for example, the relationship between marginalised communities and the mainstream) and those who see it as a way of dealing primarily with poverty, and therefore distributional.

The UK government's earliest definition of social exclusion was quite broad and limited (and this is the definition that most organisations are still using):

> a shorthand term for what can happen when people or areas suffer from a combination of linked problems such as unemployment, poor skills, low incomes, poor housing, high crime, bad health and family breakdown. (Social Exclusion Unit 2001, 10)

The importance of this definition is the flagging-up of social exclusion as 'a combination of linked problems', a recognition that it is multi-dimensional (see, for example, Room 1993) and often hard to unravel:

> Social exclusion is multidimensional, and can encompass lack of access to employment, legal redress and markets; a lack of political voice; and poor social relationships. Therefore, it is not enough to examine the issues individually, rather the links between must be explored. (Governance and Social Development Resource Centre 2006)

Versions of this definition were used – with some minor modifications – as the basis for early research into exclusion; for example, DCMS developed their work on social exclusion and libraries against a broad background definition:

> Social exclusion takes many forms. It can be direct or indirect, and can embrace both groups and individuals. Exclusion also has a geographical dimension embracing rural, urban and suburban areas alike. (DCMS 1999a, 9)

However, by 2001, the government's definition had broadened considerably:

> Social exclusion is something that *can* happen to anyone. But some people are significantly more at risk than others. Research has found that people with certain backgrounds and experiences are disproportionately likely to suffer social exclusion. The key risk-factors include: low income; family conflict; being in care; school problems; being an ex-prisoner; being from an ethnic minority; living in a deprived neighbourhood in urban and rural areas; mental health problems, age and disability. (Social Exclusion Unit 2001, 11, emphasis in original)

And, more recently:

> While social exclusion is often associated with highly marginalised groups facing extreme forms of multiple disadvantage, our approach is broader. We also include an understanding of how wider social inequality and intergenerational disadvantage can impact on the causes of social exclusion and the risk of becoming excluded.
>
> This is a deliberately pragmatic and flexible definition. One of the characteristics of social exclusion is that problems are linked and mutually reinforcing. (Social Exclusion Unit 2004, 14)

More recently still, the Social Exclusion Task Force has recognised that the issues that cause social exclusion cannot be resolved overnight – and, indeed, have long-term consequences:

Social exclusion is a short–hand term for what can happen when people or areas have a combination of problems, such as unemployment, discrimination, poor skills, low incomes, poor housing, high crime and family breakdown. These problems are linked and mutually reinforcing. Social exclusion is an extreme consequence of what happens when people do not get a fair deal throughout their lives and find themselves in difficult situations. This pattern of disadvantage can be transmitted from one generation to the next. (Social Exclusion Task Force 2009)

Work at Leeds Metropolitan University showed that there were at least seven 'dimensions' to social exclusion:

- Economic (e.g. long-term unemployment; workless households; income poverty)
- Social (e.g. homelessness; crime; disaffected youth)
- Political (e.g. disempowerment; lack of political rights; alienation from/ lack of confidence in political processes)
- Neighbourhood (e.g. decaying housing stock; environmental degradation)
- Individual (e.g. mental and physical ill health; educational underachievement)
- Spatial (e.g. concentration/marginalisation of vulnerable groups)
- Group (concentration of above characteristics in particular groups, e.g. disabled, elderly, ethnic minorities). (Taken from Percy-Smith 2000a)

In talking about social exclusion, we are focusing on the needs of groups and individuals who can be defined using the 'dimensions' listed above and who do not have access to services and facilities, or to society's decision-making and/or power structures:

There are excluders as well as victims of social exclusion, and these excluders include mainstream public services, such as health, housing and education. (Fitzpatrick 1999, quoted in Geddes 1999, 7)

Work by the World Health Organisation (WHO), published in 2003, drew together some stark, 'solid facts' which should finally dismiss any arguments that social exclusion is not a key policy issue:

Poverty, relative deprivation and social exclusion have a major impact on health and premature death, and the chances of living in poverty are loaded heavily against some social groups.

Absolute poverty – a lack of the basic material necessities of life – continues to exist, even in the richest countries of Europe. The unemployed, many ethnic minority groups, guest workers, disabled people, refugees and homeless people are at particular risk. Those living on the streets suffer the highest rates of premature death …

Social exclusion also results from racism, discrimination, stigmatization, hostility and unemployment. These processes prevent people from participating in education or training, and gaining access to services and citizenship activities. They are socially and psychologically damaging, materially costly, and harmful to health. People who live in, or have left, institutions, such as prisons, children's homes and psychiatric hospitals, are particularly vulnerable.

The greater the length of time that people live in disadvantaged circumstances, the more likely they are to suffer from a range of health problems, particularly cardiovascular disease. People move in and out of poverty during their lives, so the number of people who experience poverty and social exclusion during their lifetime is far higher than the current number of socially excluded people.

Poverty and social exclusion increase the risks of divorce and separation, disability, illness, addiction and social isolation and vice versa, forming vicious circles that deepen the predicament people face. (Wilkinson and Marmot 2003, 16–17)

In 2009, Richard Wilkinson (co-author of the WHO report) co-wrote another book of immense importance for us (Wilkinson and Pickett 2009), which argued convincingly that inequality in societies is the root cause of the majority of social, economic and health problems:

For a species which thrives on friendship and enjoys co-operation and trust, which has a strong sense of fairness, which is equipped with mirror neurons allowing us to learn our way of life through a process of identification, it is clear that social structures which create relationships based on inequality, inferiority and social exclusion must inflict a great deal of social pain. In this light we can perhaps begin not only to see why more unequal societies are so socially dysfunctional but, through that, perhaps also to feel more confident that a more humane society may be a great deal more practical than the highly unequal ones in which so many of us live now. (Wilkinson and Pickett 2009, 213)

Finally, some of the early work on social exclusion in the UK proposed that, rather than seeing 'exclusion', 'inclusion' and 'cohesion' as three separate policy strands, in fact they should be seen as a continuum:

At the exclusion end, the focus is on alleviating and eliminating the exclusion. Social inclusion adds to the exclusion focus the need both to satisfy the moral concerns of the rest of the population that people should not be excluded, and to ensure that the included do not suffer the 'spill-over' effects that can come from some aspects of exclusion such as crime or the costs of tackling exclusion. Finally, social cohesion adds to the aims of tackling exclusion and promoting inclusion the wish to do so within the context of a civil society whose cohesion is based on mutual links between people, that is, 'social capital'.

It is highly likely that, in any one local area, there will be at least some activity taking place at each point on the continuum. The strategic question is therefore not, 'on which part of the continuum should one's efforts be focused', but 'what should be the balance of efforts and connections between the different elements?' For example, should further effort be focused on social exclusion? In the end, it can be argued, it is the socially excluded who are suffering the most and so focusing solely on their needs might at least ensure that something gets done. On the other hand, if it was felt that there would be public resistance to focusing resources on the socially excluded, then social inclusion might be a more viable focus. Such concerns could be assuaged by explaining the benefits to socially excluded people or appealing to their moral sensitivities. Social cohesion would be a natural focus for people who are concerned to unify the work of tackling social exclusion into wider agendas such as democratic renewal and the development of sustainable communities and environments. In the end, deciding where to focus on the continuum will involve a balance between pay-offs, feasibility, legitimacy and the possibility of making links with other policy agendas. (Miller and King 1999, 8–9)

We refer later in this book to this 'journey'.

Social (or community) cohesion has also taken on additional layers of meaning and interpretation, and these are explored briefly below.

The European Context

At the same time as work was developing in the UK, policy was also being developed across Europe:

The Lisbon and Nice European Councils (in March and December 2000 respectively) set out a strategy for combating poverty and social exclusion in Europe. It was agreed that all member states of the European Union (EU) should aim to make a 'decisive impact' on social exclusion by 2010. The strategy is built on the Open Method of Co-ordination, which requires member states to produce their own policies within EU-level guidelines. In 2006, all EU countries, including the UK, produced annual national reports on strategies for social protection and social inclusion. (Department for Work and Pensions *c*.2006)

In order to fulfil this requirement, the UK government, together with the devolved administrations, have been producing regular National Action Plans on social inclusion (the latest is Department for Work and Pensions 2008).

Also, between 1999 and 2007, the government published an annual review of progress, *Opportunity for All*, which assessed progress against specific targets (the last report was Department for Work and Pensions 2007).

Social Exclusion and the Social Exclusion Unit

On 14 August 1997, Peter Mandelson (the then Minister without Portfolio) gave a Fabian Society summer lecture (Mandelson 1997) in which he announced that the government was going to set up a unit in the Cabinet Office to focus action against poverty and social exclusion.

The Work of the Social Exclusion Unit

The Social Exclusion Unit was launched by the government in December 1997; its remit was for England only, but parallel initiatives were developed in the other three Home Nations:

- The Scottish Social Inclusion Strategy (Scottish Office 1999)
- *Building an Inclusive Wales* (Great Britain, Welsh Office 1999)
- New Targeting Social Need, launched in Northern Ireland in July 1998 (see, for example, Northern Ireland Assembly. Research and Library Services 2001)

The Social Exclusion Unit began its work by carrying out a series of consultations and visits, through which it started to analyse why it was that, despite considerable attention having been paid to the regeneration of poor neighbourhoods (particularly since the 1960s), progress had been very slow and 'the condition of many of the most deprived areas has either not improved or in some cases, has actually worsened' (Social Exclusion Unit 1998, 34).

Some of the reasons for this were economic, some social, but it also became clear that 'Government policies and the way they have been implemented have often exacerbated these problems' (Social Exclusion Unit 1998, 34).

The lessons were summarised as:

- mainstream policies not helping, or making it worse;
- 'initiative-itis';
- too many rules;
- lack of local cooperation;
- too little investment in people;
- strategies not joined up;
- 'poor links beyond the neighbourhood' (i.e. where policy has increased detachment of certain neighbourhoods);
- community commitment not harnessed;

- 'what works' neglected (adapted from Social Exclusion Unit 1998, 38–40).

Yet, at the same time, the Social Exclusion Unit was able to identify a number of places where 'all the pieces of the jigsaw are put in place' (Social Exclusion Unit 1998, 40), and good results had been achieved.

These lessons learned were then applied via a number of new national programmes to tackle social exclusion (such as welfare reform) backed by research of the Unit; and new area-based programmes, such as the New Deal for Communities (Communities and Local Government *c*.2005).

The Social Exclusion Unit and the Policy Action Teams

The Social Exclusion Unit also identified that, despite these two initiatives, there would still be gaps where policy and coordination ought to be improved. To tackle this, the government began a process of policy development, involving 18 cross-cutting teams made up of civil servants and people with experience of working in poor neighbourhoods and dealing with the issues involved.

These 18 teams each addressed a different priority area (see below) and all investigated the following five themes:

- getting the people to work;
- getting the place to work;
- building a future for young people;
- access to services;
- making the government work better (adapted from Social Exclusion Unit 1998, 57).

The 18 priority areas were:

1. Jobs
2. Skills
3. Business
4. Neighbourhood management
5. Housing management
6. Neighbourhood wardens
7. Unpopular housing
8. Anti-social behaviour
9. Community self-help
10. Arts and sport
11. 'Schools Plus'
12. Young people
13. Shops
14. Financial services
15. Information technology

16. Learning lessons
17. Joining it up locally
18. Better information

Each of these 18 Policy Action Teams produced a report; however, libraries (and museums and archives) were barely mentioned. The PAT 10 report (Policy Action Team 10 *c*.1999) did mention museums, especially in a couple of case studies, but references to libraries are in passing, and mostly related to their potential in terms of electronic service delivery. The PAT 15 report (Policy Action Team 15 2000) mentioned libraries in its remit statement, but never again!

Nevertheless, despite this, the Policy Action Team reports heralded a new focus on the potential for libraries to tackle social exclusion, which led, for example, to the publication of *Libraries for All ...* (DCMS 1999a) and the focus by Resource/ MLA on tackling social exclusion as a key element of its work (for more about this, see Chapter 5).

Social Exclusion Unit Research

As noted above, the Unit backed its new national programmes by carrying out extensive research which provided the evidence and impetus to develop new provision urgently.

This research included:

- young people not in education, employment or training (Social Exclusion Unit 1999);
- young runaways (Office of the Deputy Prime Minister 2002);
- the education of children in care (Office of the Deputy Prime Minister 2003);
- mental health (Office of the Deputy Prime Minister 2004);
- young adults with complex needs (Social Exclusion Unit 2005).

'Taking Stock'

In 2004, the Unit published an important 'taking stock' review of progress since 1997 (Social Exclusion Unit 2004). The report concluded that whilst 'much has been achieved up to now, the scale of the problem remains large' (Social Exclusion Unit 2004, 5).

The report identified:

> five key problems that continue to drive social exclusion, and that need to be
> made priorities over the next few years if overall progress is not to be held back.
> These are: low educational attainment among some groups; economic inactivity
> and concentrations of worklessness; health inequalities; concentrations of

crime and poor quality environments in some areas; and homelessness. (Social Exclusion Unit 2004, 5)

In addition, it recognised that 'Progress made by individuals can also be fragile, and is not always sustained' (Social Exclusion Unit 2004, 5).

The Social Exclusion Task Force

In 2006, the Social Exclusion Unit was closed, and the Social Exclusion Task Force established in its place.

> [The Unit] is deemed to have lost influence since its high water mark in Labour's first term. It was then based in the Cabinet Office and reported to Tony Blair directly.
>
> Critics claim its reports have had increasingly limited impact and failed to lever open the necessary funding. Others argue its open style of working has meant it has become too sensitive to the views of pressure groups.
>
> The aim is now to get social exclusion work more deeply embedded in the relevant departments – health, education and communities. A small taskforce, partly staffed by members of Mr Blair's strategy unit and the old social exclusion unit, will be set up in the Cabinet Office to prepare a detailed action plan. (Wintour 2006)

> The aim of the Social Exclusion Task Force is to extend opportunity to the least advantaged so that they enjoy more of the choices, chances and power that the rest of society takes for granted. Social exclusion has its roots in poor early years, is compounded by the absence of basics such as a job and a home, and is often left unsolved by public services working in silos. The Social Exclusion Task Force aims to correct this. We work with the rest of government to identify priorities, test solutions, and facilitate collaboration across government. (Social Exclusion Task Force 2009)

In 2006, the Task Force published its Action Plan, *Reaching Out* (Social Exclusion Task Force 2006). The Action Plan began by celebrating the successes to date:

> This Action Plan shows that through early identification, support and preventative action positive change is possible. We can tackle problems before they become fully entrenched and blight the lives of both individuals and wider society. (Social Exclusion Task Force 2006, 8)

However, at the same time:

> Some might ask why this agenda is still important, particularly against a background of general success. The Government's view is that it is precisely

because of those successes that it is vital to do more. No civilised country should ignore the plight of the most excluded in society and no one should be shut off from the opportunities, choices and options in life which most of us take for granted. (Social Exclusion Task Force 2006, 8)

Interestingly, the underlying economic reasons for continuing with this work also came to the surface:

Tackling social exclusion also matters because failing to do so creates a cost for society. The UK has enjoyed a strong economy and growing prosperity in recent years, but we would be even more prosperous if the talents of each and every member of the community could flourish. The need today to act to ensure that opportunity is enjoyed by the whole community is ever more urgent and demands a response from government. (Social Exclusion Task Force 2006, 8)

This Action Plan, therefore, set the course for the next phase of the government's work. It identified five key guiding principles:

1. better identification and earlier intervention;
2. systematically identifying 'what works';
3. promoting multi-agency working;
4. personalisation, rights and responsibilities;
5. supporting achievement and managing underperformance.

It also identified the need for a 'lifetime approach':

System reform can take years to deliver, and results can take decades to show. We will supplement our drive for deeper reform with more focused and immediate action that we are confident will make a difference. This Action Plan establishes a range of specific proposals that we believe to be of pivotal importance throughout an individual's lifetime, both in terms of their impact on the life chances of the most excluded and in order to strengthen the case for wider reforms. (Social Exclusion Task Force 2006, 10)

Through this, it focused on the early years; children and teenagers – particularly 'children in care, teenage parents and those with the lowest educational achievement' (Social Exclusion Task Force 2006, 10) – and adults living chaotic lives.

The Task Force also carried out research into the 'multi-dimensional' aspects of social exclusion, which led to another revised definition:

Social exclusion is a complex and multi-dimensional process. It involves the lack or denial of resources, rights, goods and services, and the inability to participate in the normal relationships and activities, available to the majority of people in a society, whether in economic, social, cultural or political arenas. It affects both the quality of life of individuals and the equity and cohesion of society as a whole. (Levitas et al. 2007a, 9)

This research also identified what they called 'severe' or 'deep' exclusion:

Deep exclusion refers to exclusion across more than one domain or dimension of disadvantage, resulting in severe negative consequences for quality of life, well-being and future life chances. (Levitas et al. 2007a, 9)

As a result, the research team constructed a matrix that looked across four stages of the life course: childhood, youth, working-age adulthood and later life (Levitas et al. 2007b).

This matrix, the *Bristol Social Exclusion Matrix*, or B-SEM, contains 10 dimensions or domains of potential importance in social exclusion:

Resources:	Material/economic resources
	Access to public and private services
	Social resources
Participation:	Economic participation
	Social participation
	Culture, education and skills
	Political and civic participation
Quality of life:	Health and well-being
	Living environment
	Crime, harm and criminalisation.

(Levitas et al. 2007a, 10)

This analytical tool has been used most recently to begin to clarify the risks of exclusion that people face at different stages in their lives. The Task Force has published four pieces of research as part of its 'Understanding the risks of social exclusion across the life course' project, which identify issues faced by families with children (Oroyemi et al. 2009); young people (Cusworth et al. 2009); working age adults without dependent children (Fahmy et al. 2009); and older people (Becker and Boreham 2009).

So, Where Has Social Exclusion Got to Across the UK?

This section will look briefly at activity both UK-wide and specific to Scotland, Wales and Northern Ireland. Whilst key aspects of this agenda (e.g. social security policy and taxation) are reserved to the UK government, many of the critical policy levers are devolved to the administrations in Scotland, Wales and Northern Ireland.

From the outline given above, it is clear that, since 1997, the UK government has made some huge advances in tackling social exclusion.

However, at the same time, serious flaws in policy, omissions and, perhaps, a major under-realisation of the scale of the problem have emerged. This is, frankly, disappointing, as writers and researchers had been making it clear from the start that social exclusion was a problem that required long-term solutions: 'All of this will take time (perhaps 10 or 20 years)' (Atkinson 2000, 1050).

For example:

> The anti-poverty strategy appears to have run out of steam not because it is fundamentally flawed, but because the government has taken its foot of the pedal. (Sefton et al. 2009, 44)

And:

> Labour's agenda for tackling poverty and disadvantage among children was serious and wide-ranging, but with the benefit of hindsight, it is clear that policies did not match the scale of the challenge …
>
> In reality, very little has changed since 2004. Expenditure on tax credits and benefits, which had risen sharply in each year since 1999, has flattened out, with the expected impact on child poverty. Progress in reducing worklessness has also stalled. (Stewart 2009, 68)

Recent work by the Institute for Fiscal Studies (Brewer et al. 2009a), which tracked income inequality in Britain since 1968, has shown a continuing trend in income inequality:

> The most important drivers of increased inequality appear to be occupation – with a widening earnings gap between unskilled workers and professional/ managerial workers – and education, with increasing relative wages among better-educated members of the workforce throughout the 1980's. This finding is consistent with the idea that 'skills-biased technological change' was responsible for much of the increase in inequality – with new technologies complementing the work of skilled and educated workers, but substituting for the work of lower-skilled workers.
>
> However, our analysis also provides grounds for humility – there is still much about inequality changes over the past four decades which remains unexplained. Individuals' observable characteristics (at least the ones we have in our data) account for only a fraction of total inequality – rarely as much as half. Indeed, the unexplained ('residual') portion of inequality increases over time, suggesting that incomes have become more dispersed even within tightly defined groups. (Brewer et al. 2009b)

As noted elsewhere in this book, a recent report from the Social Exclusion Task Force (Fahmy et al. 2009) also made it clear that there are continuing problems with social exclusion: '2.6 million adults experience social exclusion' (University of Bristol 2009).

In relation to child poverty, the latest position is as follows:

> In 1999, the UK Government announced its aim to eradicate child poverty by 2020, and this pledge will soon be enshrined in legislation. Since the commitment was announced, 500,000 children have been lifted out of relative poverty (before housing costs), and a further 1.7 million children have been lifted out of absolute poverty. Despite this progress, 2.9 million children are still living in relative poverty in the UK. Two of the key reasons for this are: living in a home where no-one works – two fifths of poor children live in lone parent families, the majority of whom are without work; being in a two parent family where one adult or more works part-time. The UK Government's comprehensive strategy for tackling child poverty is based on:
>
> - Increasing employment and raising incomes: helping people who can work to move into employment and progress in work
> - Financial and material support: providing additional resources for when work does not pay, or when families cannot work
> - Improving poor children's life chances: improving opportunities and outcomes for children from low-income families. (Department for Work and Pensions 2009b, 3)

Recent research has also highlighted the major impact that poverty has had on children and their families over the last 10 years:

> This heavy hand of poverty overlays family life and permeates economic and social relationships. It makes everyday life difficult and uncertain and family equilibrium is easily destabilised or undermined by external and internal shocks. Unemployment, sickness, disability and family upheaval create circumstances of change and uncertainty for all families but the added pressures and restrictions of poverty leave deprived families highly vulnerable to instability, homelessness, debt and social retreat. The conditions of poverty make the daily demands of parenting particularly challenging, and although parents strive to protect their children and put them first this is often at great personal cost, particularly for women. (Ridge 2009, 93)

Statistics released by the government in November 2009 showed that, in England alone, some 304,000 children were identified as being in need (Department for Schools, Children and Families 2009).

As columnist Deborah Orr put it:

The progressive agenda may have faltered in many respects over recent decades. But in challenging the evils of racism, homophobia and sexism, fantastic success has been achieved. Mainstream British attitudes, in the last 30 years, have been transformed …

This is social progress, of course. But it is not the progress that the left once envisaged. On the contrary, in the same time as the argument for diversity has made such strides, the increased equality that was assumed to be part of its goal, has not materialised at all. Instead, inequality in Britain is now much greater than it was prior to the success of its various 'equality' campaigns …

Does this matter? Is it important to understand that diversity and equality are different things, and that they are sometimes even at odds with each other? After all, the rooting out of discrimination achieves social justice, whether in the name of diversity or equality. (Orr 2009)

To take one other example, whilst there have been improvements in the attainment of and provision for looked-after children and young people, nevertheless, a recent report said, damningly:

Despite over a decade of reforming legislation and initiatives, the treatment of many children in care and those leaving the care system deserves to be a source of national shame. These children too often go on to experience lives characterised by unemployment, homelessness, mental illness and addiction. (Centre for Social Justice 2008, 11)

Social mobility – or rather the lack of it – has also been in the headlines in 2009, with, for example, the publication of Alan Milburn's report on the professions (Panel on Fair Access to the Professions 2009) and the work undertaken by the Sutton Trust (see, for example, Sutton Trust 2009). Importantly, there is data to show that the lack of social mobility is having an impact on a wide range of children and young people:

The data we have seen suggests that tomorrow's professional is today growing up in a family richer than seven in ten of all families in the UK. If the growth in social exclusivity, that our report details, is not checked it will be more and more middle class children, not just working class ones, who will miss out. Take internships: they tend to go to the few who have the right connections not the many who have talent. Or careers advice in schools: the Connexions service seems to have focussed on the disadvantaged minority to the detriment of the aspirational majority. Across the board too many able children from average income and middle class families are losing out in the race for professional jobs. If the aspirations that most hard-working families have for themselves, their children and their communities are thwarted, then social responsibility and individual endeavour are both undermined. (Panel on Fair Access to the Professions 2009, 6)

However, it is also worth noting the conclusions reached by the Joseph Rowntree Foundation research (Hills et al. 2009a):

> The findings of this book will come as a disappointment to two groups of readers: those who might have hoped that a Labour government in power for over a decade would decisively reverse the gaps in society that had widened over the previous two decades; and those who – perhaps dominated by the rows over lone-parent benefits and the 10 pence tax abolition that bracket our period – were expecting to see a simple picture showing the betrayal of egalitarian ideals.
>
> The picture is more complex and nuanced. In several key respects, the UK *was* a somewhat more equal society after 10 years of New Labour government …
>
> But, at the same time, incomes at the very top – especially for the top 1 per cent, and even within it – grew much more rapidly than the average, while incomes of the poorest 10 per cent grew much more slowly. Wealth inequality continued to grow, and so did a wide range of measures of inequalities in health outcomes. (Hills et al. 2009b, 357–8)

To sum up:

> The UK's experience in the 1980s and 1990s showed that the laissez-faire strategy of hoping that rapid growth in living standards at the top would 'trickle down' to those at the bottom did not work. The last decade has shown that a more interventionist strategy of 'pump up' is hard. The period since 1997 shows that gains are possible, but they require continuous effort to be sustained. (Hills et al. 2009b, 359)

Finally, at the beginning of 2010, the National Equality Panel produced its final report (Hills et al. 2010a). The Panel had been 'set up to document the relationships between inequalities in people's economic outcomes – such as earnings, incomes and wealth – and their characteristics and circumstances – such as gender, age or ethnicity' (Hills et al. 2010b, 1):

> The report draws out some over-arching themes, including:
>
> - Inequalities in earnings and incomes are high in Britain, both compared with other industrialised countries, and compared with thirty years ago. Over the most recent decade according to some measures, earnings inequality has narrowed a little and income inequality has stabilised, but the large inequality growth between the late 1970s and early 1990s has not been reversed.
> - Some of the widest gaps in outcomes between social groups have narrowed in the last decade, particularly between the earnings of women and men, and in the educational qualifications of different ethnic groups.

- However, there remain deep-seated and systematic differences in economic outcomes between social groups across all of the dimensions we have examined – including between men and women, between different ethnic groups, between social class groups, between those living in disadvantaged and other areas, and between London and other parts of the country.
- Despite the elimination and even reversal of the differences in educational qualifications that often explain employment rates and relative pay, significant differences remain between men and women and between ethnic groups.
- Importantly, however, differences in outcomes between the more and less advantaged *within* each social group, however the population is classified, are usually only a little narrower than those across the population as a whole. They are much greater than differences *between* groups. Even if all differences between such groups were removed, overall economic inequalities would remain wide.
- The inequality growth of the last forty years is mostly attributable to growing gaps within social groups, however those groups are defined. The pattern of the last decade has been more mixed, with the effects of growing inequality within some groups offset by narrowing gaps between them.
- Many of the differences we examine cumulate across the life cycle, especially those related to people's socio-economic background. We see this before children enter school, through the school years, through entry into the labour market, and on to retirement, wealth and resources for retirement, and mortality rates in later life. Economic advantage and disadvantage reinforce themselves across the life cycle, and often on to the next generation. By implication, policy interventions to counter this are needed at each life cycle stage.
- A fundamental aim of people with widely differing political perspectives is to achieve 'equality of opportunity', but doing so is very hard when there are such wide differences between the resources which people and their families have to help them fulfil their diverse potentials. (Hills et al. 2010b, 1)

Work to Tackle Social Exclusion in Scotland

Drawing on the work that had already been started by the Social Exclusion Unit in England, in March 1999 the Scottish Office published their report (Scottish Office 1999) on the programme to promote social inclusion in Scotland, which was based on the principles of:

an underlying commitment to the empowerment of individuals and communities, and an emphasis on prevention as the most effective and sustainable way of tackling social exclusion in the long term. The report also describes the four strands of our action programme – promoting opportunities, tackling barriers to inclusion, promoting inclusion among children and young people, and building stronger communities   a programme that is opening the door to a better Scotland. (Scottish Office 1999, Foreword)

This was followed in November of the same year by their report (Scottish Executive 1999) detailing targets and milestones against which progress would be measured.

From 2000 to 2003, the Executive reported its progress against targets and milestones in the Social Justice Annual Report (see, for example Scottish Executive 2000, 2001; Scottish Government 2006).

From 2004, the social justice strategy was refocused with the *Closing the Opportunity Gap* approach:

Six Closing the Opportunity Gap objectives were launched on July 12, 2004:

- To increase the chances of sustained employment for vulnerable and disadvantaged groups – in order to lift them permanently out of poverty
- To improve the confidence and skills of the most disadvantaged children and young people – in order to provide them with the greatest chance of avoiding poverty when they leave school;
- To reduce the vulnerability of low income families to financial exclusion and multiple debts – in order to prevent them becoming over-indebted and/or to lift them out of poverty;
- To regenerate the most disadvantaged neighbourhoods – in order that people living there can take advantage of job opportunities and improve their quality of life;
- To increase the rate of improvement of the health status of people living in the most deprived communities – in order to improve their quality of life, including their employability prospects; and
- To improve access to high quality services for the most disadvantaged groups and individuals in rural communities – in order to improve their quality of life and enhance their access to opportunity. (Scottish Government 2008b)

Following a period of consultation, the Scottish Government published a new framework in November 2008 (Scottish Government 2008a), which:

sets out further priorities for action and investment to deliver improvement across four main areas:

- reducing income inequalities
- introducing longer-term measures to tackle poverty and the drivers of low income
- supporting those experiencing poverty or at risk of falling into poverty
- making the tax credits and benefits system work better for Scotland.

The Framework provides the context for future action while setting out some immediate steps. It sets out the ways in which the Scottish Government will support partners and strengthen the infrastructure necessary for successful action, and it sets out the contribution needed from wider Scottish society. (Scottish Government 2008a, 4)

Whilst there has been much progress in tackling social exclusion, there have also been growing concerns about the ability to assess the impact of the programmes, as:

Reliable and comparable information about the change in small areas is not available … Where change has come about, it can be difficult to attribute the reason for that change. It may have come about because of dedicated programmes, local mainstream programmes, national programmes or significant change in the local or national economy. It may have resulted from a significant change as a result of new build housing or demolition or from population 'churn' in the area. In many senses, if positive change is achieved, this should be welcomed without the need to allocate the reasons precisely. But understanding what has made the impact is an important part of learning about what works – and replicating this success in other areas. (Fyfe 2009, 23)

Incidentally, Andrew Fyfe identified that this was not only a Scottish issue, but a UK-wide one:

Across Britain there is a lack of solid evidence of the overall impact of geographically targeted programmes on multiple deprivation. (Fyfe 2009, 22)

In his assessment, described as 'a comprehensive analysis of the impact of devolution on social policy, based on the experience of all three countries' (Birrell 2009, 1), Derek Birrell summed up the position in Scotland as:

Scotland clearly has formulated and implemented distinctive social policies and developed coherent underpinning narratives. It has developed the capacity for policy analysis, shaping policies to match what are defined as Scotland's needs and engaging the public in policy formulation and implementation. (Birrell 2009, 184)

Most recently, the Scottish Government and the Convention of Scottish Local Authorities (COSLA) have issued a joint statement that:

> confirms the ongoing commitment of government at national and local level to addressing the socio-economic disparities that exist between our most deprived communities, entire local authority areas, and the rest of Scotland. (Scottish Government and COSLA 2009, 2)

Work to Tackle Social Exclusion in Wales

In 2001, the Welsh Assembly Government published its forward plan which set out its commitments to tackling social exclusion, to equality and to sustainable development (Welsh Assembly Government 2001). This was followed by the launch of the Communities First programme:

> [it] initially worked with 142 communities comprising of the 100 most deprived wards from the Welsh Index of Multiple Deprivation (WIMD) 2000, 32 pockets of deprivation and 10 Communities of Interest ... Following the publication of the WIMD 2005, a further 46 areas identified by the Index as being in the 10 per cent most deprived in Wales and were invited to apply for inclusion in the Programme. There are now a total of 188 Communities First areas, some of which are working with existing Communities Partnerships for inclusion in the programme and other larger areas are establishing their own Communities First Partnerships.
>
> Communities First is now moving forward into a new phase which will include a greater focus on outcomes and on addressing the causes and effects of poverty ... The vision for Communities First in its next stage has been summarised as a programme which will mobilise and enable local people to contribute to the regeneration of their communities in practical ways, in line with their local priorities and those of statutory bodies such as the Assembly Government, local authorities and health bodies. (Communities First/Cymunedau yn Gyntaf *c*.2009)

In 2003, the Welsh Assembly Government published a new strategic plan which sets out:

> our guiding vision of a fairer, more prosperous, healthier and better educated country, rooted in our commitment to social justice and to putting health and wealth creation that is sustainable at the heart of policy-making. (Welsh Assembly Government 2003, 1)

In 2007, the Labour and Plaid Cymru Groups in the National Assembly came to an agreement via the 'One Wales' policy:

Shared values, common goals and joint aspirations for the people of Wales will drive this four-year programme for government. It offers a progressive agenda for improving the quality of life of people in all of Wales's communities, from all walks of life, and especially the most vulnerable and disadvantaged.

The people of Wales, and their government, face unprecedented challenges. Working together, we have devised a programme of government which meets these challenges head on. Our ambition is no less than to transform Wales into a self-confident, prosperous, healthy nation and society, which is fair to all.

Our joint commitment to the principles of social justice, sustainability and inclusivity – of the whole of Wales and for all its people – run throughout this programme. These principles underpin the programme and are fundamental to its success.

In devising this programme, we have explicitly recognised the diversity of Wales – geographically, socially, linguistically and culturally. We propose a comprehensive programme of government, for the full four year term, which covers the whole spectrum of policy and action. (Welsh Assembly Government 2007, 5)

The Welsh Assembly Government is delivering much of this work through its Department for Social Justice and Local Government, the mission of which is to:

improve and deliver excellent public services in Wales, with a particular emphasis on safeguarding and supporting vulnerable people, combating social exclusion and reducing inequality, and promoting safe and sustainable communities; and on supporting and funding local government to deliver these and other objectives. (Welsh Assembly Government *c*.2009)

In 2007, the Equality and Human Rights Commission commissioned a review of the research literature on equality in Wales, and this was published early in 2009 (Winckler 2009). This review found it extremely difficult to assess progress:

The evidence on poverty and social exclusion is fragmented, and suffers from methodological problems e.g. high refusal rates and inconsistent definitions. Nevertheless, there is sufficient evidence to conclude that ethnic minority groups, women, disabled people, children and young people and older people experience poverty and social exclusion to a greater extent than other groups. However, there is almost no evidence on religion and sexual orientation. (Winckler 2009, iv)

The report concluded:

There is an urgent requirement to address the massive research deficit, not only by commissioning more one-off studies (much though they are needed), but through a clear strategic lead. This is necessary to ensure that the not inconsiderable effort and expenditure on Welsh Assembly Government surveys produces data that can be analysed by equality strand, and that Assembly Government-commissioned studies are sensitive to equality issues. There is also a need to ensure that research by UK government departments adequately takes account of specific circumstances in Wales and presents findings accordingly. Within government bodies, the commissioning of research needs to be done on a more systematic basis than is apparent at present, so a body of knowledge about equality in Wales can begin to be built up. Those undertaking academic research need to be encouraged to value Welsh-specific studies and to share their findings with the Welsh policy community as well as the academic community elsewhere. (Winckler 2009, 200)

Given this, it is very difficult to analyse just how successful initiatives to tackle social exclusion across Wales have been.

This has been borne out by a report by the Welsh Audit Office, evaluating the 'Communities First' programme; this shows that, whilst there have been successes (for example, successful partnerships established and local gains made), the programme is unlikely to meet its targets unless there is a 'more robust approach to programme bending' (Wales Audit Office 2009, 6):

'programme bending' – ensuring money and support from various public programmes and organisations are directed to Communities First areas. (Wales Audit Office 2009, 6)

Derek Birrell's analysis was that there had been limited development, but:

The Welsh Executive and Assembly are able to formulate policies, strategies and actions, whether different or not from the other UK countries, determined in Wales by elected representatives and aligned to the needs of the Welsh people. (Birrell 2009, 184–5)[1]

Work to Tackle Social Exclusion in Northern Ireland

The New Targeting Social Need policy (which continued previous work, following criticisms of the then Targeting Social Need policy) was introduced in 1998 'to tackle social need and social exclusion in Northern Ireland, by targeting efforts

---

1 The Welsh Assembly Government launched in December 2009 their new Community Cohesion Strategy (Welsh Assembly Government 2009b, which 'focuses on those policy and service delivery areas that research has shown can have a significant impact on how well a community gets on together – housing; learning; communication; promoting equality and social inclusion and preventing violent extremism and strengthening community cohesion' (Welsh Assembly Government 2009a).

and available resources on people, groups and areas in the greatest social need' (Northern Ireland Assembly. Research and Library Services 2001, 1).

In 2006, the Assembly adopted the 'Lifetime Opportunities' policy (Office of the First Minister and Deputy First Minister 2006) which is the government's Anti-Poverty and Social Inclusion Strategy for Northern Ireland. In its conclusions, this report stated:

> From the quantitative analysis it was evident that there had been much progress in reducing socio-economic differentials between the two main communities, which had been an explicit objective of New Targeting Social Need. However, despite the steady growth in the Northern Ireland economy and corresponding growth in employment, levels of income poverty have remained persistently high and labour market inequalities remain. Economic inactivity and benefit dependence in Northern Ireland are higher than in any other region in the United Kingdom and lone parents and people with disabilities have emerged as groups significantly more at risk of poverty now than previously. The risk of poverty is higher in rural areas and in urban areas experiencing multiple deprivation. In addition while certain areas show the benefits of intervention, other areas have become more deprived and in a core of neighbourhoods, multiple deprivation has persisted over a long period of time. (Office of the First Minister and Deputy First Minister 2006, 67)

A later announcement stated:

> The strategy outlines what will be done by the Northern Ireland Departments and the Northern Ireland Office over a period of fourteen years in achieving its overall objectives of working towards:
>
> - the elimination of poverty and social exclusion in Northern Ireland by 2020;
> - halving child poverty by 2010 on the way to eradicating child poverty by 2020.
>
> The strategy is structured into four key life stages. Early Years (0-4), Children and Young People (5-16), Working Age Adults and Older Citizens.
>   The Anti-Poverty and Social Inclusion strategy is described as retaining the key principle of New Targeting Social Need which is to direct resources within government programmes at those areas, groups and individuals in greatest objective need. (Northern Ireland Assembly. Research and Library Services 2008, 1)

Again, Derek Birrell's analysis was that:

> Social policy issues do not dominate political party agendas even if the population view health and education issues as important. (Birrell 2009, 185)

This has led to a lack of innovation in social policy and delays in introducing new policies from Great Britain.

Community Cohesion

As noted above, the term 'social cohesion' had originally been seen as part of a continuum (from exclusion, via inclusion, to cohesion), although there was also work being undertaken in the UK (e.g. Forrest and Kearns 1999) and elsewhere (e.g. Putnam 2000) that argued that cohesion was more about the 'knitting-together' of communities.

During the spring and summer of 2001, there were a number of disturbances in towns and cities in England (including Bradford, Burnley, Oldham and Stoke-on-Trent). The government's response was to establish a Ministerial Group on Public Order and Community Cohesion whose role it was to 'examine and consider how national policies might be used to promote better community cohesion, based upon shared values and a celebration of diversity' (Denham 2001).

At the same time, the Home Secretary also established a Review Team, led by Ted Cantle:

> to seek the views of local residents and community leaders in the affected towns and in other parts of England on the issues which need to be addressed to bring about social cohesion and also to identify good practice in the handling of these issues at local level. (Denham 2001; Home Office 2001b)

The Ministerial Group on Public Order and Community Cohesion initially defined community cohesion as:

> a shared sense of belonging based on common goals and core social values, respect for difference (ethnic, cultural and religious), and acceptance of the reciprocal rights and obligations of community members working together for the common good. (Home Office 2001a, 18)

In July 2005, there was a series of bombings in London, and, in the aftermath of those, questions began to be asked about the nature of British society. For example:

How can different groups:

- peacefully co-exist
- respect differences but avoid isolation and segregation

- work together to develop a shared sense of belonging and purpose? (IDeA 2008)

In June 2006, Ruth Kelly, then Secretary of State for Communities and Local Government announced the creation of the Commission on Integration and Cohesion. The Commission had the following brief:

to consider how local areas themselves can play a role in forging cohesive and resilient communities, by:

- Examining the issues that raise tensions between different groups in different areas, and that lead to segregation and conflict
- Suggesting how local community and political leadership can push further against perceived barriers to cohesion and integration
- Looking at how local communities themselves can be empowered to tackle extremist ideologies
- Developing approaches that build local areas' own capacity to prevent problems, and ensure they have the structures in place to recover from periods of tension. (Commission on Integration and Cohesion 2007, 17)

It produced its final report, *Our Shared Future*, in June 2007 (Commission on Integration and Cohesion 2007). Following this, Communities and Local Government, the Improvement and Development Agency (IDeA) and the Local Government Association (LGA) agreed a new definition:[2]

Community Cohesion is what must happen in all communities to enable different groups of people to get on well together. A key contributor to community cohesion is integration which is what must happen to enable new residents and existing residents to adjust to one another.

Our vision of an integrated and cohesive community is based on three foundations:

1. People from different backgrounds having similar life opportunities
2. People knowing their rights and responsibilities
3. People trusting one another and trusting local institutions to act fairly.

And three key ways of living together:

1. A shared future vision and sense of belonging
2. A focus on what new and existing communities have in common, alongside a recognition of the value of diversity

---

2   There is a useful summary of the development of thinking around community cohesion on the ICOCO website (Institute of Community Cohesion 2009a).

3. Strong and positive relationships between people from different backgrounds. (IDeA 2008)

IDeA suggested that:

> [The report] has shifted away from concentrating on 'race and faith' and 'tension and disturbance' to the importance of positive relations. It champions helping people fulfil their potential and feel a positive sense of belonging to an area or community. (IDeA 2008)

However, this is not everybody's view! There are still commentators who see 'community cohesion' primarily as a way of dealing with faith and race issues (e.g. Number10.gov.uk 2007; Institute of Community Cohesion 2009b); and some who have seen the notion as flawed from the start. In a lead article in *Race and Class*, Jonathan Burnett argued that 'Without doubt, the ideological basis of community cohesion is exclusionary in its nature' (Burnett 2004, 15).

Starting by examining media coverage of the 2001 riots, Burnett suggested that the image of the Asian communities involved were manipulated to fit two dangerous stereotypes: Asians as criminals, and Asians as 'fundamentalists' – both of which led to 'the emergence of a language that bespeaks the enemy within' (Burnett 2004, 7). He then argued that community cohesion was:

> established as a value-driven, theoretical perception, one that makes assumptions about the identities and beliefs of those who come under its remit. Crucially, it encompasses not only what communities do and how they act, but their self-perception and sense of allegiance ... The role of the state, then, is to regulate citizenship and moral values in the drive for cohesive communities. (Burnett 2004, 8)

What is particularly interesting for those of us who work in the public sector is that there is a belief that by having a building or other space available and used by a cross-section of a community automatically equates to community cohesion – however, recent work has begun to suggest otherwise:

> However, just because diverse individuals and groups live in a mixed community doesn't necessarily mean that they will form positive relationships with each other. In fact, the opposite can be true ... In fact, what can happen instead is that individuals and groups can end up living 'parallel lives' ... in which they share spaces but do not interact. Moreover, placing diverse communities in close proximity to each other, especially in situations of competition over limited resources, can increase the potential for conflict. This is because, without the kinds of interaction that result in positive relationships being formed, there is a high potential for people to scapegoat those who are different and blame them for the ills of the neighbourhood. (Orton 2009, 12–13)

Community Engagement, Community Empowerment, Equality and Diversity – and Other Related Policy Areas

To complete this brief survey of the policy landscape, we want to look at some separate, but related, areas of work.

Community Engagement

As Communities Scotland put it so well:

> The term 'community engagement' is everywhere. But it can often be used to mean a lot of different things.
>
>   Put simply, community engagement is the process of involving people in decisions that affect them. This can mean involving communities in the planning, development and management of services. Or, it may be about tackling the problems of a neighbourhood, such as crime, drug misuse or lack of play facilities for children. (Communities Scotland 2007)

In order to shape a working definition, many organisations have drawn on some earlier work by David Wilcox (Wilcox 1994), which sets out a 'ladder of participation':

- Informing – giving a message but don't require feedback or comment
- Consultation – allows choice between pre-determined options not an opportunity to propose alternatives
- Deciding together – views shared, options generated jointly a course of action agreed upon
- Acting Together – working with others to make decisions and carry through the action agreed
- Supporting local initiatives – supporting groups to develop and implement their own solutions. (London Councils *c.*2009)

Community engagement – allied to empowerment (see below, p. 60) – has become a key way in which local authorities and other organisations need to communicate with and involve their local communities – 'The action that agencies take to enable them to consult, involve, listen and respond to communities through ongoing relationships' (IDeA 2009a).

   Engagement has also been embedded into the latest policies to improve and modernise local government. These include (at the time of writing):

- The new performance framework which includes:
    - the National Indicator set (Communities and Local Government 2007)
    - Comprehensive Area Assessment (IDeA 2009d)
- New legal duties for local authorities, including:

- the duty to inform, consult and involve, which became a requirement via the 2007 Local Government and Public Involvement in Health Act (UK Parliament 2007)
- the duty to cooperate, for example via the Local Strategic Partnership
- New democratic duties for councils and councillors, which include:
  - the duty to respond to petitions
  - the councillor 'call for action', whereby all councillors have the powers to require local service providers to respond to an issue of concern.

Community Empowerment

'Community empowerment is the outcome of effective community engagement' (IDeA 2009b) through which:

> Power, influence and responsibility is shifted away from existing centres of power and into the hands of communities and individual citizens. (IDeA 2009a)

Community empowerment formed the keystone of the Government White Paper, *Communities in Control*, which sought to:

> shift power, influence and responsibility away from existing centres of power into the hands of communities and individual citizens. (Communities and Local Government 2009, 1)

This, plus the Local Government and Public Involvement in Health Act (UK Parliament 2007), has ensured that local authorities and their partners see community empowerment as a core activity.

Equality and Diversity

There has been an increasing volume of legislation and guidance around equality and diversity – although these two terms are frequently used without differentiating them,[3] and it is important to clarify them, as, for example, National Museum Wales has done:

> **Equality** is creating an even platform to enable everyone to access the same opportunities and is backed by legislation to prevent discrimination based on prejudices against any group.

---

3   There is a very useful briefing paper (Sanglin-Grant 2003), that looks in some depth at the confusion around the terms 'equality' and 'diversity'.

Diversity is understanding and valuing the differences in people and believing that harnessing these differences will create a productive working environment and an enriching life experience where talents are fully utilised and organisational goals are met.

Valuing diversity means valuing the qualities that different people bring to their jobs, to the resolution of problems and to the development of business opportunities – rather than judging people's ideas by the extent to which they conform to our existing values or personal preference. (Amgueddfa Cymru/ National Museum Wales 2009, emphases in original)

At the time of writing, the government is consulting on the new Equality Bill (House of Commons 2009a) (for more discussion, see Chapter 4).

The main provisions of interest to local government are:

- the introduction of new strategic socio-economic duty to reduce socio-economic inequalities
- a new public equality duty that will extend the public duties to age, sexual orientation, religion or belief, gender reassignment, also including pregnancy and maternity – consultation will follow shortly on the specific duties
- clarification that procurement can be used to drive equality – this will be included in the consultation of specific duties
- banning age discrimination for those over 18 in the provision of services, subject to further consultation on the details. (IDeA 2009c)

Conclusions

This chapter has focused on the development of social exclusion (and related policy areas) – the following chapters will investigate how public libraries have taken on this area of work.

In conclusion, we feel that the former New Labour government embarked on a journey full of good intentions; certainly made some progress across the UK (often in areas that have been little-heralded, such as some of the advances for LGBT people); but that, overall, the policies and practices to tackle social exclusion have still got a very long way to go – and, despite the current economic climate, this is not the moment to lose sight of the key aims.

Similarly, although the former New Labour government's strategies on community cohesion, community engagement and community empowerment have been launched, these critical areas have become bemired in lack of definition and drive (and, in relation to community cohesion, suspicions about the political aims of work in this area).

It is vital that we do not lose sight of the ambitious programmes to engage, empower and involve all people in developing UK society – and beware of continuing down an elitist path.

Chapter 4
Strategic Context

The aim of this chapter is to examine some of the major policy drivers which have encouraged organisations, including public libraries, to tackle social exclusion and how these connect with wider government policies and strategies. The library-specific policy drivers were covered in Chapter 2, and this chapter will focus in particular on the following key documents:

- *Communities in Control: Real People, Real Power* (Communities and Local Government 2009);
- *A Fairer Future: the Equality Bill and Other Action to Make Equality a Reality* (Government Equalities Office 2009);
- *Equity and Excellence in the Public Library: Why Ignorance is Not Our Heritage* (Usherwood 2007);
- *Identity in the 21st Century: New Trends in Challenging Times* (Wetherell 2009);
- *Who Cares About the White Working Class?* (Sveinsson 2009a);
- *Sources of Resentment, and Perceptions of Ethnic Minorities Among Poor White People in England* (Garner et al. 2009).

Taken together, these reports create a powerful message for public sector policy-makers and practitioners to consider. They combine legislative pushes and research pulls which library managers and workers should not ignore. The common thread which runs through these papers is that we must actively engage all sections of our communities in the planning, design, delivery and evaluation of library services. How this can be achieved is explored in Chapter 6. Taken together, these policy drivers create a useful framework which libraries can adapt and adopt to help them create relevant, responsive and inclusive services.

Communities in Control

A constant and growing theme of government since 1997 has been the need to put communities in control, by giving 'real people, real power'. Until quite recently this has had little impact on the way that public services are delivered, and there has been more rhetoric than reality to the government's announcements.

This mood began to change in 2008 and was signalled on 9 July when the Secretary of State for Communities and Local Government presented *Communities in Control* to Parliament. The tone was set by then Prime Minister Gordon Brown's foreword:

> In the modern world there are many challenges that cannot be met by central government acting alone – and to address those challenges effectively, we need to harness the energy and innovation of front line professionals, local government, citizens and communities. (Brown 2009b, i)

The aim of 'empowering communities and citizens and ensuring that power is more fairly distributed across the whole of our society' (Brown 2009b, i) is a modern version of the traditional Labour aspiration to shift power and resources towards working people. The added ingredient is the role of public sector workers in this process – 'the transfer of power both to front-line professionals and to users, who we want to be able to play a far greater role in shaping the services they use' (Brown 2009b, i).

The notion of staff and service users delivering services together has been given the name 'co-production' and will be explored further in Chapter 7.

In her introduction, Hazel Blears, the then Secretary of State for Communities and Local Government, said that the hallmark of a modern state should be 'devolved, decentralised, with power diffused throughout our society. That people should have the maximum influence, control and ownership over the decisions, forces and agencies which shape their lives and environments is the essence of democracy' (Blears 2009, iii).

The historical examples she gives include the Rochdale Co-operative, the Chartists and the Suffragettes. These were all very important movements, but it can be argued that none of them really succeeded in achieving the sharing of power equally among the population, regardless of age, race, ability, faith, sexuality, gender or class. They put pressure on the system, which led to reforms, but which did not fundamentally change the system.

The government wants to see 'stronger local councils, more co-operatives and social enterprises, more people becoming active in their communities as volunteers, advocates and elected representatives' (Blears 2009, iii).

The steps on this journey have, apparently, included 'devolution for Scotland, Wales and London, reforming the Lords, more investment and powers for local councils' (Blears 2009, iv). The latter has not been very apparent to some senior local government officers who have seen council control over 'big issues' such as housing and education weakened rather than strengthened, and the constant financial theme has been that of 'efficiency savings'.

This White Paper claims to take us further on the community empowerment journey and also changes 'the terms of the debate'.

In June 2009, Hazel Blears returned to a familiar theme in a valedictory ministerial speech to MPs, just two days before she resigned from the government. As the Local Democracy, Economic Development and Construction Bill received its second reading, she repeated a well-worn theme: people need a stronger voice and more influence in decisions that affect their lives. As one commentator noted:

> Who could argue with that? The problem, critics say, is that Blears had been saying little else since she was appointed almost two years ago. Community empowerment, rather than stronger local government, seemed to be her obsession. A new communities secretary will doubtless have other plans ...
>
> What else do we need? An end to the pretence that, under Blears, community empowerment made a great leap forward – her rhetoric didn't match the reality. And a loosening of Whitehall's grip on town and county halls so they can rediscover a civic entrepreneurship that delivered so much a century and a half ago. (Hetherington 2009)

So what, exactly, does the White Paper propose and how is it new or different from previous attempts to empower local communities? According to the Executive Summary:

> *Communities in Control: Real People, Real Power* aims to pass power into the hands of local communities. We want to generate vibrant local democracy in every part of the country, and to give real control over local decisions and services to a wider pool of active citizens ...
>
> We want to shift power, influence and responsibility away from existing centres of power into the hands of communities and individual citizens. This is because we believe that they can take difficult decisions and solve complex problems for themselves. The state's role should be to set national priorities and minimum standards, while providing support and a fair distribution of resources. (Communities and Local Government 2009, 1)

These two paragraphs need unpacking because of both what they mean and where they come from. If the first paragraph is taken at absolute face value, it would mean that people who currently manage public services would hand over this power and control, or at least share it, with local communities. In the library world this would mean actively involving all sections of the local community in the design, planning, delivery and assessment of library services. To date the record in this area has been patchy. Some libraries have given some control to some sections of their local communities. But this control has been carefully prescribed and managed – for example, enabling library users to select stock, but not allowing them to decide the size or allocation of the stock fund. There have also been issues of how representative the library users are in terms of the make-up of the local catchment area, and white middle-class people often predominate. So, building the capacity of working-class communities to take on power is a big issue if the government's aspiration to empower local communities is going to be realised.

It is also worth considering where this policy driver has come from. Historically the call for empowerment of the individual and the reduction of state control has been a Conservative instinct. Labour has traditionally been in favour of Big Government and central control. So, to hear a Labour government calling for decentralisation is a political paradigm shift, although Labour has consistently been in favour of the redistribution of wealth and power away from the few and towards the many. This has been a key call to action in many Labour Party campaigns since the war, although 1983 was the last time that it appeared so starkly in the election manifesto.

A clue to this paradigm shift lies in the second paragraph where government wants local people to 'solve complex problems for themselves' while the state sets national priorities and standards.

For 'complex problems' read too much demand, not enough supply and competing priorities. Government does not want to be drawn into disputes about who gets what, and prefers these to be resolved locally. But if these disputes are caused because of government policy and priorities, then surely they cannot abrogate their role. In 2009 there were some high profile examples of this in the public library domain. Swindon announced that it planned to close four libraries to make financial savings. This decision was not taken with the involvement of local people who organised an effective campaign to reverse the decision. The Taxpayers'Alliance made a Freedom of Information application to find out how the plan to close libraries was agreed. The council's proposal was that the four libraries could be run by local communities (with support). But this is not empowerment because local people were not involved in the initial decision to close the libraries – if they had been involved, they may have come up with alternative solutions, including more investment in the library service. For this to happen they would need a real say in how the council budget is allocated. This demonstrates that empowering local people to make decisions must involve them in the highest levels of decision-making, at a corporate level, including budget-setting. Instead, they were being 'empowered' to take on 'surplus' libraries which the council could no longer afford to run. This is a classic community 'dumping' exercise rather than true empowerment. But the ultimate responsibility lies with the government which allocates resources to local councils in the first place. Year-on-year 'efficiency savings' have cut council services to the bone, but the government then expects local councils – and now local communities – to 'solve these complex problems for themselves'.

The other, even more high profile case, is that of Wirral where, for the first time, the DCMS is using its full legal powers to look into Wirral's closure plans, after a long fight by local people who argued that they were not consulted. The government view on this was:

> If substantiated, this would constitute a procedural rather than a specific statutory duty failure by the council, the remedy for which would be outside the Secretary of State's powers under the Act. (House of Commons 2009b)

This alarmed campaigners who saw consultation as the central issue. This also flies in the face of the White Paper which aims to 'give real control over local decisions and services'. Swindon and Wirral can be seen as early tests of the former New Labour government's ambitions to 'pass power into the hands of local communities'. The evidence so far suggests that the government has failed this test because local people were not involved in the decision to close libraries in Swindon and Wirral, and, according to the government, the lack of public consultation is not a specific statutory duty failure. If consultation (one of the lowest forms of community engagement) is not a statutory duty, then what hope is there for communities to take real control of services and decisions which affect their lives?

The White Paper makes recommendations in several key areas and many of these are of relevance to libraries:

1. Local Councils remain crucial – the existing 'duty to involve' local people in key decisions was extended in April 2008 to include key arts, sporting, cultural and environmental organisations.
2. Supporting you in becoming a more active citizen or volunteer – a pathfinder programme will offer training and information about how to be an active citizen.
3. Providing you with more access to information – there is a great opportunity here for public libraries but they are not mentioned in the White Paper. 'We will ensure that all sections of society can enjoy the benefits of the Internet' (Communities and Local Government 2009, 4) may have implications for libraries who charge for Internet access.
4. Making sure your petitions are heard and acted upon – many library campaigners use petitions to raise awareness of planned library closures.
5. Increasing your chance to influence council budgets and policies – this is the critical recommendation, and the plan is to encourage every local council to use participatory budgeting schemes by 2012.
6. Giving you more say in your neighbourhood – more neighbourhood councils will be encouraged, and local authorities must engage more people in commissioning local goods and services, which could include library stock and ICT systems.
7. Giving older and young people a stronger voice – a review of older people's engagement with government and schemes to encourage young people to vote and participate more.
8. Enabling you to hold those with power to account – the visibility will be raised of the overview and scrutiny function in local government, which includes the planning and performance of public libraries.
9. Providing you with redress when things go wrong – it is important that every local authority has a system of accessible interactive contact for citizens to raise concerns.

10. Making it easier for you to stand for office – backbench councillors will be given more powers, and people who serve in a range of civic roles will be given time off work for their public duties.
11. Ownership and control – 'we want to see an increase in the number of people helping to run or own local services and assets, and to transfer more of these assets into community ownership. These assets might include community centres, street markets, swimming pools, parks or a disused school, shop or pub' (Communities and Local Government 2009, 10). Libraries were not on the list but community asset transfer has already been piloted by some authorities with varying degrees of success.

The White Paper concludes by saying that 'there are no limits to the capacity of the British people for self-government, given the right platforms, mechanisms and incentives. Empowering citizens and communities is an urgent task for us all' (Communities and Local Government 2009, 10). One of the reasons for this urgency is the strong link between community engagement and community cohesion, and this will be explored in the next section.

A Fairer Future

According to Harriet Harman, former Minister for Women and Equality, in her foreword to *A Fairer Future: The Equality Bill and Other Action to Make Equality a Reality*:

> The Government is and always has been, the champion of equality in public policy and in our democratic institutions. Equality is not just right in principle, it is necessary for:
>
> • Individuals: everyone has the right to be treated fairly and the opportunity to fulfil their potential. To achieve this we must tackle inequality and root out discrimination;
> • The economy: a competitive economy draws on all the talents and ability – it's not blinkered by prejudice; and
> • Society: a more equal society is more cohesive and at ease with itself.
>
> Everyone has a stake in creating a fair society because fairness is the foundation for individual rights, a prosperous economy and a peaceful society. Fairness and equality are the hallmarks of a modern and confident society. (Harman 2009, 1)

The former New Labour government has been proud of their strong legal framework and their record on fighting discrimination and against inequality. Over the last 40 years the Labour Party has introduced laws both to create and respond to change in society and to promote civil rights and equality. Their record includes, for example: the first Race Relations Acts back in the 1960s; the steps towards equality for women in the Equal Pay and Sex Discrimination Acts in the 1970s; strengthening rights for disabled people in the 1990s; and the introduction of civil partnerships in 2004.

They claim that 'Britain is now a fairer and more confident nation because our commitment to greater equality has been at the heart of public policy' (Harman 2009, 1).

And yet, despite all this activity, some recent research has indicated that Britain has become a more unequal society since Labour came to power. The report by former cabinet minister Alan Milburn recognises that: 'Britain's got talent – lots of it. It is not ability that is unevenly distributed in our society. It is opportunity' (Milburn 2009, 7).

Britain is one of the least socially mobile countries in Europe:

> although only 7 per cent of the population attend independent schools, well over half the members of many professions have done so … For example, 75 per cent of judges, 70 per cent of finance directors, 45 per cent of top civil servants and 32 per cent of MPs were independently schooled. (Panel on Fair Access to the Professions 2009, 17)

Only 29 per cent of students – and just 16 per cent of the Russell Group of universities – come from lower socio-economic backgrounds, even though they make up 50 per cent of young people.

The *Guardian* (22 July 2009) editorial commented:

> Sometimes the obvious needs to be stated. Britain is an unequal society. The elite look after their own. Poverty traps people from one generation to another … It is uncomfortable to be told such truths: behind its modern veneer, British society is determined by who you know, and who your parents are … But effort and merit are not rewarded as they should be. In some regards, poor children born in 1958 had better prospects than those born five decades on. This was, of course, one of the problems that Labour won power to tackle. The conclusion of the panel led by a former Labour cabinet minister, Alan Milburn, is that the party has failed. (*Guardian* 2009)

Perhaps the new Equality Act 2010 will succeed in making Britain a more equal society, but it was introduced at the very end of the former New Labour government and may not be fully implemented by the coalition. Yet the need for such an Act is very clear because:

- Despite progress since 1997 to reduce the gender pay gap, women still earn, on average, 22.6 per cent less per hour than men …
- Less academically able, but better off children, overtake more able, poorer children at school by the age of six;

- The gap between the employment rate of disabled people and the overall employment rate has decreased from 34.5 per cent to 26.3 per cent since 1998, but disabled people are still more than twice as likely to be out of work than non-disabled people …
- If you are from an ethnic minority, you were 17.9 per cent less likely to find work in 1997 than a white person. The difference is still 13 per cent …
- One in five older people are unsuccessful in getting quotations for motor insurance, travel insurance and car hire … and
- 6 out of 10 lesbian and gay school children experience homophobic bullying and many contemplate suicide as a result. (Government Equalities Office 2009, 6)

If progress is not stepped up:

- the pay gap between men and women will not close until 2085; and
- it will take almost 100 years for people from ethnic minorities to get the same job prospects as white people. (Government Equalities Office 2009, 6)

The Bill is needed to streamline the law and help people to understand their rights and help businesses to comply with the law. This is necessary because:

- The discrimination laws have helped us make progress on equality, but because they have been developed over more than 40 years, they have become complex and difficult for people to understand and navigate;
- There are currently nine major pieces of discrimination legislation, around 100 statutory instruments setting out rules and regulations and more than 2,500 pages of guidance and statutory codes of practice.

The Bill will replace this thicket of legislation with a single Act, which will form the basis of guidance for employers, service providers and public bodies. (Government Equalities Office 2009, 7)

This includes local authorities and public libraries.
    The Equality Bill will:

1. introduce a new public sector duty to consider reducing socio-economic inequalities;
2. put a new Equality Duty on public bodies;
3. use public procurement to improve equality;
4. ban age discrimination outside the workplace;
5. introduce gender pay reports;
6. extend the scope to use positive action;
7. strengthen the powers of employment tribunals;
8. protect carers from discrimination;

9. protect breastfeeding mothers;
10. ban discrimination in private clubs; and
11. strengthen protection from discrimination for disabled people. (Taken from Government Equalities Office 2009, 8)

The new Equality Bill has some significant implications for public libraries which will need to take its provisions into account with regard to a wide range of issues, including:

- Involvement and Consultation – libraries will need to take reasonable steps to consult and involve employees, service users and interested others (or their representatives where appropriate). Involvement should initially encompass the evidence-gathering activities, analysis and review of functions which form part of the objective-setting process (and reviewing these in future years). Equalities and Human Rights Commission (EHRC) guidance will follow.
- Procurement – when libraries are setting out equality objectives, and the steps to achieve them, they will need to include how it will be ensured that equality factors are considered as part of public procurement activities to deliver those objectives. They will also need to consider the use of equality-related award criteria where they relate to the subject matter of the contract, and are proportionate. Finally, they will need to consider incorporating equality-related contract conditions where they relate to the performance of the contract and are proportionate. Very small-scale purchases that fall below the thresholds set by the Public Sector Directives will not be affected by the specific duties but large-scale contracts, such as the purchase of books and other goods, could fall within the remit of the Act.
- Equality Schemes – libraries will need to ensure that these schemes are part of core business planning and embedded within service plans. Monitoring and reporting will also be against the service plans.
- Equality Impact Assessments – libraries will need to demonstrate evidence of the impact on equality of policy and service design, and the difference effected.
- Training – libraries will need to provide appropriate training to staff so that the duties of the Act can be met.
- Employment Monitoring – libraries will need to have a range of data pertinent to local circumstance, need and assessment. There will be a requirement to report on the gender pay gap.

Libraries will also need to consider what action they can take to reduce the socio-economic inequalities people face. According to the Equality Bill:

We know that inequality does not just come from your gender or ethnicity; your sexual orientation or your disability; your age, or your religion or belief.

Overarching and interwoven with these specific forms of disadvantage is the
persistent inequality of social class – your family background or where you were
born. (Government Equalities Office 2009, 9)

It was refreshing to see the former New Labour government acknowledge that social
class still holds a powerful grip over people's lives. When they came to power in
1997, they created a whole range of synonyms for social class, including social
exclusion. But talk of social class itself was almost taboo and the Marxist analysis of
power and society was dismissed as being out-of-date and irrelevant in the modern
'post-capitalist' world. It was only at the very end of the former New Labour
government, and in the wake of a serious financial crisis which has shaken the very
foundations of capitalist wealth and power, that social class at long last came back
onto the political agenda. Not only is social class a key strand of the equality agenda
but also *the* most important determinant of success and social mobility:

- Class trumps ability – less academically able but better off children overtake
  more able poorer children at school by the age of six; and
- Class trumps gender when it comes to life expectancy – while women
  generally have longer life expectancy than men, since the early 1980s poorer
  women can now be expected to live less long than rich men. (Government
  Equalities Office 2009, 9)

The Equality Bill will place a new duty on government ministers, departments and
key public bodies such as local authorities and NHS bodies to consider what action
they can take to reduce the socio-economic inequalities people face. The duty will
affect how public libraries make strategic decisions about spending and service
delivery. It will enshrine in law the role of public libraries in narrowing gaps in
outcomes resulting from socio-economic disadvantage. How the socio-economic
duty could work:

- A public library service could evaluate the library membership process and
  find that some families in social housing were having difficulty navigating
  the system and gaining a library card. The library service could then target
  people living on housing estates to help them with the application process.
- A public library service could review how accessible its services are. It
  discovers that residents from deprived neighbourhoods find it difficult
  to travel to the local library because of infrequent public transport, low
  car ownership rates and high parking costs. The library service decides to
  work in partnership with local transport providers to develop a strategy to
  tackle this, which could include introducing a free or subsidised shuttle bus
  service to the library from pick-up points around town.
- A public library service decides to do more to tackle health inequalities in
  deprived areas so allocates money from its core budgets to target areas with
  the worst health outcomes.

The Equality Act 2010 is the first piece of equality legislation in over 40 years to deal specifically with the issue of social class. Of course, it will not eliminate the class system which creates class-based inequalities in the first place. But it will make people aware of these inequalities and public bodies will have to demonstrate what steps they are taking to reduce the opportunity gap between the haves and have-nots. This renewed focus on the white working class is to be welcomed even though it has partly been driven by the fear factor created when the British National Party (BNP) won two seats to the European parliament in June 2009.

On 3 August 2009, former Communities Secretary John Denham announced that white working-class estates are to be targeted in a government drive to tackle the threat of right-wing extremism:

> About 100 of the most deprived neighbourhoods in England will be involved in the programme, which could include open discussion meetings to allow residents to air grievances about housing and immigration without being accused of racism, and a requirement on councils to be more transparent about their social housing policies.
>
> The plan comes after years in which the far-right BNP has made inroads into traditional Labour strongholds …
>
> Mr Denham said that some of those backing the BNP were 'undoubtedly people who have voted Labour in the past' and that the government has launched a 'sustained and visible campaign' to re-engage with white working class communities.
>
> 'Very few people would actually see themselves as white supremacists or white fascists', he said.
>
> 'But we know that those communities are the ones that often say no-one's speaking up for us. That's a sense populist parties can exploit.
>
> I think that there has been a concerted effort over the last 10 years to target resources at the most deprived communities. But I think, if we're honest about it, the extent to which that work has really engaged a lot of local people has been patchy'. (Roberts 2009)

In other words, the government needs to pay more attention to the needs of the white working class, and this was explored in *Who Cares About the White Working Class?* (Sveinsson 2009a).

The foreword to this report by Dr Kate Gavron is hard-hitting and straight to the point in describing the problems created by a class-based society:

> the most disadvantaged working class people of whatever ethnic background, roughly the poorest fifth of the population, are increasingly separated from the more prosperous majority by inequalities of income, housing and education. By emphasizing the virtues of individual self-determination and the exercising of 'choice', recent governments have in fact entrenched the ability of the middle

and upper classes to avoid downward social mobility and preserve the best of life's goods for their own children. Moreover, the rhetoric of politicians and commentators has tended to abandon the description 'working class', preferring instead to use terms such as 'hard working families' in order to contrast the virtuous many with an underclass perceived as feckless and undeserving. (Gavron 2009, 2)

Equity and Excellence

This notion of the 'deserving' and 'undeserving' poor can be traced back to the Poor Law, and it was particularly evident during the Victorian period. As the opening speeches of many public libraries made plain, these philanthropic institutions were created to control the reading habits of the 'deserving' working class and were designed to turn 'the people from Alehouses and Socialism' (cited in Corrigan and Gillespie 1978).

The following is typical of the motives behind public library provision, as expressed by Gladstone at the opening of St Martin-in-the-Fields Public Library in February 1891. Public libraries were part of a movement using 'every direct and indirect agency for the right education of the masses', to ensure 'the free circulation of a sound and healthful literature'. Above all, libraries were designed to occupy that 'idle time' which remained 'as real leisure' after work, sleep and eating:

> There is the competition of evil soliciting visibly and sensibly in the good streets through which he passes. There may also be a competition of good in beneficial institutions. His leisure may be employed in these libraries. I express to you the most earnest desire of my heart to be that prosperity and success in social and moral improvement may attend increasingly from year to year in the progress of this library. (Greenwood 1891, 69)

The aim was to keep the working class out of pubs where they could read newspapers and hear 'penny dreadful' readings which were often of a seditious nature. Museums and libraries were part of the Victorian strategy of distracting and indoctrinating the masses, while it is no accident that parks (which were designed to literally contain and control their movements) were linked to local barracks via wide and well-lit roads, so that troops could be sent quickly to quell any disturbances.

This notion that we should only help those who are prepared to help themselves is still strongly embedded within the professional library culture. On the surface it appears as a debate about whether public libraries should stock popular music, DVDs and computer games. But, at a deeper level, it is an expression of cultural values whereby the dominant reader – white, middle-class, female and middle-aged – is the preferred library user.

The question of who deserves a library service was raised by Bob Usherwood in his recent book *Equity and Excellence* (Usherwood 2007):

> It needs to be recognised Britain is now subject to the behaviour of the members of an amoral and apolitical section in society who are neither deserving nor poor. It is a group that is against learning, anti intellectual and, in the words of one commentator, 'despise browns and blacks (especially if they are making something of their lives) and also education, enlightenment and internationalism' (Alibhai-Brown 2007). Sometimes identified by the inelegant label 'Chav', members of this group raise issues that are uncomfortable to address. However, their attitudes are contrary to all the public library stands for and the profession must be prepared to confront them. (Usherwood 2007, 99)

Here Usherwood aligns himself with those who denigrate so-called 'Chav culture' at every opportunity. This is at best cultural elitism and at worst classism, as evidenced by the range of anti-Chav hate websites which have been developed in recent years.

An example of this negative stereotyping is provided by Usherwood when he quotes a 'teacher's final cry of despair':

> The only building that causes confusion is the library. Red brick and modern, its purpose clearly mystifies and actually evades most Chavs. Occasionally, they can be spotted muttering and pointing in its direction whilst wheeling little Courtney Dakota back home from some Tartrazine flavoured juice and unsupervised play. Consequently, the library remains unvisited, un-graffitied and untouched. Because no one knows what the fuck it is. (An electronic discussion group cited in Usherwood 2007, 99)

Usherwood refers to 'Chav' as an 'inelegant label', but it is much worse than that – it is a term of abuse which is as offensive to some working-class people as 'nigger', 'Paki' and 'pikey' is to black, Asian and Traveller people. If this level of invective was directed at ethnic minorities, older people or those with disabilities, then the perpetrator would quite rightly be in danger of breaching equalities legislation. However, when it is the white working class who are being attacked, they are 'fair game' and there is no one to defend them, not even the liberal intelligentsia. This constant denigration might be the cause of some of the 'arrogance' which some white working-class people develop as a defence against constant attacks on their lifestyles and values.

As for 'Chavs' not wanting to use public libraries, who can blame them, given the attitude of the teacher above and her fellow professionals in public libraries. From their inception, public libraries have reflected the interests and values of the middle class, and have failed to identify, prioritise and meet the needs of the masses. Public libraries were part of that growing middle-class commitment to working-class education in the late eighteenth and early nineteenth centuries, which was totally different from their ideals in middle-class education, but was rather a means of ensuring that the lower classes would acquiesce in middle-class aspirations.

Adam Smith epitomised this English bourgeois viewpoint regarding working-class education in *The Wealth of Nations*: 'An instructed and intelligent people besides are always more decent and orderly than an ignorant one … less apt to be misled into any wanton or unnecessary opposition to the measures of the government' (Smith 1785).

For Smith, as well as for the vast majority of the political and intellectual elite at the time, the schooling of the working classes was always to be subordinate and inferior to that of the middle classes, designed to contain and pacify rather than to educate and liberate.

As William Lovett, the working-class campaigner, argued in the early nineteenth century: 'Possessors of wealth … still consider education as their own prerogative, or a boon to be sparingly conferred upon the multitudes' (Lovett 1967, 114).

Writing about the introduction of state education for all, 100 years after the publication of *The Wealth of Nations*, Jane Miller asserts that 'the provision of education for working class children was thought of by and large instrumentally, rather than as likely to contribute to the life possibilities of the children themselves' (Miller 1992).

When the English state schooling system was set up in the late nineteenth century, the intention of the dominant classes was still to police and control the working classes rather than to educate them. So any notion of education as liberatory has always been tempered by the ruling elite's instrumental view of education as a form of control of the working class.

In his survey of the rise of education systems in England, France and the United States, Andy Green (1990) singles out England as the most explicit example of the use of schooling by the upper classes to dominate the lower classes.

Jack Common put it well when he talked of the alienation which the working class feel towards education and schools:

> School, which is the Council school, is in origin quite alien to working class life. It does not grow from that life; it is not 'our' school, in the sense that other schools can be spoken of by the folk of other classes. The government forced them on us and school in working class life expresses nothing of that life; it is an institution clapped on from above. (Common 1938, 60)

Exactly the same can be said of public libraries. They are middle-class institutions 'clapped on from above' to control working-class reading habits. They appeal to those of the 'deserving poor' who have aspirations of social mobility, but they remain irrelevant to the vast majority of the proletariat. A group quoted by Muddiman (1999b) told researchers:

> I think you're flogging a dead horse here, because people in this room don't really use a library and I don't think whatever you call it you're not gonna get us through the door. It's because we don't read the fact that we don't go really. (MVA 1998, 8)

The authors of this book were part of the team which carried out the research that was published in *Open to All? The Public Library and Social Exclusion* (Muddiman et al. 2000a, 2000b and 2000c). We concluded that the working class use public libraries but only a small section has benefited:

> The numerical evidence suggests that it is [a] minority of the working class who are socially, educationally, or intellectually aspirational who particularly value and use public library services. (Muddiman 1999b, 184)

If 'Chavs' are not using library services, then we must find ways in which to engage with the white working class, discover what their needs are and redesign services to meet those needs. If we give up on the white working class then we will abandon the opportunity to develop fully inclusive and needs-based public libraries. In the same way that no sustained effort was made to implement comprehensive education, there have been few systematic attempts to involve active users, lapsed users and non-users in the creation of community based libraries.

Usherwood reaches a different conclusion:

> In times of limited resources we need to ask if the profession should attempt to provide specifically for people who choose to exclude themselves and, all the evidence suggests, are never likely to use what the service can legitimately offer. Obviously, they should be given every chance to engage with the service but not at the expense of people who can and want to benefit from what a library provides. (Usherwood 2007, 99)

So if you are aspirational you deserve a public library service, but, if you are a 'Chav', you do not. We do not agree with Bob Usherwood's analysis, and one of the reasons this book was commissioned was to respond to some of the arguments found in *Equity and Excellence*. Indeed, rather than abandoning that section of the working class who need libraries the most but use them the least, we believe that the future of public libraries depends on our ability to engage with excluded and marginalised communities, including the white working class.

Identity in the Twenty-First Century

Judging by the increasing level of recent research into social class, it appears that more people are becoming aware of its importance and relevance.

Table 4.1   Changes in perception of class, 1964 and 2005

Year	Working class	Middle class	Classless
1964	65%	30%	5%
2005	57%	37%	6%
Variance	**- 8%**	**+7%**	**+1%**

Anthony Heath is lead researcher on the project 'Individualisation and the decline of class identity' (the results of which have just been published in *Identity in the 21st Century: New Trends in Changing Times* (Wetherell 2009)) that claims to be the first systematic investigation into subjective attitudes to class in the UK, and how they have changed over five decades. 'I've done lots of work before on what you might call objective views of inequality, such as educational attainment and patterns of social mobility. But there's never been much empirical evidence on class identity' (quoted in Arnot 2009).

Along with John Curtice, a professor at Strathclyde University, Heath analysed the British Social Attitudes survey of 2005, as well as scouring a whole series of the British Election Surveys conducted after every general election since Wilson's narrow win in 1964. Each has a section that asks: 'Would you say that you belong to any social class? In which case, which class is that?' After the 1964 election, 65 per cent of respondents described themselves as working class and 30 per cent as middle class. Only 5 per cent felt classless. Surprisingly, perhaps, the classless category had increased by only 1 per cent by 2005. Those who saw themselves as working class had contracted to 57 per cent, while middle-class respondents had expanded to 37 per cent (see Table 4.1).

The balance between the working and middle classes has not varied significantly over a 40-year period, which suggests that, despite all the social progress made since the 1960s, the class system has remained relatively static.

Indeed, other evidence suggests that social mobility has declined and so the working- and middle-class proportions are likely to stay around the 60/40 level for some time. This has huge significance for social policy and the planning of public services. Public libraries should be increasing their efforts to engage with the working class who still make up two-thirds of the population.

Heath's subjective study of social class has discovered that the issue is not straightforward or easy to define and classify:

> There are now huge inequalities of wealth within the middle class. At the same time, the working class links that once formed an anchor for the Labour Party have been severed. (Arnot 2009)

One striking aspect of the project is the tendency of some of those in professional and managerial positions to claim that they are still working class:

> Our research officer on this project went to some respondents' homes to ask some more in depth questions. What came over from that is the lasting impressions that people retain from childhood. One said: 'If you've not been brought up middle class then you're not the real deal.' (Arnot 2009)

Who Cares About the White Working Class?

Many people are not comfortable with the notion of class and, as Kjartan Sveinsson (2009a, summarising Bottero 2009) has noted, the term was dropped in 1997 by New Labour who favour terms such as 'social exclusion' and 'hard working families'. Sveinsson also points out that the white working class are often portrayed as the victims of multiculturalism, but the real issue is the class system itself, which controls access to power and resources:

> the plight of the white working class is constructed – by the media, politicians and anti-immigrant groups – as either the fault of immigrants and minority ethnic groups, or the cultural deficit of the underclass itself, or both, while leaving the hierarchical and highly stratified nature of Britain out of the equation. (Sveinsson 2009b, 5)

> Socially, Britain remains dominated by class divisions, with class identities relatively similar in shape and strength as they were 40 years ago. (Sveinsson 2009b, 4)

In addition:

> If we really want to understand disadvantage, we need to shift our attention from who fights over the scraps from the table, to think instead about how much the table holds, and who really gets to enjoy the feast. (Bottero 2009, 7)

The white working classes are discriminated against on a range of different fronts, including their accent, their style, the food they eat, the clothes they wear, the social spaces they frequent, the postcode of their homes, even their names – witness the earlier scornful reference by a teacher (who should know better about bullying) to 'Courtney Dakota'.

> 'Class' is about unequal resources and status, and the social hierarchies to which they give rise. (Bottero 2009, 8)

The working class make up around half of the working age population but the power and influence of this group – and the attendant social respect – has been reduced by the decline of manufacturing industry and the loss of many well-paid skilled manual jobs.

'Class' is about how, and why, some people have *more* – more opportunities, more resources, more prestige or social esteem – whilst others have *less*. (Bottero 2009, 10, emphasis in original)

It is important to remember that class is about relative inequality, and is an inherently comparative concept. It is not just about what a group has, or where it stands in society, but about what it has or where it stands in relation to others. It is easier and more comfortable to focus on the characteristics of the excluded (hence the obsession with 'Chavs') rather than the processes of exclusion (the class system and class inequality). Instead of trying to divide and rule the working class into the deserving and undeserving poor, we should be using public libraries as front-line trenches in which the class war can be fought – and won.

As institutions of informal learning, public libraries should be proactive in the campaign to close the educational achievement gap between working-class and middle-class boys. The media tends to focus on the low achievement of white working-class boys and compare this to the educational achievements of other ethnic groups. But, as David Gillborn (2009) points out, the achievement gap between white working-class boys (24 per cent) and black African boys (33.7 per cent) is only 9.7 per cent compared to a difference of 32 per cent between white working-class boys and white middle-class boys (56 per cent). This indicates that the problem of low educational achievement among white working-class boys has more to do with class than race. Once this analysis has been made and is clear, the question we should ask is – what have been the attitudes and actions of those with the power and resources to effect change? And this includes those who control power and resources in public libraries.

Symon Hill has also pointed out that the term 'white working class' creates a focus on race and a diversion from the real issue, which is social class:

The expression 'white working class' implies that this is a group for whom race is important. Nearly every time I hear the phrase, it is linked to an assumption that working class white people are racist. Nor is this attitude found only on the political right. I've belonged to many leftwing campaigning movements that have included individuals with staggeringly prejudiced perceptions of working class people as racist, as well as sexist and homophobic.

This is not the reality. The BNP has won council seats from the Tories as well as Labour. I grew up in a white working class family that was not especially political, but it was clear to me from pretty early on that the people who differed from me the most were those who had plenty of money while my family scraped by – not people whose skin happened to look a bit different.

To combat the BNP, we need to emphasise that the most important division in society is not racial – it is the division between the very rich and the rest of us. Patronising comments about the 'white working class' serve only to reinforce the rhetoric of race while subtly distracting us from the realities of class division. (Hill 2009)

As Diane Reay notes:

> what is surprising is that some of the white working classes still make an enormous effort to succeed educationally in an educational system that holds little prospect of a positive academic outcome. The same two barriers that were present at the inception of state schooling still exist. The working classes continue to have access to relatively low levels of the kind of material, cultural and psychological resources that aid educational success. Most can neither afford private tuition and the enriching cultural activities that many middle class parents invest in for their children. Nor do they have the same degree of confidence and sense of entitlement that the middle classes possess in their interactions with schooling. (Reay 2009, 24)

Public libraries can help to lift both of these barriers: libraries can provide good quality educational resources and cultural activities; and libraries can build confidence and self-esteem by reflecting and affirming working-class culture and achievements.

Kate Gavron concludes:

> life chances for today's children are overwhelmingly linked to parental income, occupations and educational qualifications – in other words, class. The poor white working class share many more problems with the poor from ethnic communities than some of them recognise. All the most disadvantaged groups must be helped to improve their joint lot. Competition between them, real or imagined, is just a distraction. (Gavron 2009, 2)

We agree with this analysis and feel strongly that public libraries can be a catalyst for making this happen.

Perception and Resentment

With the media's constant tendency to present class-based issues as race related issues, it is not surprising that the white working class has developed some resentment towards and negative perceptions of ethnic minorities. These issues were explored in a report compiled for the National Community Forum, *Sources of Resentment, and Perception of Ethnic Minorities Among Poor White People in England* (Garner et al. 2009).

> The aims of this report, following from the literature review on perceptions of ethnic minorities among 'poor white' people in England, were:

1. to gather data on two not necessarily connected things: the sources of resentment, and perceptions of ethnic minorities among people resident on estates in four places in England
2. to attempt to unpick these perceptions
3. to identify suggestions to facilitate integration
4. and to put forward some recommendations for moving community cohesion and integration forward on this basis.

The four selected sites were relatively mono-cultural 'white' urban spaces with different migration experiences: Castle Vale (Birmingham); Netherfield, Beanhill and Coffee Hall Estates (Milton Keynes); Halton Housing Trust in Runcorn and Widnes; and the Abbey Estate in Thetford. (Garner et al. 2009, 5)

Forty-three people in these communities were interviewed about their local areas, national concerns, and integration:

The data needs to be understood against the context of changing understandings and interpretations of racism. Popular understandings of racism contain two misleading messages. Either the focus is solely on discourses of superiority (abusive and/or intimidating language) and violence, which is part of the story but not all of it, or secondly, it is seen as purely a matter of individual prejudices. However the concept of 'institutional racism' (a set of practices and processes at a level above that of the individual) has been recognised in British law since the 1970s. Moreover, racism is not only about physical, but also about cultural difference. White people can become the objects of racist discourse because of cultural reasons. In British history, Jews, Irish Roman Catholics and Eastern Europeans have been through this experience. (Garner et al. 2009, 5)

The four selected sites on which this report focuses had specific histories of migration and community development, which are important in the way the people there respond to minorities and the issues of immigration and integration.

Runcorn/Widnes has virtually no history of immigration, Castle Vale is a relatively white area of a city in which 30 per cent of the population are black and minority ethnic, and Thetford has a recent experience of European migrants (notably Portuguese and Polish workers).

In terms of development, the sites also differed: we found that in those where social and environmental conditions were better, there was, as a general rule, less apparent hostility to minorities. In Milton Keynes, where some of the accommodation was of very poor quality, the feelings of resentment and abandonment were nearer the surface. Another contextual point was the frequency and type of contact with black and minority ethnic people. Overall, few of [the interviewees] had frequent contacts with ethnic minorities. Some had a particular friend or acquaintance, and a few others worked in more multicultural settings. (Garner et al. 2009, 5–6)

The important local issues in each area differed, both in substance and priority:

> While anti-social behaviour figured in each of the areas, it was much more prominent in Thetford and Runcorn/Widnes than in Milton Keynes and Castle Vale. Poor living conditions were an issue for Milton Keynes but scarcely at all for redeveloped Castle Vale, where worklessness, litter and sustaining the gains of regeneration were the most important topics. Anxieties over benefits and entitlement on a very local basis exercised the minds of people in Runcorn, and were mentioned by a few people in Castle Vale, yet not as a pressing concern for most. Only in Milton Keynes did immigration and integration appear to be serious issues. The pattern seemed to be that morale was lowest and therefore identity-related anxieties at their highest, where the material conditions (housing and economics) were worst. (Garner et al. 2009, 6)

The important national issues raised were very varied. The rise in food and fuel prices was commented on and anti-social behaviour was regularly referred to as being 'everywhere nowadays'. The economy was seen purely as a national phenomenon. There was no particular pattern in terms of topics, except that the important national issues were often seen through the lens of local ones. One national topic of interest however was that of 'political correctness' which was mentioned by interviewees as a barrier to freedom of self-expression or of honest exchange.

> By far the most frequent context for referring to ethnic minorities [was] that of perceived competition for resources – typically housing, but also employment, benefits, territory and culture. In Coffee Hall (Milton Keynes), feelings of anxiety around housing were so acute that respondents claimed they had voted against the regeneration of the estate (which meant pulling down all breeze block houses and rebuilding them with new and better materials) because they feared that their necessary displacement during building work would result in them losing their places on the estate to immigrants. (Garner et al. 2009, 6)

A woman in Runcorn was quoted as saying:

> 'you've now got towns which were predominantly white and now they're not. And you're expected to get on and not cause any waves, not look at people differently and be accepting. But at the same time how can you be accepting when they're taking your house off you?' (Garner et al. 2009, 7)

The second theme focused on the conditions for becoming, or being accepted as a full member of society. This was most often expressed during talk of integration and cohesion. The main two arguments used [were] 'when in Rome' (people who come here must adapt to 'our way of life'); and the necessity for contributing in order to earn membership. This earning process can be undergone by something as simple as joining in community activities, or by making wider efforts to integrate, or paying into the welfare system. (Garner et al. 2009, 7)

But the onus for integration in these perspectives:

lies entirely with immigrants. There are also more nuanced appreciations of difference in terms of length of residence and degree of acculturation already achieved. Indeed there is a strand of this discussion that insists on integration as a two-way process, and that everyone must 'be flexible'. Anxieties about other topics might well be attached to this type of reasoning. From them are drawn conclusions: there is an almost unbridgeable difference between particular kinds of people and the playing field is tilted toward minorities because they can do things white people are not allowed to get away with. (Garner et al. 2009, 7)

This leads to frustration among the majority population who feel constrained by the limits of 'political correctness'.
    According to the interviewees:

it is the white working class who are the biggest victims of social change. Some of the conversations included examples of how people perceive unfair situations in which minorities are advantaged; either directly or indirectly. From a variety of stories, two are indicative. One is about a community 'clean up day' in which members of all ethnic groups had taken part on an estate. After the event, a city councillor managed to get funding for a day trip as a reward – but only for the Asian participants. This story was commented on as having 'destroyed the ethos' of what they were trying to achieve by the original activity.

    Another set of stories relates to the perception that incoming migrants are treated advantageously. A typical view in Thetford, for example, was that 'they seem to be getting what we've worked all our lives for and can't get'. This was interpreted as especially unfair when contrasted with the 'elderly who haven't got anything, can't afford to pay heating, worked all their lives and get nothing', and with 'single mums who have to live in hostels', while 'foreigners are in nice cars and have big houses'. (Garner et al. 2009, 7–8)

Many interviewees felt that resources were being 'given away' to minorities and that white people were the victims of discrimination. Some 'key recurrent emotional themes' were identified:

resentment; betrayal; abandonment; loss; defensiveness; nostalgia; unfairness and disempowerment. Local and central government are identified as doing the abandoning and betraying, while the communities experience loss and disempowerment. (Garner et al. 2009, 8)

Social class emerged as a very important focus for people's identities:

> people are very aware of the results of class differences in terms of life chances. Seeing the hostility around resource allocation only between the white working-class and ethnic minorities is a one-dimensional view. There is also intra- and inter-class resentment without which, the position of the respectable, employed working-class makes no sense. (Garner et al. 2009, 8)

However:

> Among the negative attitudes toward ethnic minorities were a minority of positive comments and empathy regarding their predicaments as asylum-seekers, and migrant workers doing jobs the British don't want to do, or providing services the British can't provide. There were also suggestions for activities that would encourage integration, but these were set against a context of criticism of government intervention in such a field, with people arguing that integration cannot be imposed. (Garner et al. 2009, 8)

> The contexts from which the interviewees were speaking differed in terms of: local black and minority ethnic populations and histories of migration; levels of economic and environmental development; and the type of frequency and quality of contacts with black and minority ethnic people. 'These contexts strongly inform, if not determine, people's attitude toward a number of issues, including perceptions of black and minority ethnic people.' (Garner et al. 2009, 9)

The conclusions which emerged from this research have strong implications for public libraries which have an important and sometimes unique position within local authorities as value-free, democratic public spaces. Public libraries are used by a wide range of local people and can be used as spaces where communities can be encouraged to meet and understand each other better. It is unlikely that these encounters will happen naturally and spontaneously, and so they will need to be enabled and facilitated by skilled community engagement and development workers. Taking the research findings as a call for action, here are some ways in which public libraries can change perceptions of ethnic minorities among poor white people, and thereby reduce feelings of resentment and promote community cohesion.

The importance of the local: the quality of the physical and social environment determined whether local issues were considered important.

This meant that in three of the four sites, immigration and integration were scarcely perceived as local issues at all. Local conditions are still very significant framing factors for any relationships between groups of people. This [does not mean] that an improvement in the physical and economic conditions of estates will necessarily lead to the disappearance of all hostile attitudes to minorities. There is a cultural element to racism that will be more difficult to erode. However, the processes of democratically-based local development appear to contribute to the narrowing of the scope for the type of competition, and vulnerability to such competition that seem to pervade much of what [was heard] in these interviews. (Garner et al. 2009, 9)

The great strength of public libraries is that they are community-based, or at least based in communities. The quality of the public library – from its physical fabric to the range and quality of its book stock and services, and the skills and empathy of its staff – can help to improve the quality of the physical and social environment. Just the sheer physical presence of a public library on a 'run down' estate can help to give the area a lift as it is evidence that someone cares about the local people. By their very nature public libraries cannot be said to be 'owned' or 'taken over' by one part of the local community, to the detriment of another part. The public library belongs to everyone and can become a focus of community pride and 'togetherness'.

Social Class as Part of Identity

People experience their social position through a number of lenses, and an important one (necessarily in a project that focuses on the 'white poor') is social class. People in this research seemed happy to refer, unprompted, to themselves and communities as 'working class', and the concerns they focused on were seen through a set of experiences that are clearly marked by class. (Garner et al. 2009, 9)

As has been shown by earlier discussions in this chapter, social class is a key determinant of library use and non-use. Typically, middle-class people tend to use public libraries more than the working class do, compared to the proportions of these classes within the population. In some areas the public library is dominated by white middle-class people, and this can make it an alien and uncomfortable environment for working-class people. Interestingly, research by Patrick Roach and Marlene Morrison (Roach and Morrison 1998) has indicated that many black and ethnic minority people also do not feel comfortable in public libraries. So here, yet again, we find that the real difference is not between white working-class people and black and ethnic minorities; the real difference is between the white working-class and middle-class people. The mission of public libraries is to transform themselves into welcoming environments where the white working class and black and ethnic minorities can feel at home.

'Assimilation' or *'integration'?*: all the interviewees were asked what integration meant to them.

> It emerged strongly that a majority understood 'integration' as meaning minorities giving up identity and merging with the local one, i.e. 'assimilation'. (Garner et al. 2009, 9)

In other words, most people think 'integration' means 'assimilation'.

Public libraries are safe spaces where the benefits of integration can be tested and demonstrated. A good starting point is to take a historical perspective which demonstrates how the local area has benefited from previous waves of new arrivals. There are few parts of the UK where the genes of local communities do not contain traces of earlier waves of migrants. Public libraries can also make some interesting cultural connections through family and local history. Gypsies, for example, have lived in England for over 500 years and can be regarded as one of our oldest ethnic minority groups. Yet they share many cultural similarities with new arrivals from Romania, and public libraries can bring these communities together to demonstrate and celebrate this shared cultural identity.

Political Correctness

> There are different ways in which this idea is used to describe obstacles to communication. At present, the function of stories about political correctness appears to be to recast the power relations pertaining to the situations described so that the white majority assume the role of victims. There is a need to sort what is genuinely unhelpful to dialogue, on the one hand, from what is actually protecting groups of people from abuse, on the other. (Garner et al. 2009, 9)

The campaign against political correctness is often driven by the populist media, such as the red-top daily newspapers. The editorial and opinion columns of newspapers like the *Sun*, *Daily Mail* and *Daily Express* are full of diatribes against 'trendy liberal ideas'. But these overt attacks on political correctness are often a convenient device to conceal more covert assaults on minority groups. Newspapers cannot condemn these groups directly because of anti-discrimination legislation, and so they use political correctness as a proxy.

For example, on 16 November 2009, the *Daily Express* editorial was headed 'Government strikes new blow against family values'. This was a comment on the National Academy for Parenting Practitioners (NAPP) whose director of research Stephen Scott was quoted as saying 'Lesbians make better parents than a man and a woman'. The *Daily Express* described the NAPP as 'the sort of new-fangled charity that receives taxpayer-funded grants and in return churns out fashionable and politically correct claptrap'. The editorial then becomes more sinister: 'Have they really studied enough cases over a long enough period to be sure that same-sex parenting does not risk inflicting psychological harm that becomes apparent in later life? And why is Scott silent on what research says about children brought up by gay men? Could it be that the story there is not so rosy?'. Predictably the blame is put on 'hard-line feminism' and 'public-sector socialists' who 'have long wanted to marginalize husbands and fathers. They will not be happy until families headed by mums and dads who are married to each other are an endangered species' (taken from: *Daily Express* 2009).

So here we have an article purportedly about family values and political correctness, but which is really a vicious attack on gays and lesbians, with an implication that they are a danger to children. A daily diet of this kind of ignorance and bigotry can lead to physical assaults on members of the gay and lesbian community. The role of the public library (which the *Daily Express* would regard as 'public-sector socialists') is to present positive and constructive viewpoints about so-called 'alternative lifestyles'. This can be via LGBT book collections and celebrations of Gay Pride and LGBT History Month, for example. This enables people to see both sides of the story and to recognise that minority groups have far more to fear from accusations of political correctness than the mainstream majority.

Competition for Resources

> Where immigration and integration are discussed in depth as problematic, there was a focus on real or perceived competition for resources: housing, benefits, jobs, territory and national culture. The implications of this for the political capital that can be accrued by the Far-right are very grave. [The] white interviewees' responses to minorities are far from universally negative. In fact everything from indifference, through empathy, a desire for more and better engagement, to anxiety was registered in these interviews. People express a desire for equality and a level playing field, not only in economic terms, but also in terms of ethnic groups (and even sections of ethnic groups). [It was suggested that] there is injustice and unfairness because the same rules do not seem to apply to everyone. However, the assumptions about who is entitled to resources seemed to lean toward a racial base, with local variations. (Garner et al. 2009, 9–10)

Public libraries, by their very nature, can demonstrate the benefits of sharing resources, rather than competing for them. A well-stocked and managed public library will provide resources for the whole community and will respond to need as well as demand. A needs-based library service will be flexible in its response to changing community requirements. The redirection of resources should not be presented as taking them away from one part of the community and giving them to another, as this is divisive and plays into the hands of far-right extremists. Instead it should be demonstrated that, by meeting the needs of one part of the community, it is also possible to improve services for other library users.

Another role which public libraries can play is that of 'myth-buster'. The real or perceived competition for resources can create urban myths such as 'all asylum-seekers are given new houses, jobs and cars'. These myths are supported by the popular media which regularly run banner headlines that stir up fear and resentment about immigration, for example. Public libraries can counter these half-truths by providing validated and accurate public information. Leaflets and web-based resources can be produced, using official sources, to dispel these myths – pointing out, for example, that asylum-seekers are not allowed to work until their status is resolved.

Although public libraries are not specifically mentioned in the report, they are a well-positioned vehicle for delivering the four principal recommendations:

1. There should be shared and consistent approaches at all levels of government. For example, a lead officer should be appointed at local authority level. Public libraries cannot and should not attempt to solve the challenges of community cohesion alone. This is best achieved via partnership working with a wide range of public, private, voluntary and community-sector agencies. Within these partnership arrangements public libraries can take the lead role in coordinating a shared and consistent approach.

2. The information deficits around immigration and resource-allocation should be reduced. 'The poor quality information available on which to base opinions is exacerbating people's sense of loss and frustration, therefore improving communication and making processes transparent can help address this issue' (Garner et al. 2009, 10). If information is power, then public libraries are an important source of that power. They are in a unique position to provide the widest range of unfettered and unmediated high quality information, available free at the point of need and demand. In addition to this important role of being an impartial source of community information, they can also play an important part in communicating this information, and sometimes interpreting it to meet local needs. Beyond the role of information provider, public libraries can also give advice, guidance and support and be advocates for the communities which they serve.

3. A working definition of integration should be established 'through concerted dialogue involving community groups, black and minority ethnic people and non-government organisations, as well as local authorities and central government ... Current understandings of this major policy concept are variable, and many tend toward assimilation rather than integration. Using dialogue to address what people really want and how to go about it, [public libraries can] focus on the shared solution of a problem, and provide opportunities for initiatives to develop from the ground upwards

as well as from the top down, which is not presently the case' (Garner et al. 2009, 10).

4. 'Political correctness' is widely regarded as a negative force, and so it is necessary, via dialogue, to evaluate 'exactly what people mean when they say this, and then attempt to sift what is helpful from what is less so' (Garner et al. 2009, 10). Public libraries can enable and facilitate the process of dialogue which is both a mechanism and part of the process of integration. Public libraries can help to lessen the scope for misunderstandings and to shrink the basis for the narratives of unfairness, while forming some bonds between people and communities that are not currently communicating.

In conclusion, it is essential that public libraries engage with all sections of their local communities, particularly non-users, the socially excluded and those who are at risk of exclusion. Some of these individuals and communities feel deserted and let down by national and local government. Such engagement is even more necessary at a time of economic recession and the rise of the British National Party, who seek to exacerbate community tensions to advance their electoral fortunes. The white working class are a key target group and should not be labelled as 'hard to reach' or even 'unreachable'. They certainly do not use public libraries anywhere near as much as middle-class people. Rather than denigrating 'Chavs' and treating them as the modern-day undeserving poor, we need to understand their fears, anxieties and needs and ensure that their voice is heard when we plan, design, deliver and evaluate library services.

Chapter 5
Tackling Social Exclusion

Introduction

In the previous chapters, we have looked at the historical background to and development of public libraries' work to tackle social exclusion. In this chapter, we examine critically what public libraries have been doing since 1997, assess key lessons learned from this experience, and lay the ground for the final chapter which will look at 'where next?'.

Public libraries' progress in tackling social exclusion is quite hard to assess, partly because there has been an enormous number of exciting developments in the last 10 years or so; partly because, despite this, advocacy for the role that public libraries can play has been relatively low-key; and partly because, at the time of writing, libraries are beset – along with the rest of local government – by a range of economic and political issues which threaten to undermine the good work that has been developed.

This chapter begins by skimming through developments since 1997, and then begins to assess progress made by public libraries in tackling social exclusion (and sustaining this work).

The Build-up After 1997

Chapters 2, 3 and 4 have set the scene historically; discussed what social exclusion is; and set the work in public libraries in its pre-1997 context.

Despite some major innovations in policy and delivery, public libraries were distinctly downbeat by 1997:

> Library services have been rationalised, reinstitutionalised and, like a 'business', required to demonstrate a degree of utilitarian efficiency. What looms as a result is a community librarianship with little sense of its ideals and a drift towards private provision and technological extinction. (Black and Muddiman 1997, 113)

What happened next?

Annual Library Plans

In 1998, DCMS introduced Annual Library Plans; every public library authority in England had to complete one, and they included information about the library service, reviews of past performance, and strategies and targets for the current and future years.

The first two reviews of the Plans (in 1998 and 1999) showed that public libraries were still having problems coming to grips with social exclusion. For example, the 1998 review found:

> Social inclusion was scored poorly … we have found many individual initiatives that are clearly directed at one or more minority groups, but what seems to be lacking is a comprehensive review of social inclusion, from a library service standpoint, and a co-ordinated response. (DCMS 1999b, 7)

The 1999 appraisal looked even more critically at libraries' performance in relation to tackling social exclusion:

> 6.3.2 54 authorities were assessed as 'Good' in relation to social inclusion policies overall; 73 were assessed as 'Satisfactory'; 19 were assessed as 'Poor' and 3 were assessed as 'Inadequate' for this section. (DCMS 2000)

Once again, it is surprising that so few authorities were assessed as 'Good' in relation to this policy area in view of the request from the DCMS to show how these policies were being taken into account in library planning. Of greatest concern is that the social inclusion dimension of access policies for the location and availability of libraries was considered by only 60 of the 149 authorities.

> 6.3.5 The low level of consideration of social inclusion relating to access policies is a matter of concern. (DCMS 2000, 19–20)

In addition:

> In 2001, the Government launched the Public Library Standards. The aim of the Standards was to help create a clear and widely accepted definition of a Library Authority's statutory duty to provide a 'comprehensive and efficient service', and set for the first time a performance monitoring framework for public libraries. Since then there has been a significant increase in library opening hours, improvements to stock and ICT provision, an increase in user satisfaction and visits. (DCMS 2008a, 3)

However, disappointingly, these new Standards did not attempt to evaluate public libraries' impact, but, rather, concentrated on 'traditional' inputs.

Libraries for All

As noted in Chapter 3, the Social Exclusion Unit was launched by the government in December 1997, and set up the 18 cross-cutting Policy Action Teams which produced a series of reports; however, these reports barely acknowledged the role of libraries, except for the report of PAT 15 identifying (in its remit statement only, not in the report itself!) public libraries as potential 'shared access points' (Policy Action Team 15 2000, 2).

Despite that, DCMS established a working group[1] that produced a consultation document, *Libraries for All* (DCMS 1999a), which identified the role that public libraries could play in tackling social exclusion (with case studies).

The report began by identifying some of the barriers which people face in trying to use libraries, and grouped these as:

- Institutional
- Personal and social
- Related to perceptions and awareness
- Environmental

The report's main recommendations were that:

1. Social inclusion should be mainstreamed as a policy priority within all library and information services
2. Library authorities should consider what specific services need to be tailored to meet the needs of minority groups and communities
3. Library authorities should consult and involve socially excluded groups in order to ascertain their needs and aspirations
4. Libraries should be located where there is a demand, but should build upon existing facilities and services wherever possible
5. Opening hours should be more flexible and tailored to reflect the needs and interests of the community
6. Library and information services should develop their role as community resource centres, providing access to communication as well as information
7. Library authorities should consider the possibilities of co-locating their facilities with other services provided by the local authority
8. Libraries should be the local learning place and champion of the independent learner
9. Libraries should be a major vehicle for providing affordable (or preferably free) access to ICT at local level
10. Library and information services should form partnerships with other learning organisations
11. Library authorities should consider whether some services aimed at socially excluded people might be more effectively delivered on a regional basis. (DCMS 1999a, 5)

---

1 John Pateman was a member of this working group.

The report also encouraged libraries to adopt a strategy based on the following six-point plan:

- Identify the people who are socially excluded and their distribution. Engage with them and establish their needs
- Assess and review current practice
- Develop strategic objectives and prioritise resources
- Develop the services, and train the library staff to provide them
- Implement the services and publicise them
- Evaluate success, review and improve. (DCMS 1999a, 5)

The final results of the consultation were published in 2001, following parallel consultations with the museums and archives sectors (DCMS 2001).

Public Libraries, Ethnic Diversity and Citizenship

In 1996, the University of Warwick commenced an 18-month study to investigate how public libraries have engaged in response to ethnic diversity. The final report was published in 1998 (Roach and Morrison 1998).

In her foreword, Margaret Kinnell Evans emphasised the importance of this piece of work:

> There has never been a greater need for research which explores the role of the public library and its relationship to citizenship. All the evidence of recent work suggests that library services are not achieving the widespread support across the community that was the major aim of their nineteenth century founders. (Evans 1998, 1)

She also cited the Aslib *Review* (Aslib 1995) which, she said, 'found that whole groups in the community were not being served effectively, despite the overall positive image of libraries' (Evans 1998, 1).

The study involved a literature review, a postal audit and four extended case studies. The key findings from the research were:

1. The public library service has not yet managed to engage fully with ethnically diverse communities;
2. A social distance exists between the public library and ethnic minority communities which tends to exclude ethnic minority citizens whilst preserving professional autonomy;
3. There is a clear lack of vision and leadership on ethnic diversity and racial equality matters within the public library service;
4. Across the public library service there is a lack of coherence in strategies to identify and track changing needs of ethnic minority communities and

in those strategies which seek to engage ethnic minorities in debate on the future of public library provision;

5. The public library is not yet central to or sufficiently supportive of the social and community networks established by ethnic minorities;

6. The structure, culture and ethnic profile of the public library service is restrictive in terms of service access and denies ethnic minorities a stake in the public library system;

7. The public library service has failed to account fully for its progress in respect of race equality whilst current performance systems are largely colour-blind;

8. The resource pressures on the public library service coupled with current uncertainty regarding the loss of special funds may present further challenges to ethnic minority engagement and inclusion. (Roach and Morrison 1998, 6–7)

Patrick Roach and Marlene Morrison concluded:

> it may be argued that the principle of 'universality' as expressed in the Public Libraries and Museums Act of 1964, rather than enabling, actually defeats equality by imposing a standard based on the needs of the most powerful or influential groups within society whilst failing to recognise the needs of less powerful or influential groups. In this way it has been possible for individual public library services to promote access for all whilst continuing to deliver, at best, colour blind (or, at worst, ethnically biased) service provisions. (Roach and Morrison 1998, 165)

The authors also published a set of baselines for good practice (Morrison and Roach 1998), which some public libraries (such as those in the London Borough of Enfield) began to use to reassess their services.

Open to All?

In 1998, the then Library and Information Commission (subsequently Resource, and now the Museums, Libraries and Archives Council) commissioned a research project, 'Public library policy and social exclusion', as part of its 'Value and impact of libraries' programme.

The project was based at the School of Information Management, Leeds Metropolitan University, and was carried out in partnership with the London Borough of Merton (Libraries); Sheffield Libraries, Archives and Information Services; and John Vincent.

The research was carried out between October 1998 and April 2000, and consisted of three main elements: researching and writing a set of Working Papers; a survey of all public library authorities in the UK; and eight case studies.

It was published in three volumes in 2000: Volume 1 (Muddiman et al. 2000a) contained the overview and conclusions of the research; Volume 2 (Muddiman et al. 2000b) contained the survey, case studies and research methods; and Volume 3 (Muddiman et al. 2000c) contained the 16 Working Papers.

The research project made over 50 recommendations, looking at all areas of public library provision. These recommendations have certainly stood the test of time, and we thought that it was important to reiterate them – they are included as the appendix to this volume.

Whilst other pieces of library research had tended to have a small blaze of publicity and then disappear, *Open to All?* was successfully launched by Mo Mowlam MP – who had contributed the foreword to the report (Mowlam 2000, vi) – in July 2000 and, as well as gaining considerable, continuing press coverage, also led directly to a number of key developments.

These included:

- the setting up of the Quality Leaders Project;
- the setting up of The Network;
- involvement in other developments.

The Quality Leaders Project

A number of the Working Papers (e.g. Vincent 1999; Durrani 2000) produced as part of the 'Public Library Policy and Social Exclusion' research reiterated issues of racism and the need for libraries to take some form of positive action to support BME staff and potential staff. Leading on from this, Shiraz Durrani (London Borough of Merton) and Paul Joyce (University of North London) investigated options (Durrani and Joyce 2000), and, with support from the Library and Information Commission, carried out a pilot project, looking at how library services could be enhanced to meet better the needs of black and Asian communities. Following full evaluation (Bartlett 2001), the Quality Leaders Project was launched; and, in 2002, was developed to become the Quality Leaders Project-Youth [QLP-Y].

> The QLP-Y project is designed to address social exclusion of young people from libraries and other services, through developing partnership between library services, youth services and community groups.
>
> Its aim is to create opportunities for young people to participate in society and to develop their creativity, reading and life skills, through developing staff skills and innovative services responsive to the needs of young people. (The Network c.2007)

This work was also evaluated (Pitcher and Eastwood-Krah 2008), and led to the development of a new strand of work, 'Skills for a globalised world: relevant skills for public library staff' (The Network 2009a):

The QLP experience suggests that the combination of work-based learning, supported by an academic approach, will lead to a significant level of skills development, unlikely with an entirely work-based or entirely university-based approach. By supporting staff to develop services/management skills within their own work-based context, learning opportunities aim at enhancing staff motivation and confidence and re-engaging workers with a learning agenda, facilitating further progression both academically and professionally. (Durrani and Smallwood 2009, 2)

The Network

Formed following a seminar in February 1999 (as part of the dissemination and publicity for the research project, 'Public library policy and social exclusion'), The Network continues to run courses, seminars and conferences; to publish a monthly Newsletter (and e-bulletins in between); to coordinate a number of email lists; and to advocate the role of libraries, museums and archives in tackling social exclusion and working towards social justice.

The Network has worked on a number of specific projects, such as 'Welcome To Your Library' (Welcome To Your Library 2009), and working with the Paul Hamlyn Foundation to promote the role that libraries play in supporting children and young people in care (see, for example, Vincent 2004).

Launched nationally at the Public Library Authorities Conference in Torquay in October 1999, The Network has, at the time of writing, some 136 organisational members, plus a growing number of individual members.

Member organisations and individuals use The Network to:

- ensure that their services are well placed to meet national, regional and local objectives on social justice;
- share expertise and good practice;
- make enquiries of other Network members;
- work with other Network members to benchmark services (e.g. library services in the East Midlands have worked with John Vincent to draw up a 'distance-travelled' benchmarking tool as a way of assessing how well their work with children in care is developing);
- receive relevant information to keep abreast of developments and promote their work as part of integrated service planning and delivery;
- receive in-house training at reduced cost;
- draw on the consultancy skills of a range of practitioners, for example on development strategies and policies: currently this is happening around refugee education.

The Role of the Museums, Libraries and Archives Council

After setting up the 'Public library policy and social exclusion' research project, and publishing the results, Resource (and its successor body, the Museums, Libraries and Archives Council [MLA]) took a real lead in developing approaches to tackling social exclusion (and investigating other social policy areas). For example, they:

- Initiated public library developments via the 'Framework for the future' implementation plan (Museums, Libraries and Archives Council 2003).
- Supported further research into the role of libraries, museums and archives in tackling social exclusion (e.g. via: Museums Libraries and Archives Council 2003; Book Marketing Ltd 2004).
- Consulted widely and produced guidance and toolkits (e.g. Hopkins 2000; Museums, Libraries and Archives Council 2004b; Kerley no date, *c*.2004) and, in 2003–4, the major 'Disability Portfolio' (all 12 guides are available to download from Museums, Libraries and Archives Council 2008b) to support work in libraries (and museums and archives).
- Organised training courses, for example for representatives from the MLA Regions, and supported a series of courses (run by the Research Centre for Museums and Galleries and The Network) on tackling social exclusion, which were run regionally; they also evaluated the effectiveness of these (Resource 2003).
- Introduced their 'New Directions in Social Policy' strand in 2005 (Hylton 2004; Linley 2004; Weisen 2004; Burns Owen Partnership 2005).
- Seed-funded The Network on a one-off basis to support the provision of training, the production of the regular newsletters, and the extension of The Network's coverage to museums, galleries and archives.

Other Developments

In addition, members of the 'Public library policy and social exclusion' research team were involved in (or advised) a number of other pieces of work which continued to ensure that its recommendations were taken up and acted upon. These pieces of work included:

- The parallel assessment of work to tackle social exclusion in archives (National Council on Archives 2001).
- The Social Inclusion Advisory Group to CILIP, which reported in 2002 and which emphasised that 'CILIP should lead the mobilisation of the LIS sector's response to social exclusion and diversity' (Social Inclusion Executive Advisory Group to CILIP 2002, 32).
- The cross-sectoral research which led to publication of *Mapping Social Inclusion in Publicly-funded Libraries in Wales* (Grimwood-Jones 2003).

This report identified a number of key issues to be resolved: cross-sectoral and partnership working; access issues; staffing and training; raising the profile of libraries; measuring impact. Following the publication of this report, many of these began to be implemented, for example the establishment of cross-authority consortia (e.g. for training) and the production of cross-Wales public library publicity.

What Happened Next?

Many public libraries embarked on a wide range of initiatives to tackle social exclusion; as noted above, this was spurred on by a number of factors, including:

- Tackling social exclusion had become a UK government and local government priority, emphasised, for example by *Framework for the Future* (DCMS 2003) and the Shared Priorities between central and local government (Local Government Association 2002).
- Organisations such as MLA emphasised the need to tackle social exclusion.
- External funding became available, assisting in the development of these services.
- There was a considerable emphasis on training and staff development in order to gain the necessary skills to build inclusive services.
- Library staff who were committed to tackling social exclusion saw an opportunity to develop community-based service provision.

Within the scope of this book, it is possible only to give a flavour of this exciting period.

Policy Development

Many public libraries examined their existing policies and practices, and created approaches to making their services more inclusive.

A key example was Leicester Library Service. In 2000, their situation looked bleak:

> We appear to be losing some support for traditional uses and reaching insufficient numbers of adults and children living in the most disadvantaged areas and communities in the city, who are in great need of the resources and services libraries provide. (Leicester City Libraries 2000, 3)

The then Head of Service, Patricia Flynn, gained support of local councillors to undertake a review of their library service, using social inclusion as the focus for the review. This led to a complete overhaul of provision, particularly the important re-focusing of the service on the needs of BME communities (and the highly symbolic re-siting of the Asian language materials close to the entrance to the central library).

As a result, tackling social exclusion became embedded in all their work (for example, their work as a partner in 'Welcome To Your Library' was developed as part of the mainstream library service), and the library service began to contribute actively to council-wide priorities and targets.

As a Best Value inspection found in 2002:

> the Best Value Review 'Achieving Inclusion' provided excellent prospects for improvement because it has a 'clear and ambitious vision for the future; a robust improvement plan, improvements which are realistic, timetabled and resourced, innovative use of partnership and external funding and strong commitment to change from Councillors and staff.' (Leicester City Libraries 2003, 1)

Work with Priority Target Groups – Libraries Change Lives Awards

CILIP has hosted the Awards since 1992, when they were originally called the Community Initiative Award – since 1998, they have been known as the Libraries Change Lives Awards (LCLA).[2]

The Award highlights and rewards good practice in any innovative library and information projects which:

- Change lives
- Bring people together
- Involve user communities
- Demonstrate innovation and creativity
- Develop staff and services. (CILIP 2009c)

The winners and finalists are a roll-call of exciting and innovative pieces of work (for the winners and finalists 1992–2008, see CILIP Community Services Group 2009). They also encompass work with many of the key socially excluded groups, so we are using these as an indication of the range of work developed in public libraries (although, of course, they are not comprehensive). They include:

- *Adults with learning difficulties*: It's My Life, Enfield Libraries and Enfield Disability Action – finalist 2005 (CILIP 2009e); Bradford/Care Trust Libraries Partnership Project – winner 2008 (Brown 2009a; CILIP 2009i).
- *Black and minority ethnic communities*: The Northamptonshire Black History Project, Northamptonshire Racial Equality Council (lead agency) and Northamptonshire Library and Information Service (community partner) – winner 2005 (CILIP 2009e); Multicultural Development Service,

---

2   John Vincent was a judge for the LCLA 2009–10 and 2010–11.

Lincolnshire County Council Library Service – finalist 2006 (CILIP 2009b).

- *Children with Autistic Spectrum Disorders*: Across the Board: Autism support for families, Leeds Library and Information Service – winner 2009 (CILIP 2009a).
- *Community engagement via IT*: Nunny TV, North East Lincolnshire Library Service – finalist 2008 (CILIP 2009i).
- *Health/bibliotherapy*: Read Yourself Well, East Ayrshire Library, Registration and Information Services – finalist 2007 (CILIP 2009g).
- *Looked-after children and young people*: Caring about Reading, Leicestershire County Library Services – finalist 2003 (CILIP 2009j); The Edinburgh Reading Champion Project, City of Edinburgh Council – finalist 2009 (CILIP 2009a).
- *Refugees and asylum-seekers*: Welcome To Your Library, Camden Libraries, Leicester Libraries, working with London Libraries Development Agency – winner 2007 (CILIP 2009g).
- *Travellers*: The Mobile Library Travellers Project, Essex County Council Libraries – winner 2004 (CILIP 2009d).
- *Visually impaired people*: eye2eye: the visually impaired IT project, Portsmouth City Libraries – winner 2003 (CILIP 2009j); Large (Leeds Always Reading Group for Everyone), Leeds School Library Service – finalist 2007 (CILIP 2009g).
- *Young people – excluded and vulnerable children and teenagers*: Sighthill Library Youth Work, Edinburgh City Libraries and Information Service – winner 2006; and Books on the Edge, Blackburn with Darwen Borough Council – finalist 2006 (CILIP 2009b).

Work with Priority Target Groups – the DCMS/Wolfson Fund

The DCMS/Wolfson Public Libraries Challenge Fund (see, for example, Wallis et al. 2002) was established in 1997 to give £3 million per year for three years to projects to enhance library services in England, and supported much work to tackle social exclusion.

Examples of the kinds of work funded were:

- *Bibliotherapy* – Kirklees, a local project, targeted at users in poor health.
- *Black Inc.* (initially Black Lines) the London Borough of Brent, a local project, targeted at African-Caribbean and black British communities.
- *Cool Books* – Gatehouse Publishing Company, a national project, targeted at prisoners.
- *Fully Booked* – Cheshire County Library, a local project targeted at adults aged 65 and over in need of support and care.
- *Reading Lifelines* – a consortium project led by Bolton Metropolitan District, a regional project targeted at socially excluded 16–25 year olds.

- *Reading Opportunities for Looked After Children (ROLAC)* – Gateshead Metropolitan District, a local project, targeted at looked after children and their carers.
- *Southampton Storysacks* – Southampton City, a local project targeted at socially excluded people of all kinds.
- *Stories from the Web* – a consortium project led by Birmingham City, a national project targeted at children and young people.
- *Talking Cumbria* – Cumbria County Library, a local project targeted at the visually impaired.
- *Traveller Outreach* – a consortium project led by Sutton with Merton, a local project targeted at Travellers.

Work with Priority Target Groups – Paul Hamlyn Foundation Reading and Libraries Challenge Fund

The Paul Hamlyn Foundation (PHF) launched this Fund in 2003:

> The Reading and Libraries Challenge Fund is intended to effect long-term change to the way libraries and other institutions work with young people and others with limited access to books and reading. (Paul Hamlyn Foundation *c*.2007)

There were three streams:

- 'Right to Read' – access to books and reading for children and young people in public care.
- 'Free with Words' – access to books and reading for prisoners and young offenders, e.g. Prison Reading Champions (Prisoners' Education Trust 2009).
- 'Libraries Connect' – focused on communities, such as refugees and asylum seekers, which are not benefiting from the services public libraries offer. Work funded included: The Reader Organisation (health and bibliotherapy); Nottingham City Library and Information Service, and Welcome To Your Library Phase 2 (refugees and asylum-seekers); Blackburn with Darwen Borough Council, and Partners for Change (for a brief summary, see The Reading Agency 2005) (young people).

Some 45 of the funded projects were in the 'Right to Read' stream (which had been set up in 2001, following a successful pilot, to support children and young people in care, and which became a part of the Reading and Libraries Challenge Fund); an interim evaluation report, which gives a real taste of this work, was published in 2007 (Griffiths et al. 2007).

Work with Priority Target Groups – Big Lottery Fund

In 2006–7, the Big Lottery Fund invited bids from a 'pot' of £80m, which had been created:

> to fund libraries that are more than traditional library services and worked with their communities to:
>
> 1. invigorate libraries as centres of wider community learning and development and learning based activities
> 2. create, improve and develop library spaces that meet the needs of the whole community
> 3. be innovative and promote good practice in the ways libraries are designed and run. (Big Lottery Fund no date, *c.*2007)

Some 58 applicants were successful, and these library services:

> worked with their communities to identify the activities that they would offer, that would best meet the needs of those communities. Many different opportunities were identified, including reading groups, writing groups, language classes, family learning activities, art and museum exhibitions, cultural activities such as drama, health activities such as well-being classes, information seminars about local volunteering or other opportunities, work experience library gardens, and outreach activities into more remote communities. (Big Lottery Fund no date, *c.*2007)

At the time of writing, the exciting range of new developments is starting to appear (see, for example, Big Lottery Fund 2009).

Work with Priority Target Groups – the National Year of Reading

The National Year of Reading (NYR) ran from January to December 2008 in England (see Thomson 2009) and Wales (see Welsh Books Council 2008; Arad Consulting 2009).

In England, the NYR aimed to increase reading activity overall, but with specific emphasis on a number of key target groups:

a. white working-class boys (defined as being on free school meals)
b. families from socio-economic groups 2DE – particularly fathers
c. Key Stage 3 children, especially boys
d. Bangladeshi and Pakistani children
e. newly-arrived East Europeans
f. dyslexic children and visually impaired children
g. looked after children
h. adults seeking 'skills for life' (Thomson 2009, 5).

Undoubtedly, the NYR was an overall success: for example, '2.3 million new library members through the first ever national promotion of library membership … 23,000 more boys taking part in The Summer Reading Challenge' (Thomson 2009, 28). The evaluation report includes a number of small case studies of good practice in public libraries in England.

However, the NYR work also threw up a number of challenges which still need to be addressed, for example the lack of:

> historic data about the engagement of the target groups with libraries. Some libraries have found establishing membership numbers a real challenge. Only 65 (44 per cent) services could provide information on the breakdown of new members into adults and children/young people. Not all services collect ethnicity data for new joiners. No services are able to supply comprehensive data on some specific NYR audiences, for example, white working-class boys or looked after children, as it would be inappropriate to ask for such information at the time of joining. (Thomson 2009, 75)

These factors severely inhibited many libraries' engagement with the NYR priority groups.

Libraries' approaches to their users were also challenged:

> There are therefore lost opportunities inherent in the view that 'we are here to serve everyone so we will not target anyone'. The risk is that little is done to attract new readers, and the existing user-base continues to be the same in character … Readers are not all the same. The same messages and the same service will not appeal to all, even to all readers who appear to be in the same group. (Thomson 2009, 49)

The evaluation report also highlighted issues around literacy:

> The challenge the nation faces in improving literacy is not exclusive to the more excluded groups of society – that is, those who are less likely to join in education, libraries and so on, or who are less likely to feel that these services are really for them. However, there is a disproportionate concentration of lower literacy rates amongst the poor, the disaffected, the newly-immigrant, those for whom English is a new or second language, the imprisoned and the otherwise disadvantaged. These groups were a logical focus for the NYR and, as we have seen, they often need to start their journey into more reading at a point quite distant from the sort of reading they believe schools and libraries mainly offer. (Thomson 2009, 47)

In Wales, the NYR had three main thrusts:

- Give a Book Week: a campaign 'using images of personalities and prominent figures in public life to generate positive publicity' (Arad Consulting 2009, 5).

- Reading Communities: Barry and Llanelli.
- 08 Clubs: '50 reading clubs across Wales, with over 500 children and young people involved – the vast majority boys' (Arad Consulting 2009, 6).

In addition, every library authority in Wales was given a small additional sum to spend on reading promotion activities.

According to the evaluation, the work with libraries was successful. For example:

> A number of library services reported increased numbers of people attending events and an increase in the numbers of registered borrowers, including children and young people. Local authorities also reported an upward trend in the number of children taking part in, and completing, the Summer Reading Challenge.
>
> … There is some evidence that the additional funding enabled libraries to try out activities that would not have been part of their usual programme of activity and, as such, the relatively small sums of money enabled them to think more creatively.
>
> … The extra funds made a contribution to partnership working at a local level. Around half of the local authority areas set up a Year of Reading steering group which, in some cases, drew together a diverse and impressive list of partners. New partnerships were also created and others strengthened as a result of delivering the activities. (Arad Consulting 2009, 7)

Work with Priority Target Groups – Other Initiatives

This is just a sample of some of the other initiatives that were developed:

- Work with new communities (refugees, migrant workers and others) (Lincolnshire County Council Culture and Adult Education 2008; Ngyou 2009; Southend Borough Libraries. Community and Diversity Team 2009).
- Work with older people – brief case studies and descriptions of initiatives are included in the recent 'good practice guide' (Sloan and Vincent 2009).
- Work with housebound people, for example Falkirk's 'Home Sound', a project to provide adapted CD players and spoken word resources for sight-impaired and physically disabled homebound library members to borrow (SLAINTE: Information and Libraries Scotland *c*.2009).
- Development of work with prisoners, ex-prisoners and their families (see, for example, Cashman 2009).
- Work to support 'Skills for Life', development of Basic Skills, ESOL (e.g. Southend Borough Libraries. Community and Diversity Team 2008).
- Provision of information to support homeless people, for example the project involving seven London library authorities (Outside Story 2009).

Staff Development and Training

Finally, the period since 1997 has seen a real growth in training around broad and specific areas of social inclusion and social justice.

The need for training of library staff had been identified during the 'Public library policy and social exclusion' research project:

> public libraries also need to ensure that they have high quality training in place for all their staff. This should include thorough induction training, as well as in-depth training in all aspects of service provision, particularly focusing on tackling social exclusion. (Muddiman et al. 2000a, 53)

The need for resources for staff training in social inclusion issues was highlighted by the DCMS (DCMS 2001); and the Demos report (Demos 2003) for the then Resource spelled out the very real skills gap – and that different kinds of people were needed to work in libraries (and museums and archives). CILIP too, in the report of its Executive Advisory Group (Social Inclusion Executive Advisory Group to CILIP 2002), stressed the importance of training and leadership.

The MLA Workforce Development Strategy (Museums Libraries and Archives Council 2004a) highlighted a number of key areas where staff development and training were required, including new audience development and service delivery skills.[3]

However, as John Vincent has noted:

> Interestingly, whilst these areas clearly relate to the training required for tackling social exclusion, nothing specific about training in diversity, inclusion (or wider political awareness) appears to have been identified at this stage. Indeed, whilst there has been considerable investment in training to meet two strands of *Framework for the Future* (Department for Culture, Media and Sport 2003) – the people's Network and reader development – there has been less focus generally on the third strand which includes tackling social exclusion. (Vincent 2009b)

Partly to fill this gap, The Network has organised a series of training courses over the last 10 years, working with organisations such as the MLA, CILIP, 'library schools', and also working in local authorities directly (in 2007 and 2008, The Network ran/spoke at some 30 training events each year; in 2009, 25).

---

3   Interestingly, in the latest revision of this Strategy (Museums, Libraries and Archives Council 2009), MLA have shifted the focus to the make-up of the workforce itself, prioritising: leadership development; widening entry routes; increasing the demographic diversity of the workforce; e-skills development. These are all vital, but do not necessarily focus on tackling social exclusion for library users (and non-users).

The training needs of library staff – particularly in relation to tackling social exclusion – were again highlighted in recent research by Kerry Wilson and Briony Birdi (Wilson and Birdi 2008), and we take a closer look at this in Chapter 7.

The Legacy

Overview

So – after all these developments and initiatives, have public libraries fundamentally changed their approach? What is the legacy of all this work (and expenditure)?

It is clear that public libraries have changed, and this section begins by looking at some of the specific developments and assessing their impact. This is then followed by our overall evaluation of progress and achievements, plus a link in to Chapter 7 which looks at what needs to be done next and the way forward.

Context – The Policy Framework

For a number of reasons, social inclusion/social justice appears to have slipped down the DCMS/MLA agenda. As background to a paper at Umbrella 2009 (Vincent 2009d), John Vincent looked at how social justice and community cohesion were covered on the DCMS and MLA websites. A quick search revealed nothing on the DCMS site; the MLA website had nothing specific, although there was a couple of references in the Action Plan for Public Libraries:

- Put the community at the heart of developing and delivering services, engaging with people and responding to their needs.
- Embed excellence, creativity and diversity; innovate and adapt to new working methods. (Museums, Libraries and Archives Council 2008d, 2)

Obviously, 'talk' at government level at the time of writing is almost entirely about the financial crisis and public expenditure cuts; although 2010 has been designated the European Year for Combating Poverty and Social Exclusion (Department for Work and Pensions 2009b), thinking and actions are not being related to it.

In addition, the MLA suffered in the last round of the Comprehensive Spending Review, and, as a result, has had a major restructuring which has led, so far, at least, to less focus on this area of social policy.

The Lack of Evidence, Especially Targeted to People Outside the 'Library World'

Early in 2009, the DCMS published the important, final report of BOP Consulting's analysis of the impact that public libraries were having. This highlighted the urgent need for libraries to provide reliable evidence, and to present it in language that is understood by funding bodies, government departments, and other partners. (There will be greater consideration of this key report in Chapter 7).

As noted above, the evaluation of the NYR showed that, sadly, even at a fairly basic level, public libraries were unable to provide 'historic data about the engagement of the target groups with libraries' (Thomson 2009, 75).

Fortunately, some NYR development work by public libraries did hit others' targets; Leeds Metropolitan University carried out an evaluation of the National Year of Reading in Yorkshire against the Generic Social Outcomes and the National Indicators. They found that there was:

> considerable evidence of NYR related activities in supporting the three primary social outcomes 'Stronger and Safer Communities', 'Health and Well-Being' and 'Strengthening Public Life'. (Rankin et al. 2009, 19)

In relation to the National Indicators, they similarly found that:

> the evidence gathered from the case study authorities held 'Stronger communities' to be their most important issue. Obviously the 'Use of public libraries['] (N 9) was very strong, but also 'Belonging to neighbourhood' and 'People from different backgrounds' were significant. The evidence shows that they had the needs of 'children and young people', 'adult health and wellbeing' and tackling exclusion and promoting equality inherent in what they do. (Rankin et al. 2009, 21)

In addition, work is, at last, being developed to highlight the contribution that public libraries can make, for example by the MLA (Museums, Libraries and Archives Council 2008a); CILIP's 'Campaigning toolkit' (CILIP 2009k); and the Society of Chief Librarians' 'Libraries Inspire' campaign (Society of Chief Librarians 2009). In addition, The Network has been advocating the positive role that public libraries (and others) can play, for example in a recent response to the Centre for Excellence and Outcomes in Children and Young People's Services (C4EO) (Vincent 2009a).

The Legacy of the Libraries Change Lives Award

As noted above, over the 17 years of the Award, some outstanding work by libraries and their partners has been recognised. Many built on this recognition by using the prize money to take their services to new levels: for example, the 2001 winner, the London Borough of Merton Libraries (for 'Refugee resources collection and service'), used the money to develop more in-depth work with refugees (which, in turn, allowed Merton to become part of the pilot stage of 'Welcome To Your Library'). Other winners' or finalists' work was pioneering, and acted as a catalyst to drive forward library initiatives, for example the 1995 winner, Sunderland Libraries and Booktrust, for Bookstart; and the 1998 winner, Wakefield Libraries for the Pontefract Library Readers' Group, which inspired the reader development movement.

An immense amount of hard work has gone in to developing the LCLA, and, clearly, the winners, finalists, and those who submitted their work for consideration have also put a huge effort into this. Yet, somehow, some of these worthy projects never quite made their mark beyond their winning year. Why was this?

Part of the issue was, in earlier years, the lack of 'reach' of the Award beyond a fairly narrow audience (librarians!); what was needed – and has become a much more successful feature of the LCLA – was publicity and a way of 'hitting the headlines', showing that these pieces of work really do transform people's lives. This approach has begun to pay off, with, for example, the 2009 Awards getting a much higher profile (including building on the popularity and 'name' of Sir Andrew Motion).

Secondly – and this is a theme that runs through this legacy section – part of the reason has to be that many of the nominations were projects. They were time- or resources-limited, and were not destined to continue much beyond their year of fame. This too has been addressed in recent years, with a much greater insistence that winners and finalists should be sustainable pieces of work, not only in themselves but also as pieces of work that can be replicated easily elsewhere. The 2009 winner, Leeds Library and Information Service's 'Across the Board: Autism Support for Families' (CILIP 2009a), is just that, a sustainable piece of work which can also be easily rolled out across other public library services at very little cost.

The Legacy of External Funding

The Paul Hamlyn Foundation's 'Reading and Libraries Challenge Fund' (RLCF) has been assessed, and the final report is due to be published in 2010. The report makes it clear that there has been significant progress in those libraries involved in the RLCF, and highlights some of the key lessons learned:

- The importance of library staff's having a sophisticated understanding of users' needs:

  > it was critical that staff be willing and able to invest time continuously towards listening effectively to users' needs, and how they varied and changed. It is no surprise that the amount of time required was often underestimated. The value of going through this process was strengthened further when those working on projects were effective in sharing the knowledge and insight gained. (Carpenter 2010, 9)

- The importance of staff training.
- Ensuring that consultation with and engagement of users were clear and full.

- The importance of improving access and welcome (particularly by involving people from local, target communities).
- The importance of building and maintaining partnerships; those projects that demonstrated successful partnership working included the following:
  - Providing support to community organisations to help them meet their own objectives and giving them a better understanding of what libraries do.
  - Mutual understanding of different organisational cultures alongside flexibility and willingness to adapt to changing circumstances.
  - Clear objectives and clarity about roles and responsibilities of different partners in formal and informal project steering groups and any joint project work.
  - A strategic approach, with strong multi-agency commitment to tackling specific priorities and developing a recognised role for the library service and specific projects.
  - Exchanging and sharing skill-sets with partners in other sectors such as health, in order to co-develop strategy and project work and adopt a more reflective approach.
  - Addressing with partners the options for sustaining work in the long-term at the earliest opportunity. (Carpenter 2010, 14–15)

Yet, at the same time, the report identifies a number of key issues and gaps (for example, lack of sustainability, poor project management, lack of leadership), and has pulled out the following key issues:

Learning from delivery of projects

- Evidence from project work shows that most new ideas have come from staff working at or near the frontline, as well as from working across sectors and boundaries, with communities and partners with different backgrounds and skills.
- Long-term success is contingent on vision, effective ownership and planning, and real motivation and proactive commitment at *all* levels to: work creatively and collaboratively; be open to learning; exchange good practice; and move away from a service-led model.
- Flexibility is required. What is relevant and appropriate in one location may not be right in another, and public libraries need to be in a position to make decisions based on evidence about their local population.
- Local authorities have tended overall to be hierarchical and risk-averse, with structures that militate against innovation and create departmental silos. Public libraries are not immune from this and it poses a challenge for the sector.
- Bold change may be viewed as too risky by local authorities. They may be content to see a library service coasting if that service is perceived as

a small part of council business, if it is not currently failing in relation to national indicators and satisfaction levels, and if the perception of what would be gained from the changes is seen as limited.

- The lack of space and incentive for developing foresight, reflection and creative thinking, combined with pressure to meet delivery targets, has led to timid, incremental improvements, rather than stepping back and asking more radical questions.
- A more profound systemic transformation is needed than what a project can achieve alone, but that transformation needs to draw on learning from innovative project and partnership work. Catalysts and leaders are needed to nurture new ways of working.
- Heads of library services have a critical role in making change happen, but they need appropriate supporting infrastructure, tools and programmes to help them engage with local communities and ensure that communities really are at the heart of delivering services.
- Libraries do not have to play a lead role in partnerships, but do need to be able to articulate and define much more clearly what their contribution is, with evidence to back this up.
- Libraries need to have a clear vision of what they want to achieve, and to plan and deliver to new audiences in a way that demonstrates their public value.
- Lack of clarity of purpose has tended to leave public libraries at the periphery of local government concerns, with too much emphasis on processes and not enough on demonstrating how they are able to transform lives.

Wider impact

- The lack of articulation of a clear, shared vision and purpose within the sector is reflected in a lack of understanding and recognition in the external policy environment of the wider role and value of public libraries.
- Strong leadership and direction is needed within government to generate a renewed sense of impetus and purpose, and to drive improvement. There are already national strategies and policy frameworks in place that can help place public library work into context – for example in relation to community empowerment.
- Advocating for and positioning public libraries across central and local government is essential to opening up opportunities and resources for strategic long-term partnership working – for example in relation to citizenship and integration.
- Champions at every level in and outside the sector are vital, as are constructive critical friends in positions of authority with no direct connection to library service delivery. They can challenge and support, refresh debate about the future, provide different perspectives and stimulate new ideas and ways of thinking.

- Partnerships need to be part of a long-term phased approach to change management, for example to enable cross-sector skills-sharing and opportunities for funding to test and develop new ways of working.
- There needs to be a clear analysis of the skills and diversity needed in the library service of the future. This needs to be coupled with far more opportunities for staff that are eager to acquire the necessary leadership, management, communication and people-skills needed for a dynamic and outward-facing service. (Carpenter 2010, 18–19)

Between 2002 and 2006, the Laser Foundation (Laser Foundation 2007) funded some major public library initiatives. These included two studies (Leadbetter 2003; Coates 2004) which, whilst not specifically about social justice, did raise key issues about public libraries – and opened up a debate about their role and governance, a debate that is still rolling on at the time of writing! The initiatives also included two ground-breaking community engagement initiatives: the Birchfield Library Community Consultation Project (Birmingham City Council 2007) which should be better known; and Bolton Libraries' arts-based consultation, 'What do you want? A library service for the future', the legacy of which has been a growth in innovative ways of engaging with local communities, especially people who may not regularly use public libraries.

The Reviews of the Public Library Service

As noted elsewhere in this book, 2008–9 saw the publication of two reviews of public libraries (Davies 2008; All-Party Parliamentary Group on Libraries, Literacy and Information Management 2009) – and a further instalment in the DCMS Modernisation Review (DCMS 2009b)!

The two completed reviews pointed out key issues facing public libraries – particularly in their governance and sustainability – and the DCMS Modernisation review covered the same territory. As we shall discuss in Chapter 7, unless there is a clear direction and leadership for public libraries from now on, these three pieces of work are in danger of being added to the stacks of other public library reports, unread and unused.

Other Assessments

In 2008, the MLA published a research report which 'has established a baseline which the MLA and Big Lottery Fund will use to evaluate the programme in future years' (Taylor and Pask 2008, 5).

The purpose of this research was to evaluate current levels and quality of community engagement, and to identify and disseminate good practice, and to assess the effectiveness of the Communities Libraries programme. It looked at six case study authorities (five Communities Libraries Programme funding recipients and one 'counter example' case study).

The overall conclusion was very positive:

> We found that the case study authorities are, despite capacity challenges, working hard to take advantage of what they recognise as a significant opportunity to transform not only the individual libraries receiving programme funding, but also their entire services. We feel that they are on the whole on course to achieve significant positive results. (Taylor and Pask 2008, 5)

However, at the same time, the research identified six areas for improvement, which show that some key areas were still under-developed:

- Vision and goals
- Community segmentation
- Organisational transformation
- Effective communications
- Real social networks
- Methods and metrics (i.e. the development of a methodology around 'what works' and ways of measuring this impact).

In his recent book about public libraries, lecturer and writer David McMenemy has been critical of progress:

> It would seem then that while public libraries have a clear identification with a mission towards social inclusion, research indicates that much work remains to be done to ensure this is the case. (McMenemy 2009, 52)

Finally, John Vincent recently evaluated provision for BME communities (Vincent 2009c) and concluded:

> There have been immense changes in the past 40 years, not only in UK society generally, but also in public libraries' provision for BME communities specifically. Many public libraries have built strong links with their local communities, creating (often iconic) places where people come together; they also recognise the importance of diversity, and are looking beyond the notion that people are simply one-dimensional (for example Black) to seeing people as belonging to many communities.
>
> Yet, at the same time, some of the problems that Claire Lambert[4] identified are still with us – the desire for someone else to solve issues for us, the lack of real communication with parts of our communities.
>
> Finally, this brief analysis of events over the past 40 years has also highlighted a major failing by public libraries and public library agencies so far – the lack of engagement in wider public policy. There has been a number of opportunities

---

4   The author of the original article (Lambert 1969) which this one was reassessing.

when libraries could have engaged – for example around citizenship, race relations, migration, diversity – showing how they contribute to these wider agendas, even taking a bold stand to start debate (on how to break down the 'mono-cultural' approach to communities noted above, for example), and working with partners to demonstrate their value to society, yet examples where this has happened are few and far between. (Vincent 2009c, 144)

So, What Progress Has Been Made Since 1997?

There certainly has been some extraordinary, innovative and imaginative work undertaken in the last 13 years, which has really begun to remove barriers to the take-up of library services for people who are socially excluded (and, as in all good practice, this has then had a positive impact on library services for everybody). Some examples of this are given above, and many public libraries can feel justifiably proud of the role they have been playing and the impact they have had.

A handful of public libraries have gone even further, and have begun to change the very core of their services, moving towards the kinds of provision recommended in *Open to All?* (Muddiman et al. 2000a):

- Long-term strategies for tackling social exclusion, which involve:
  – Targeting priority needs and resources
  – Secure and sustainable funding
  – Advocacy and innovation, including proactive outreach, advocacy and intervention
  – Monitoring and evaluation.
- The scope to take positive action (for example, in developing training and the recruitment of staff with necessary skills and experience)
- Undertaken community profiling and/or needs analysis to help determine local needs and priorities
- Involved local communities in the setting and development of social exclusion strategies and prioritising actions
- Embedded their social exclusion strategy within other policy priorities, for example, equality and diversity, community engagement, community cohesion
- Taken the opportunity to challenge and overhaul existing procedures.

A greater number of public libraries have made some advances in this area, but the work is localised (in a Social Inclusion Team, or similar) and is not taken on and understood right across the service. Initiatives are not necessarily rooted in any fundamental, wholesale change, the staff as a whole are not on board, and the work is often not sustained beyond the life of short-term projects.

A very small number of library authorities appears to have paid lip-service to social justice whilst it was politically expedient so to do, but, more recently, have begun to gravitate to other 'priorities', such as new IT projects, income-generation, and massive building projects, leaving social justice behind.

As we have attempted to show throughout this book, there are a number of reasons for this:

- national issues, such as lack of vision and leadership;
- political issues, such as lack of party political commitment to the provision of properly-funded library services;
- local issues, such as lack of engagement of local people, including politicians;
- professional issues, particularly around what public libraries' purpose should be and what kinds of people work in them.

As a residue from the last 13 years, there are also some issues that are unresolved – or which have not yet been tackled – and we look at all of this in Chapter 7.

What Are the Major Issues That Have Not Yet Been Tackled?

These are going to be looked at in more depth in Chapter 7, so, for now, here is just a list of key points:

- Whilst projects are valuable for testing the feasibility of particular approaches, the continual bidding for funding (often for short-term pieces of work) has led to a 'project culture' in libraries – and across local government – which often leads to short-termism.
- As a result, a lot of vital work is not mainstreamed …
- … and funding is not re-directed towards priority areas.
- Staff may not be 'on board'.
- Staff may not hold shared values – or they may hold values that are not compatible with the library service's aims at all.[5]
- Lack of leadership.
- Lack of understanding by and support from politicians …
- … and this may mean that library initiatives are thwarted by vocal minorities.

---

5 For a discussion of values, see Vincent 2008.

Chapter 6
Developing a Needs-Based Library Service

The language of needs has become a dominant concept in the contemporary discourse on public libraries. At the Public Library Authority conference in October 2009, then Culture Minister Margaret Hodge emphasised that libraries must be able to demonstrate how they are responding to and meeting community needs:

> The answer, of course, is to remember your core purpose and raison d'etre, but most of all to provide a service that people want and will use. Most of the people, most of the time. Yes, there can very often be a tension between local need and existing provision …
>
> The '64 Libraries Act … anchors the 'comprehensive and efficient' delivery of a local service to the desires and requirements – or 'needs' – of local people. And, from this, it requires local authorities to seek out and understand what those local needs are.
>
> Not what the council reckons the people want. Not guesswork. Evidence.

She then went on to say that:

> the wise and enduring library service will be the one that responds to public need …
>
> If we make our service popular; if we ensure it is well and widely used, it will be much more difficult to chop it when times are tough …
>
> We need to offer young people something new and distinctive …
>
> CILIP's guidelines on 'What makes a good library service' [(CILIP 2009f)] … are a fantastically useful reference work for our thinking … The CILIP principle that 'local library services need to be continually refreshed and improved to respond to the adapting needs of local communities' sounds, on one level, like a sort of Trotskyite 'permanent revolution' but is, I believe, absolutely spot on. And I wholeheartedly commend CILIP's ten point checklist to you all, as sheer practical common sense. (Hodge 2009)

The first point on this CILIP checklist is: 'Does your library service … have a library strategy which meets the needs of the local community?' (CILIP 2009f, 4). The existing dominant paradigm of universal provision does not work for socially excluded communities. In order for their needs to be met, a targeted approach is required. While public libraries remain a statutory service (under the 1964 Public Libraries Act), they will continue to provide a universal service to those who live, work or study in the local authority area. But within this universal model, it is possible to take a targeted approach and to direct resources to meet the requirements of people who need libraries the most but use them the least. In this way, libraries can be made more relevant to non- and lapsed users while, at the same time, improving services for existing users. The need to balance universal and targeted services was explained by Andrew Motion in the following exchange with Tim Buckley Owen:

> [Tim Buckley Owen]: The government has been frequently criticised for seeing libraries as useful vehicles for implementing social policy rather than being repositories and presenters of literature, knowledge and culture. Do you think there's a conflict here?
>
> [Andrew Motion]: To cherish those orthodox values, which I absolutely do, in a way that doesn't allow other kinds of development to occur within what a library might be is just silly, and not embracing life as it is lived. So let's make proper connections between what a library is traditionally able to offer and what other aspects of a community's work might be – whether it's literacy projects or job seeking or whatever – partly because the synergies between these things can be very productive, and partly because it's a way of getting people to come into libraries who might not otherwise go over the threshold in the first place. (Buckley Owen and Motion 2009)

So it is not a case of developing universal or targeted services, but both simultaneously with a deliberate and sustained focus on community needs to create a win-win situation for the whole community. This is what we call a needs-based library service.

What is a Needs-Based Library Service?

A needs-based library service is characterised by the following ten key features:

1. A needs-based library service is predicated on the assumption that everyone has needs and everyone has different needs. Therefore a needs-based library service is a universal concept which can be applied to any library service in any circumstances at any time.
2. A needs-based library service has the appropriate strategy, structure, systems and culture which enable it to identify, prioritise and meet community needs.

3. A needs-based library service involves and engages the whole of the local community in the planning, design, delivery and evaluation of library services.

4. A needs-based library service does not have customers, but stakeholders, who own a stake in the library service because they pay for it through their taxes, and they have a say in its control and management via their locally elected representative.

5. A needs-based library service is both democratic and accountable. Stakeholders include staff, partners, suppliers, service users, lapsed users and non-users.

6. A needs-based library service is a new way of thinking and a new way of working. It is about hearts and minds, attitudes and behaviours, as well as policies and services. It is a framework and infrastructure which enables and facilitates organisational change. It is a whole service approach to meeting needs, a holistic transformation, a revolution.

7. A needs-based library service can be summed up in the phrase 'From each according to their ability (staff), to each according to their needs (community)'. In other words, a needs-based library service gets the most out of its staff (through workforce development); and takes positive action to meet the greatest needs (through community development) in the community.

8. A needs-based library service is not a new concept. It is part of a historical tradition and continuum which started in the mid-nineteenth century. Public libraries were founded to educate the poor and disadvantaged. They were not established for the rich or the middle class. They were not intended to be neutral, universal or open to all. They were targeted, focused and pro-poor. They were an early form of positive action (not discrimination). Developing a needs-based library service is a return to this tradition and these values of self-help and self-improvement for those who need us the most but use us the least.

9. A needs-based library service is not a return to Victorian values in the sense that public libraries were established primarily as a means of social control – to control the leisure time and reading habits of the poor; to keep them away from pubs, gin houses and penny dreadfuls; to stop them reading and discussing 'seditious literature'. Social change and improvement was a secondary consideration.

10. A needs-based library service is primarily about social change – enabling, facilitating and empowering individuals and communities; giving them the information they need and helping to level the economic, social and political playing fields of life.

The essential elements of a needs-based library service are strategy, structure, systems and culture. Strategy needs to be informed by the corporate objectives of the local authority, which are in turn influenced by the local Sustainable Community

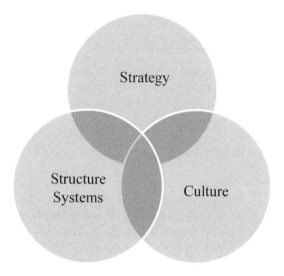

Figure 6.1   The essential elements of a needs-based library service

Strategy. The next step is to develop new staffing and service structures to deliver this strategy. Long hierarchies need to be replaced by flatter matrix structures, and outreach should be replaced by community development. All existing systems, procedures and processes should be reviewed to ensure that they are consistent with a needs-based approach to service delivery. Finally, and most importantly, the organisational culture must change in terms of ways of working, attitudes, behaviours and values.

The essential elements of a needs-based library service are shown in Figure 6.1. The overlap between these elements is critical because they must all be mutually reinforcing – for example, the Structure and Culture must be able to deliver the Strategy. A needs-based library service occurs at the centre of this diagram, where all three elements come together.

Here are two examples of the kind of changes that are required to develop a needs-based library service.

The first change is a shift from customer orientation to customer care. Customer orientation comprises a range of techniques for dealing with customers – this can include giving a welcoming smile, wearing a name badge or picking the telephone up within three rings. Customer care is about going the extra mile (or kilometre) and having the skills to understand and assess the needs of library users. It is about recognising that customers are not all equal in their life experiences and chances; so we should not treat all of our customers equally, but in a way that meets their individual needs. This challenges some deeply held professional library paradigms around issues such as equality, fairness and neutrality.

The second example is a shift from libraries that are based in communities to community-based libraries. Most libraries are based in the community, but not all libraries are community-based. There should be a positive and dynamic relationship between the library and the people who live in the neighbourhood. In community-based libraries, there is a clear organic connection between the work of the library and the needs of the local community. Everyone in a community-based library is needs-focused and working to tackle social exclusion and disadvantage in the local area.

Strategy

The first stage in the transformation process must be the development of a robust strategy and a clear vision which all stakeholders can sign up to. Strategy development should be an inclusive process and actively involve staff, councillors, partners, suppliers and all sections of the local community, including socially excluded people. This will require creative and non-traditional approaches to community engagement to make sure that everyone is involved in the process. Consideration should also be given at this early stage to the success criteria and performance indicators which will be used to determine if the strategy has achieved its objectives and how to measure if it has had a positive impact on local communities. This requires a focus on outcomes rather than outputs and these must be generated via dialogue with local people.

An inclusive and holistic strategy will start the process of cultural change within the organisation and will prevent the service from being diverted and distracted. The strategy will also provide a common platform and language for everyone involved to work from, and so it is important that it is written in an appropriate style with straightforward language and no management jargon. The look and feel of the strategy should be accessible, with colour, pictures and quotes to bring it to life. The strategy should also be reviewed on a regular basis to make sure it is working and relevant to changing needs.

The strategy should indicate the direction of travel of the service and how it relates to priorities around tackling social exclusion and working towards social justice.

Structure

The next stage in the process of developing a needs-based library service is to remodel the staffing and service structures to enable them to deliver the strategy. It is likely that significant changes to the existing structures will be required. For example, if a library is in the wrong place or too small to deliver the strategy, it might be necessary to redirect these resources into a different part of the service – one which can deliver the strategy. Similarly, if the staffing structure cannot deliver the strategy, it also needs to be changed. The staffing structure must be fit for the purpose. It must contain the right number of posts, with the right job titles, job descriptions, person specifications and competencies to deliver the strategy. Some jobs may need to be completely redesigned to reflect the new service direction and the skills required to deliver them.

Changing the structure will also help to change the organisational culture. All cultures are based on language and so, by changing the language we use, we also start to change the culture. For example, many traditional library structures are based on the old professionalisms of children's, lending and reference work. Staff within each of these areas were regarded as specialists and had little, if any, involvement in other service areas. Thinking of libraries in these ways is no longer relevant or helpful. It is more likely that the new strategy will be based on themes such as Inclusion, Learning and Regeneration. If so, then these terms should appear in the staffing structure and job titles.

But one set of specialisms should not be replaced with another. So, although a member of staff's primary responsibility might be Inclusion, they should also have secondary responsibilities for Learning and Regeneration. This will encourage multi-skilling and will produce a more flexible workforce. It will also increase the portfolio of transferable skills that each member of staff has and should improve their job satisfaction, employability and progression. If the service is targeting socially excluded people, all staff should have community development (rather than outreach) in their job descriptions. This will make it clear that community development is the job of all staff and not just those in 'Special Services' or 'Equal Access'. The aim is to make community development a normal part of activities. There are a number of ways to achieve this.

A good starting point is job titles, job descriptions, person specifications and competencies. If community development is not built into the design of a post then the post-holder can turn around and say that 'community development is not my job'. Community development should appear in everybody's job description from Library Assistant to Head of Libraries. It should be clear from a person's job title and job description exactly what it is that they do – and what can be expected from them. Job descriptions should not be long lists of duties – but a focused description of the key responsibilities and tasks of the post. And these should be public documents for users and non-users to see. In that way library staff become accountable to the communities they serve, as well as to their employers.

Service structures also have to be reviewed to ensure that they are meeting needs. These structures have grown up and been changed over time to suit local circumstances and budget pressures. Because change is carried out in this piecemeal fashion, and not always for the right reasons, there can be some perverse outcomes. There may be too many libraries for a geographical area to sustain. The London Borough of Hackney, for example, had 14 branch libraries in what is a very compact inner London authority. These were built before the local government reorganisation in 1965 which combined smaller urban and rural councils into 32 London boroughs. Instead of rationalising the number of service points at the point of administrative reorganisation, they were all retained, creating an over-supply in terms of established demand. This was compounded by the proximity of libraries which were located close to each other within the new borough boundaries. Some were literally on opposite sides of the same road, and there are stories of mobile library staff waving at each other from vehicles which stopped in the same street.

Reducing the size of a library network is always a challenging task because of the emotional support which people feel for their local library (even if they do not use it) and campaigns organised by the media and well-known and well-connected residents. The benefits of changing the service structure must be made clear to all concerned, and the change process must actively involve local communities, including the socially excluded. When this happened in Hackney, it became possible to close seven library buildings which were not fit for purpose, and redirect their resources into improving the rest of the library network. Today Hackney has a new state-of-the-art Central Library in Mare Street, a joint public-college library at Shoreditch, and plans for new libraries at Dalston and Clapton.

Sometimes the problem is under-provision when the service structure is too small to meet community needs. This can happen in some large rural counties which have small populations that are spread thinly over a vast geographical area. Lincolnshire faced this challenge when it carried out a Fundamental Library Review in 2007. The solution was to cluster district (large), neighbourhood (medium) and community (small) libraries into Group Offers (complemented by mobile libraries) which would ensure reasonable access to library services throughout the day and across the week. The Mobile Service was also re-designed to create fewer but longer community stops (to aid partnership working and ICT access) and increased targeted provision to children and older people's settings.

The key questions to ask when reviewing your service structure are is it fit for purpose, affordable, sustainable and able to meet your council objectives? If any service cannot answer 'yes' to most of these criteria, then serious consideration should be given to re-providing the service in a different way. If this need for change can be identified through a transparent and inclusive process, then there is a much higher probability that real transformation can be achieved. This also assists the journey of cultural change and reinforces the impact of strategy development and staff restructuring.

Systems

The third stage in developing a needs-based library service is to assess all existing policies, procedures and processes to ensure that they are consistent with the strategy, service and staffing structures. Many traditional library systems have created barriers which deter non-users from accessing services. Membership and joining requirements, for example, are often quite onerous and bureaucratic. New members are asked for proof of both address and identity. Tickets are only posted to known addresses. For those who are unable (e.g. Travellers) or unwilling (e.g.

refugees) to give their personal details to the authorities (often for good reason), this can be a problem. It was widely reported at the time that the Poll Tax was introduced that library records would be accessed to provide evidence in court against defaulters. Anecdotal evidence indicates that this deterred some people from joining their local library, particularly in working-class communities.

Old systems need to be replaced with new ways of working such as self-issue and partnership working. These can have a huge impact on cultural change. Staff and users can have a relatively fixed view of what a library is and how it operates, and they may not be aware that there are ways of doing things which are different from what has been practised for the past 150 years. The Radio Frequency Identification (RFID) system of self-issue is a good example, because it challenges the very core of received wisdom – that libraries need counters where books are issued, renewed and discharged by staff. RFID offers the opportunity to break free from these archaic practices and liberate staff to meet community needs. Counters take up lots of space in libraries and create physical barriers between staff and service users. The process of checking in and out books is repetitive and time-consuming. RFID allows service users to control these processes and be in charge of their reservations and fines. Staff can then walk the floor of the library looking for people to help, particularly those who are not confident or habitual users. This creates a win-win situation for staff and customers and people are voting for it with their feet – typical success rates in RFID libraries are 80–90 per cent use of the self-issue system.

Partnership working is another powerful way to shift culture and challenge systems and procedures. Partnership work is challenging but can be very productive and beneficial to all concerned. The basis of a good partnership should be shared objectives, values, power and resources. Short-term partnerships can be formed for pragmatic reasons (such as to access external funding), but long-term sustainable partnerships have to be based on more than just a healthy financial bottom line. It is fairly common these days for library services to be delivered in partnership with a wide range of organisations in the public, private, community and voluntary sectors. Indeed, one test of a needs-based library service should be that it is based on some form of partnership working because the stand-alone library is no longer feasible or desirable.

Lincolnshire Libraries have formed a number of useful partnerships with district, parish and town councils, for example. A joint Public Library and Community Access Point (CAP) was built at Mablethorpe (Mablethorpe and Sutton Town Council no date, *c*.2009), which combines a modern, open-space public library with an East Lindsey District Council customer contact point. This joint arrangement has enabled opening hours to be extended, which benefits both sets of service users. Staff have been trained in library and CAP work, and customers are encouraged to use both services. Usage in terms of interactions and issues has increased substantially and CAPs have also been established at Coningsby and Tattershall Libraries.

Joint public and school libraries are common in countries such as Australia, but less established in the UK. That is starting to change as Extended Schools and Children's Centres begin to come on-stream. The benefits of a shared facility are obvious, and the joint public library at Branston Community College near Lincoln is a case in point. The library is used by the school community – teachers and students – during the day, and, at evenings and weekends, it is open for community use (Branston Community College no date, *c*.2008). A less obvious, but equally successful, partnership has been forged with Lincolnshire Fire Service which has a number of retained fire stations which are infrequently used. These are in prime locations with meeting spaces and good ICT, and so it is a relatively small step to incorporate a library into the building. A similar arrangement has been developed in West Berkshire and at Salford's Pendleton Gateway (Salford City Council 2009) where the library shares a building with a GPs' surgery and health centre respectively.

But the most innovative models of shared service delivery are those which involve the voluntary and community sectors, because these create a real bridge between libraries and their local communities. When Crowland Cares (Crowland Cares 2009), a community group in a small isolated rural town, lost its premises, the offer was made to share space in Crowland Library which was struggling to maintain its opening hours. This partnership arrangement has enabled the library to stay open at times when staff are not available, and Crowland Cares volunteers run the library. This has benefited Crowland Cares (who now have a secure base) and the local community (who have guaranteed opening hours). It has also developed awareness and understanding of older people who are the Crowland Cares client group.

A systematic approach needs to be taken to reviewing, changing and possibly eliminating unhelpful or redundant processes. Embervision, a library training and consultancy organisation (Embervision 2006), recommend a lean thinking approach which places barriers to access into three categories: paper walls (processes which can be changed immediately); partition walls (processes which need permission to be changed because they have policy implications); and brick walls (processes which are dependent on legislative and other changes). Involving staff in this work enables them to make changes to their local libraries, which they did not think was possible – such as de-cluttering notice boards and lobbies.

Culture

The final and most important stage in developing a needs-based library service is to develop an organisational culture which can support and deliver the strategy, service and staffing structures, and systems. Culture change can take many years to achieve, depending on how long the current culture has been embedded. This could take 3–5 or even 10–15 years to change. But the process of cultural change can be accelerated through a combination of service action-planning, performance management and workforce development.

This long-term approach to culture change is linked to another important factor, sustainability. Work with ethnic minorities and other excluded groups needs to be brought in from the margins (funded by short-term grants and staffed by project workers) and put at the centre of what libraries do (mainstream-funded and delivered by permanent staff). It is no good raising expectations in the community and starting the process of meeting those expectations, only to stop when the money runs out and committed staff move on. We need to be working in excluded communities for the duration and be setting targets for the next five, 10 or 15 years, in the same way that the government has set a 20-year target for eradicating child poverty.

Social exclusion objectives and targets should appear in the Library Service Action Plan and individual Library Development Plans. These should then be translated into team and staff objectives. Targets should be set and performance reviewed as part of the appraisal process.

Libraries need to measure the impacts and outcomes of their needs based approach and collect evidence which proves that they are improving the quality of life of the communities they serve. These success criteria and performance measures are best developed in consultation with those whom the services are targeted at and who should be fully involved in the planning, design, delivery and monitoring of library services.

Targets could be set, for example, to increase active membership, particularly among target communities (young people, men, ethnic minorities). Targets for increased issues (to arrest the decline of the last 10 years) and visits (in line with Public Library Service Standards) could also be set. The National Indicator for Public Libraries (NI9) is not helpful because it counts only those people over 16 who say that they have used a library in the last 12 months, but it is possible to use a range of proxy measures to support this indicator.

For example, making it easier for people to join a library (by lowering or eliminating ID requirements) enables you to ask People's Network users to have a library ticket; you can then monitor library use in terms of book issues and People's Network usage, and extrapolate from visitor figures how many people have used the library services and for what purposes. It is also possible to measure the contribution which libraries can make to other National Indicators, including Community Cohesion (NI1).

Needs or Reads?

There are two schools of thought that are currently dominating the media and professional debate about the future of public libraries in the UK. One school says that libraries should go back to basics and focus on core services (particularly book borrowing) and making library buildings fit for purpose. This is about the modernisation of the traditional library service. The other school of thought says that there should be less emphasis on books and buildings (as evidenced by the fall in issues and visits) and more focus on meeting community needs through community engagement and development. This is about the transformation of libraries into needs-based services.

These two schools of thought are reflected in the three national reviews of public libraries which were launched in 2008: UNISON's *Taking Stock: the Future of our Public Library Service* (Davies 2008); the All-Party Parliamentary Group on Libraries, Literacy and Information Management, originally chaired by Lyn Brown MP (All-Party Parliamentary Group on Libraries Literacy and Information Management 2009); and the DCMS Library Modernisation Review (DCMS 2008b).

As its title suggests, *Taking Stock* focused on core traditional library services: 'Central and local government need to ensure that libraries have sufficient funds to maintain and develop an attractive book stock. They also need to be able to provide the traditional range of services, in terms of children's, reference and local studies sections' (Davies 2008, 4).

The All-Party Parliamentary Group on Libraries, Literacy and Information Management (2009) had a stronger emphasis on the community leadership and governance of public libraries. One of its key lines of inquiry was:

> Should local communities have a greater say in decisions about the public library service?
>
> For many commentators, the concept of a library at the very heart of a community is a powerful vision. Is this local focus reflected appropriately in local governance and consultation arrangements? Are there other mechanisms for engaging local people in service planning and delivery? (All-Party Parliamentary Group on Libraries, Literacy and Information Management 2009, 6)

The Department of Culture, Media and Sport 'Library Modernisation Review' also had a focus on community-led library services, as indicated by the following key objective: 'To explore and make recommendations on innovative models of service delivery that make libraries increasingly responsive to the needs of their communities and that involve users in their design' (DCMS 2008b).

While the public and professional debate has become polarised between Reads and Needs, the weight of political opinion seems to be coming down firmly on the side of Needs. This is evidenced by government publications such as *Communities in Control: Real People, Real Power* which

> aims to pass power into the hands of local communities. We want to generate vibrant local democracy in every part of the country, and to give real control over local decisions and services to a wider pool of active citizens … We want to shift power, influence and responsibility away from existing centres of power into the hands of communities and individual citizens. This is because we believe that they can take difficult decisions and solve complex problems for themselves. (Communities and Local Government 2009, 1)

Table 6.1   Fall in number of active borrowers, 2000/1 and 2006/7

Year	Population	Active borrowers	% of active users
2000/1	59.1 million	17.2 million	29%
2006/7	60.9 million	13.0 million	21%

Users, Lapsed Users and Non-users

The number of active library borrowers in the UK decreased by 24.3 per cent between 2000/1 and 2006/7 (Davies 2008, 22) and the number of active library borrowers has fallen from a third to a fifth of the total population (see Table 6.1).

Public libraries are only actively used by some 21 per cent of the population, and the much-touted figure of 60 per cent is a myth. An average of 48.5 per cent of adults may say that they have used a public library in the past 12 months (Museums, Libraries and Archives Council 2008c), but the reality is that less than half that number have a library ticket which they use on a regular basis. Even this national average figure of 48.5 per cent masks some very alarming local statistics, including Barnsley (37.9 per cent), North Lincolnshire (38.2 per cent), Plymouth (38.1 per cent) and Stoke on Trent (37.6 per cent) (DCMS 2009a).

Those who do actively use libraries are fairly homogenous in terms of race, class, age and gender. They tend to be white, middle-class, middle-aged and female. This has been described as the 'dominant' reader – a person whom many library staff identify with in terms of language, culture, attitudes, beliefs, values and behaviour.

Active library borrowers make regular and full use of library services. As noted above, they comprise 21 per cent of our communities. They are the core of everything we do. They are the focus of all or most of our efforts. We are always asking users what they like about the service – the CIPFA Public Library User Survey (CIPFA Social Research 2009), for example – and what else they would like. Their typical response is to ask for more of the same, which tends to reinforce the status quo. These are people who use public libraries the most but may need them the least.

Passive library users make occasional and limited use of library services. They comprise 27 per cent[1] of our communities. They include lapsed users and those who are 'easy to reach'. They might have a library ticket but do not use it very often. Or they may have used the service in the past but stopped doing so when it no longer met their needs or when they could get their needs met elsewhere – by buying books or accessing the Internet at home, for example. This group can be easily reached with some minimum effort on our behalf (via some effective and

---

1   We have reached this figure by deducting the 21 per cent active users from the 48.5 per cent figure for those who have used the library service at least once in the previous year.

targeted marketing, for example). These are people who make some use of the public library and who have some needs. Incidentally, there is another category of lapsed users – those who visited a library once, but were treated so badly by the staff that they never go back!

Non-users have never used libraries (maybe for generations) and never will, unless we reach out to them, engage with them, identify their needs and involve them in the planning, design, delivery and monitoring of our services. They comprise some 52 per cent[2] of our communities. They include the so-called 'hard-to-reach' and 'unreachable'. These are people that need libraries the most but use them the least. There are also those non-users who, following on from the 1980s/1990s, believe that they can just buy everything they need, and therefore do not want free lending services.

We need to know more about our active, lapsed and non-users. A simple count of visitors does not go far enough. We need to know who these visitors are, where they live, their ethnicity, class, occupation, gender, age, why they use the service, what they use it for, and so on. Many library authorities do not capture all of this data. Staff are reluctant, and regard it as intrusive, to ask library users too many 'personal' questions even though most people don't think twice about giving their most intimate details (including income) to supermarkets, insurance companies, etc.

We need to adopt and adapt this private-sector, market-research approach so that we know exactly who is (and who is not) using our services. We can then target our resources more accurately to meet the needs of those who already use us (the minority) and start to make efforts to reach out to those who do not use us (the majority).

Public libraries were established 150 years ago to meet the needs of 'the deserving poor'. They have, to different degrees and at different times in history, met some of those needs. But what they have never succeeded in doing is to meet the needs of the 'undeserving poor' – in modern language, the homeless, the unemployed, Travellers, asylum-seekers, refugees, migrant workers, ethnic minorities, and so on. When forced to consider the needs of those who do not make up the core 21 per cent of library users, public libraries focus their attention on the 'easy-to-reach' – that 27 per cent of passive and lapsed users who can be easily persuaded to come back to libraries. Some of these people have been attracted back by the People's Network, for example, but this is now in need of a refresh, and visitor figures are starting to go down again.

But at that point many efforts stop. Most libraries do not engage with the 52 per cent of non-users who are labelled as 'hard to reach'. As noted above, some non-users have been tempted into library buildings by the People's Network, but they still do not make full use of the range of services which libraries provide. The People's Network is not being managed to target and meet their needs. And there is an increasing and disturbing tendency to charge for People's Network access,

---

2   100 per cent less 48.5 per cent.

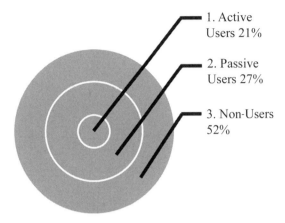

1. Active
   Users 21%

2. Passive
   Users 27%

3. Non-Users
   52%

Figure 6.2   Exclusive paradigm

to meet income targets rather than to meet needs. This is creating a two-tier People's Network for the haves and have-nots – which is the exact opposite of what was intended by government and the New Opportunities Fund. To make matters worse, in some authorities, the People's Network is censored by clumsy filtering mechanisms, and the hardware is now out of date, with no provision made to refresh it.

Figure 6.2 shows the proportions of active, passive and non-users, represented as concentric circles. In this exclusive paradigm, most effort is put into active users (1). Any spare capacity is invested in attracting passive users (2). But little or no effort is made to engage with non-users (3). The direction of travel is from the centre outwards, but there is no significant penetration of the outer circle. A strategy based on this approach is unlikely to increase total library usage beyond 48 per cent (active plus passive users).

As *Open to All?* (Muddiman et al. 2000a; 2000b and 2000c) made clear, libraries must cease putting all their efforts into existing users and start to focus on the needs of lapsed and non-users. It is possible to develop new services for socially excluded people without at the same time alienating the core user group on whom the current performance depends. To do so, it is necessary to include current users in the change process. They must understand that, within constrained resources, it is necessary to target and redirect budgets and services to meet the wide range of needs within our communities.

Core users are generally able to appreciate concepts such as equity and social justice. As well as these altruistic motives, there is also an element of self-interest – the included know that there will be a price for them to pay (both financially and in terms of crime, etc.) if social exclusion is not tackled. An inclusive library service does not only benefit the previously excluded – it benefits the already included as well. A service that is more closely tailored to meet the needs of its communities is

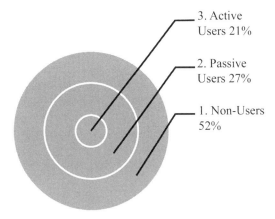

3. Active
Users 21%

2. Passive
Users 27%

1. Non-Users
52%

Figure 6.3   Inclusive paradigm

likely to provide better services, stock, premises, staff and opening hours to all of its users, old and new.

Figure 6.3 shows how an inclusive paradigm would reverse the flow of effort. The direction of travel is from the edge of the outer circle and works inwards. Non-users (1) are now the focus of attention, with spare capacity being invested in passive users (2), and least effort is put into active users (3). A strategy based on this approach is likely to increase total library usage beyond 48 per cent and could potentially grow to 80 per cent or more (achieved in Scandinavia and Cuba).

Tackling social exclusion and promoting social inclusion are steps on the continuum which leads to community cohesion and social justice. Public libraries can make interventions and add value to each of these stages. One area in which public libraries have some expertise is community engagement. There are a number of challenges to be addressed if government policies to promote community engagement are to be genuinely inclusive of newcomers as well as more established communities.

Community Engagement and Community Cohesion

Community engagement and community cohesion are both current public policy priorities. But there have been gaps in our understanding about how to promote community representation in ways that take account of diversity and population change. The Joseph Rowntree Foundation commissioned some research into *Community Engagement and Community Cohesion* (Blake et al. 2008) which explored:

- whose views were being heard and whose were not;
- what were the barriers to being heard and how they could be overcome;

- how these barriers could be addressed in ways that would promote community cohesion, rather than increasing competition within and between communities. (Blake et al. 2008, i)

This research included focus groups, direct observations and over 100 interviews with community activists, local authority officers, councillors and professionals from voluntary sector organisations in three local authority areas: Coventry, Newham and Oldham. The research identified ways in which new communities can be involved effectively, together with more established communities, thereby increasing cohesion and mutual solidarity. The key findings were as follows:

- The views of new arrivals, as well as those of established communities, need to be heard and resources allocated with visible fairness. New communities are keen to get involved and to have their views heard.
- The research identified challenges about who speaks for whom when new communities are represented. Informal networks can provide valuable ways for local authorities to communicate with new communities, but traditional leaders do not necessarily represent the voices of women or younger people.
- New communities are diverse themselves. But despite this diversity, new arrivals experience a number of common barriers, such as lack of information, difficulties in the use of English, lack of time, or barriers to recognition, making it more difficult for them to get involved or be heard.
- These barriers are exacerbated by the growing fluidity and fragmentation of governance structures. This complexity poses problems enough for established communities who are already used to navigating their way around. For new arrivals the shifting landscape of service provision and governance is even more bewildering, making community engagement correspondingly more problematic.
- The most appropriate way of engaging new communities, who may be dispersed across local authority areas, is not necessarily at the neighbourhood level. In addition, some of their concerns, such as jobs and language skills, may not be managed at neighbourhood level. Community engagement structures are needed at other levels too.
- Concerns about racism and prejudice were identified as barriers affecting engagement in structures of governance. However, more positively the research has identified a range of examples of promising practices addressing these challenges, involving new communities as part of wider strategies to promote cohesion. Community development support emerged as an important factor here. (Joseph Rowntree Foundation 2008b, 1)

The government is committed to promoting community engagement. But services are being delivered by an increasingly diverse range of providers, with correspondingly diverse opportunities for user and community involvement. There is growing concern about how to join up these different structures of local governance, through Local Strategic Partnerships (LSPs), for example. But there has been less focus upon the implications of engaging service users and communities effectively when communities are themselves diverse, with differing needs and priorities. Globalisation has been associated with increasing migration, although these changes are difficult to measure, owing to gaps in the available data. This poses major challenges for the community engagement and community cohesion agendas. (Joseph Rowntree Foundation 2008a)

Public libraries are part of the fabric of local communities and have their 'ear to the ground' in terms of gathering intelligence about community concerns and challenges. This puts libraries in a unique position to help develop both human and social capital at a neighbourhood level. Libraries can take the lead role in coordinating the efforts of service providers to create a consistent and coherent approach which local communities can understand and engage with. Libraries can be part of the glue which sticks together interventions planned and delivered via LSPs. Libraries can map local communities, gather data about them and identify the different needs and priorities of community groups.

New communities want their views to be heard, and they want to participate. For many new arrivals, 'being heard' means being recognised, having a safe space to meet, providing mutual support and gaining the knowledge, confidence and skills to engage more widely. 'Being heard' also means being listened to with respect, knowing that resources are being allocated with visible fairness. Established communities typically share this view of community engagement, and they also face problems in getting their views heard, but newer communities find it even harder.

New communities face practical barriers, such as lack of information (exacerbated by the fluidity and fragmentation of governance structures), personal barriers such as difficulties in the use of English or a lack of time to participate due to working long/unsociable hours, and barriers to recognition (e.g. newer communities often do not have formally constituted community organisations and so are not being consulted and are not eligible to receive public funds).

Groups particularly at risk of not having their views heard effectively were asylum seekers and refugees, and new migrant workers from the accession states, such as Poland. Amongst these groups, women and younger people were identified as having even less chance of being listened to than older men. Meanwhile some established minority communities, and some established white working class communities, had been less successful than others in making their views heard.

> These findings highlight the importance of linking strategies that promote community engagement with strategies that promote community cohesion. Otherwise, the result could be increased competition for scarce resources between established communities and newer arrivals. (Joseph Rowntree Foundation 2008a)

Public libraries can provide platforms for new arrivals to be heard and can be vehicles for them to participate through. Libraries can recognise new arrivals by stocking relevant books and organising cultural events. Libraries provide safe places where new arrivals can meet each other and members of the local community. Libraries can support new arrivals and provide them with knowledge, confidence and skills to engage more widely. Libraries can provide free information which explains how 'the system' works, and they can offer gateways into adult learning, including language courses. Libraries can facilitate the formation of community groups which enable new arrivals to self-organise and bid for resources.

Some library authorities have initiated innovative projects which have received national awards in recognition of their success in supporting asylum-seekers and refugees (Merton) and migrant workers (Lincolnshire). These projects have ensured that all sections of the new arrival communities, including women and younger people, were given a voice and listened to. They have also made efforts to engage established communities, including the white working class, to build community cohesion and to avoid competition for attention, recognition and resources.

> The research also highlighted the importance of continuity and sustainability in governance structures. In two of the three local areas studied there had been recent changes in neighbourhood-based structures. Participants spoke about how difficult it was to know how and where to make their views heard; this fluidity in structures exacerbates these difficulties.
>
> Much of the emphasis on community engagement has been directed at the neighbourhood. But the research found that neighbourhood forums aren't necessarily the most appropriate levels for some issues. The Olympic development in east London was an example of this in the Newham case study; transport infrastructure was another example. The neighbourhood level is particularly problematic for communities that are geographically dispersed across towns and cities, as many new arrivals are, and given that many of their concerns – e.g. jobs, refugee/asylum status and language skills – are managed outside the neighbourhood. (Joseph Rowntree Foundation 2008a)

Public libraries tend to have relatively stable governance structures – other organisations may come and go, change their names or vary their catchment areas, but public libraries stay in the same location and offer community-based services which have endured for over 150 years. This makes them trusted, respected and valued by local communities because they are not 'here today and gone tomorrow'.

Libraries may also be regarded as having no 'political agendas' and to be equitable in how they approach and serve local communities (although, of course, as we have argued elsewhere in this book, these statements can be called into question). Libraries often work best at neighbourhood level, but they can also meet the needs of wider communities, whether these are defined by common interest or geography. In rural locations, for example, mobile libraries can visit dispersed communities, and libraries can also organise initiatives and services on a regional and sub-regional basis.

The research identified a range of approaches that would enable newer community members to be heard, whilst promoting strategies for community cohesion and social solidarity. Public libraries were not specifically referenced, but these approaches have been developed by many library services:

- welcome packs providing information about where and how to access services and how to express users' concerns;
- outreach work to engage with new arrivals, including outreach work with informal leaders and networks;
- community development support, from both statutory and voluntary sector anchor agencies, including support to enable new groups to constitute themselves formally and so gain increased recognition;
- ways of challenging negative stereotypes, used most effectively when part of wider strategies to promote increased understanding between communities;
- shared events, including community festivals, sports events, outings and welcome events as part of wider strategies to promote community cohesion. (Joseph Rowntree Foundation 2008a)

In Lincolnshire, new arrivals areas have been established in places such as Spalding and Boston, which have large migrant worker communities. Welcome packs are provided to new arrivals, which contain key information about local services, and how to access support, guidance and advice. The Access Team organises outreach activities and provides a first point of contact for new arrivals. The Community Engagement Team offers community development support and capacity-building opportunities. This team has also developed links with a range of informal networks and fledgling organisations. They have actively tapped into these networks rather than waiting for new communities to come to them. This has led to the formation of a New Communities Forum, supported by senior council members, as a two-way channel of communication. Bourne Library invites new arrivals to social events where they can meet local people and develop a shared understanding of each other's cultural backgrounds. Most neighbourhood and community libraries organise community festivals which celebrate diversity via food, music and sport.

Both established and new communities face challenges in terms of who speaks for whom. Outreach work with informal leaders and networks may reach the 'movers and shakers', and these key individuals can and do play key roles. But this research also found evidence of the importance of ensuring that other people can also be heard, including women and younger people ...

Local councillors play key bridging roles. Political parties can do much to encourage representation from new communities as well as from more established communities. Local councillors can benefit from support to enable them to perform this role, facilitating community engagement in the context of wider strategies to promote community cohesion and social solidarity ...

Governance structures have a key role to play in challenging racism and promoting community cohesion. Minority communities expressed anxieties about racism, based upon experiences of harassment and discrimination. Suspicions about unfair access to resources can also fuel resentments against newcomers, highlighting the importance of visible fairness through accountable forms of governance ...

Community engagement policies have not yet taken sufficient account of increasing diversity and population turnover in modern Britain. The fragmentation and fluidity of structures of governance pose additional challenges. This research has identified a number of barriers that need to be addressed if new communities are to have their views heard alongside those of more established communities.

The research has also identified a number of promising practices, ways of reaching out to engage with new arrivals whilst promoting agendas for community cohesion and social solidarity. These cannot simply be transplanted from one area to another without adjustment, of course. But there are implications here for government as well as for local authorities, local strategic partnerships and the voluntary and community sectors. (Joseph Rowntree Foundation 2008a)

Public libraries can take the following actions:

- Build on the Local Government White Paper *Strong and Prosperous Communities* and the *Action Plan for Community Empowerment* by ensuring that the impacts of demographic change as a result of migration, population turnover and increasing local diversity are taken into account in the design of policy, guidance and initiatives relating to citizenship, community empowerment, community engagement and community cohesion.
- Include representatives of new communities, refugees and other mobile communities not currently represented by mainstream community organisations and groups in [library] strategies and structures to implement community engagement and empowerment.
- Prioritise the provision of reliable and standardised data on the population turnover experienced by a community, in order to facilitate effective [library] service planning, user and citizen involvement, and equitable resource allocation ...

- Ensure that community and citizen engagement strategies take account of diversity and the dynamics of population change and turnover.
- Provide clear and comprehensive guides to services and the criteria for allocating resources fairly and transparently, with welcome packs for new arrivals, explaining where and how service users' concerns can be addressed, and including information about how to get involved.
- Develop proactive communication strategies, including challenging negative stereotyping within and between communities.
- Provide community development support to new community organisations, groups and informal networks, both directly through [library workers] and indirectly through [partnerships with] third sector anchor organisations, ensuring that equalities issues are prioritised.
- Support the organisation of shared events, including community festivals, sports events, outings and welcome events, as part of wider strategies to promote community cohesion and community engagement.
- Recognise the limitations of neighbourhood participation structures and support the complementary development of effective [regional and sub-regional] structures ...
- Work proactively with new communities, including working through informal networks, whilst taking account of equalities issues, ensuring that all views are effectively heard, including relatively marginalised groups such as young women and young men.
- Act as hosts to support new arrivals, including supporting them to develop and gain recognition for their own community organisations and groups.
- Respect, support and facilitate new communities in exercising their rights to self-organisation, rather than speaking on their behalf. (Joseph Rowntree Foundation 2008a)

Although libraries did not feature in the case studies used in this research, there are many library services which operate what the report calls 'promising practices' with regards to new arrivals. In places such as Lincolnshire, the library service is reaching out to enable diverse voices to be heard effectively. And there are examples of initiatives and responses that are geared towards the reduction of competition within and between communities, and the promotion of community cohesion, mutual trust and social solidarity, backed by sustainable strategies to promote community development.

From Outreach Services to Community Development

For these strategies to work, libraries must move away from providing passive outreach services which tend to be planned, designed, delivered and evaluated by librarians. Outreach needs to be replaced by the development and implementation of community development strategies which are centrally important to local governance strategies (including the LSP) more generally. This shift from outreach to community development is explored further in Chapter 7. And these community development strategies need to be delivered by community development workers, who will need a different skill-set to traditional librarians. The need for 'the right "man" for the job' is also examined in Chapter 7.

These community development workers will be able to identify and work with informal networks as well as with more established organisations and groups within the voluntary and community sectors, taking account of issues of equalities, accountability, democratic representation and social justice. Partnership working is key to the success of community development, and libraries will need to work with a wide range of partners including the following:

- Local Strategic Partnerships, with responsibilities for bringing different sectors and interests together to develop strategic approaches to providing services to meet local needs.
- Local thematic partnerships such as Crime Reduction Partnerships which include members of voluntary and community groups.
- Neighbourhood Forums, bodies set up as part of service decentralisation by local authorities and their partners.
- New Deal for Communities (NDC) boards which manage regeneration programmes in many of the areas with high levels of diversity and population churn.
- Primary care services, foundation hospitals, GP clinics, adult care services and Local Involvement Networks (LINks).
- Sure Start, which is mandated to reach out and engage the most disadvantaged young children and their parents.
- School governing bodies, which provide elected places for parent representatives.
- Housing associations, which have taken over much of the remaining stock of local authority housing departments and which cater for the most disadvantaged and recent arrivals.

Libraries can also play a lead role within the 'place-shaping' agenda by acting as a voice of the whole community and an agent of place. Libraries can make creative use of their services to promote the general wellbeing of a community and its citizens by:

- helping to build and shape local identity;
- representing the community;
- contributing to the cohesiveness of the community;
- understanding local needs and preferences and making sure that the right services are provided to local people;
- working with other bodies to respond to complex challenges;
- anticipating, understanding and helping to manage and facilitate change within their locality and take responsibility for the wellbeing of 'place'.

Libraries must also provide both 'voice and choice'; in other words, service users and residents are given opportunities to have more power and control over the library services they use, to play an active role in service design and delivery, and to express their views and preferences. 'Voice and choice' can operate at a community or an individual level. For example, community groups are enabled to prioritise the mix of library services in their neighbourhoods through a local user forum. At an individual level, users are able to engage directly with their local library to tailor the service to fit their circumstances. Both avenues – the community and the individual – are key to more responsive library services and increased citizen satisfaction in their locality.

Under the provisions of the Local Government and Public Involvement in Health Act 2007 (Great Britain 2007), library services have a 'duty to involve' residents and others and give them greater influence over service decisions and delivery. User views will be included in the locality based inspections and Comprehensive Area Assessments; and the National Indicator Set – from which Local Area Agreements are drawn – contain several measures of citizen and user satisfaction. Libraries must look beyond National Indicator 9 (use of public libraries) and demonstrate, with evidence, how they are contributing to other National Indicators, including those which measure Community Cohesion, Volunteering and Positive Activities for Young People. These indicators include:

- the percentage of people who feel they can influence decisions in their locality;
- the percentage of people who believe people from different backgrounds get on well together in their local area;
- the percentage of people who feel they belong to their neighbourhood;
- the perception that people in the area treat one another with respect and dignity. (See Communities and Local Government 2007)

Libraries should also engage with Local Involvement Networks (LINks) to influence health and social care services (NHS 2009), and with young people. The Ten Year Youth Strategy (Department for Schools Children and Families/HM Treasury 2007) requires councils to actively engage with young people about their needs and issues. Libraries should reach out to the disadvantaged, marginalised or socially excluded, as well as the 'more vocal' residents and communities in the way they design and manage the 'voice and choice' arrangements. Giving everyone a voice and choice is particularly challenging in areas of super-diversity and rapid population change.

Libraries will have to improve their intelligence on local needs and priorities. Research and consultation with a wide range of community interests – including new residents and recent migrant communities – will be essential if libraries are to 'segment' their market and target and design services that are responsive to the different interests at ward and neighbourhood level as well as measure different satisfaction levels. Specifically, they should address the disadvantages that individuals experience because of their gender, race, disability, age, sexual orientation, religion, belief or social class and build more cohesive, empowered and active communities. Libraries will need performance indicators which can measure these impacts, and this is discussed in more detail in Chapter 7.

This model of change relies on service users and residents being organised and engaged so that they can take part in the user involvement, community governance and partnership arrangements that are central to a needs-based library service. Where particular groups are not well-organised or visible, it is the task of community development workers to seek them out, engage with them and provide organisational capacity. This will help migrants and new communities to be recognised as citizens, residents and/or service users and will ensure that their needs and views are taken into account.

Public libraries have always been faced with the need to make decisions about the distribution of resources in the face of competing priorities and claims. In future, this decision-making will need to be more transparent and have to demonstrate that it is fair and accountable – towards what the Commission on Integration and Cohesion has described as 'visible social justice' (Commission on Integration and Cohesion 2007). While transparency can help to defuse tensions between competing demands, there are some significant challenges involved in achieving this in practice. When this is achieved, public libraries can play an important role in building bridges within and between new communities and more established communities.

Chapter 7
Where Next?

There are three major themes running through this book and, in this final chapter, we want to draw these together to begin to chart a roadmap for how public library services could be developed.

These themes are:

- the need to put social justice at the heart of what public libraries are about;
- the vital need for leadership and direction for services …
- … and, as a result of both of these, the development of proper needs-based library services.

They are clearly interwoven themes, but here we will try to separate them and deal with each in turn.

Social Justice at the Heart

What we hope has become clear from this book is that public libraries have created some amazing services which truly meet the needs of local communities. Yet, at the same time, they are prey to the vagaries of 'boom or bust', and – as has been demonstrated by our glimpse of the longer-term outcomes of the Libraries Change Lives Award and the externally-funded projects – such work is equally likely to disappear without trace.

What is also clear is that public library services currently mean 'all things to all people', demonstrated by the very varied approaches taken in the collection of essays just published (at the time of writing) as the latest stage in the DCMS Review of Public Libraries (DCMS 2009b, 3). The danger in this approach is actually that libraries end up becoming 'nothing to nobody'!

We would argue that it is this lack of a real 'core' that has led to many public libraries becoming sidelined, being used as political 'footballs', failing to contribute to a wider agenda, failing to be recognised as important partners in key developments, and has also led to some public library staff not being 'on board' (or even being hostile to the local community).

Public libraries need urgently to re-focus, so that, wherever they are located, they develop provision, together with the local community, that starts with social justice objectives. This, we argue, would then lead naturally to the development of needs-based library services.

Yet, as we write this, we can also hear the voices of those who disagree with this approach, saying 'But libraries shouldn't serve a social purpose', 'This is all too political', even 'We're primarily about lending books – not to do with all this!' There will also be arguments that, in some small town or village library, there are not any social justice issues – people just want books and information!

Public libraries do have the potential to be powerful forces in the fight for social justice, just as they have shown in their work to support, for example, refugees and asylum-seekers, unemployed people, young people with autism, looked-after young people, and so on. However, at the same time, as Kerry Wilson and Briony Birdi have shown, they also have the potential to be a destructive force:

> Despite claims of low-level resistance *not* directed towards social inclusion policy or excluded groups themselves, respondents did reveal evidence of antagonism towards certain initiatives and a wide range of groups within the social inclusion agenda. When giving details, respondents would invariably refer to 'older members of staff'. Comments reflect prejudices towards certain groups, and a worrying distinction between deserving and non-deserving users of public library services:
>
> 'Would you want your council tax to go up to pay more for libraries to train people to do these things [work with disaffected children and young people] … should that not be done by, I don't know, parents at home, things like that … Because it always seems to be the bad ones that get the attention and money spent on them … not the good child that comes in, who's nice, gets on with things, asks for help and is genuinely a nice child' (North East [Focus Group])
>
> 'I have had problems with LGBT issues from staff and users … if the gay collection is very in your face the users get a bit uptight … I was aware of one member of staff who would carefully move the pink paper … I once worked in a library that put Gay Times in a brown envelope, that was three or four years ago, I don't know if they do it now … but there are still pockets of resistance on occasion.' (East of England [Focus Group])
>
> 'We've had issues over providing women-only desks for female Muslim users … we've had to keep a record of how many male and female members of staff are working on each desk at any time … it gets silly' (West Midlands [Focus Group]) (Wilson and Birdi 2008, 97)

Would it not be simpler to harness this energy and work with the community towards agreed social purposes?

We would also argue that, by now, people should have learned that there is nothing that is not political! The 1970s mantra of 'The personal is the political' may sound old-fashioned, but it clearly showed that everything that affects our daily lives can be construed as having a political basis. So – public libraries are not actually politically 'neutral', but carry political 'loads' from, for example, the ideology of their local authority, the sources and selection of their library materials and what 'producers' have decided to publish, and so on. If your library never includes images of BME people in its displays, or major events (such as LGBT History Month) pass unmarked, wherever the library is located, is this not sending a powerful message to visitors to the library about just who is considered display-worthy?

It is surely our role, in public libraries, to understand the 'bigger' and 'smaller' political pictures and to recognise these in all our dealings – for example, does that man who says he speaks on behalf of a group of refugees really represent them all? What are the political issues here? Working in libraries, we need to be fully aware of and understand the political complexities of our local communities; a politically naïve approach often leads to confusion – or worse!

With this understanding of what it means to be political, then libraries should be unashamedly political!

Here is as good a place as any to emphasise that we are not advocating the turning away of existing users or people who do not (immediately) fit into a socially excluded group. Of course a public library has a duty to provide services for these groups – but, when it comes to prioritising service delivery, then the social justice purposes should surely win out. Part of our skill (and leadership – see below, p. 145) has to be in arguing the case convincingly as to why resources are limited and therefore choices are made, some of which may reduce some services (e.g. the number of bestsellers purchased) in favour of greater support for our social justice work.

Work with socially excluded communities is time-consuming and often lengthy (it takes time to build up levels of trust with a Traveller community, for example). However, there is ample evidence to show that, whilst short-term, project-based work may be valuable for evidence-gathering and building a case, what is actually required is a long-term commitment with appropriate resources. Sadly, libraries simply do not have the resources to work with every community, so will need to prioritise the groups to concentrate on. Without this, we are going to see a continuing of the 'boom and bust', and also a growing recognition by social excluded communities that libraries do not really have anything to offer. Mainstreaming this work is critical.

Libraries never have been just about book-lending, as we have seen from our brief look at the history of the UK public library; public libraries today provide a vast array of services and facilities, and, pine though we might for a mythical 'golden age', we actually need to embrace these – where they meet our social justice ambitions.

As library services such as Suffolk and Gloucestershire have shown, small rural communities still have tremendous needs for library services beyond the basic book-lending, and, just as there will not be any part of the UK, no matter how remote, that now does not reflect in some ways the diversity of UK society, so public libraries also need to reflect this in their work, wherever they are.

As will be clear by now, this is not some new, radical approach, but one that has been recognised and cited as key to public libraries' role and survival over many years, most recently by 'library leaders' in their papers for *Empower, Inform, Enrich* (DCMS 2009b). For example:

Kathy Kirk, Interim Head of Culture and Community Services, Worcestershire County Council:

> Libraries have a key role in promoting change and presenting the friendly face of political rhetoric on such things as social cohesion and the economy, they are the focal point for cohesion in action. (DCMS 2009b, 32)

Miranda McKearney, Chief Executive of The Reading Agency:

> Libraries' reading role should be of profound interest to local authorities because of its impact on the population's literacy levels, educational progress, employability, well being and sense of community. (DCMS 2009b, 34)

CILIP's Chief Executive, Bob McKee:

> Modern times make the core purpose of libraries more important than ever, as is shown by the upturn in library use during the current economic downturn.
>
> Libraries reach into every neighbourhood and every family, giving free access for everyone to all of the world's knowledge whether of the intellect or of the imagination, whether in print or online, all mediated by skilled and helpful library staff. That core purpose addresses some of the most pressing challenges facing our society. With seven million people in Britain lacking basic literacy skills, at least six million excluded from access to digital technology, and over four million experiencing multiple social and economic deprivation, libraries should be central to our strategies for literacy and learning, digital inclusion, regeneration, equality of opportunity, and personal well-being. To fit libraries for the future, government needs to recognise the contribution they can make to key policy objectives.
>
> Where libraries have risen to these challenges – and have invested in strategic planning, improved opening hours, better buildings, skilled staff, and an in-depth range of print and digital resources – the graph of library use is rising, not falling. (DCMS 2009b, 36)

Fiona Williams, President of the Society of Chief Librarians:

> Members of the Society of Chief Librarians consistently deliver these changes on behalf of local people. SCL would propose that public libraries are already making themselves fit for the 21st century. They are making themselves fit for the communities within which they work by being relevant to today's needs. That means access to jobs and careers advice, tackling literacy through reader development, improving health through information and bibliotherapy,

supporting digital literacy and serving as an access point for all national government and local council services ...

Partnerships in health, education, business and the economy, basic skills, literacy, elderly care, social inclusion and others are helping improve people's lives every day. (DCMS 2009b, 64)

There is also a grave danger that, without this core at our heart, public libraries will get diverted by whatever is the newest wagon to roll by! We are living at a time of immense, speedy growth of technology – particularly communications, but also library-based technology, such as RFID – all of which is leading to rapid change. This technology is certainly valuable and important, but is not an end in itself; it should be used to improve services and access for socially excluded people. It is exciting that public libraries are experimenting with Twitter, blogs and other 'Web 2.0' developments, but these must have a barrier-breaking role, increasing access to libraries for people who never normally use them (or see that they could play a part in their lives).

The Vital Need for Leadership

In its set of consultation questions, *Empower, Inform, Enrich* (DCMS 2009b) asked how we can ensure that the library service 'attracts and nurtures leaders with the ability to drive improvement, engage in partnerships and innovate services' (DCMS 2009b, 75).

In their response, The Network said:

> There are already leaders within libraries, who demonstrate the abilities outlined in the question – the issue often is whether they are allowed to use them! Unfortunately too, where library managers show a high level of leadership qualities, they are often quickly recruited to elsewhere in the local authority. This reflects, in our opinion, that the leadership issues are not actually solely libraries', but are also being faced across local government as a whole. This is obviously a much wider issue, but it is worth noting that local government is altogether risk-averse and uncreative – so it's no wonder that many library staff either follow their peers' lead or find themselves stifled by the bureaucracy. (The Network 2009b, 11)

So – the issue is not necessarily that there are not 'library leaders', but that they are sometimes prevented from leading!

However, we see there being three levels at which strong, committed leadership is vital:

- pan-UK, national;
- regional;
- local.

Pan-UK, National

As has been shown by the latest instalment of the DCMS Modernisation Review (DCMS 2009b), and noted above, there is not currently a clear direction for public libraries in England (and, if we add to this current criticisms of the 1964 Public Libraries and Museums Act, then in England and Wales). In Scotland, Wales and Northern Ireland (where culture is a devolved power), there have been major initiatives to develop public libraries and resource them properly, but, generally, there is a lack of clear vision about libraries and their purpose.

At the time of writing, there are strong arguments being put for the development of some kind of English (or UK) national library development agency – these arguments are very persuasive, but it would need to be absolutely clear which body had responsibility for which area of library provision (otherwise, we may remain with the current, rather unclear position).

We would argue that, however this is taken forward, there needs to be national leadership that places the social justice and community-led agendas at the heart of public libraries.

Regional

In England, there are nine government regions, each with a clear regional agenda. Whilst there have been some excellent examples of work with these (particularly by some of the former MLA regional offices), nevertheless we think that more could be done to ally public library initiatives with those of the government regions.

A regional approach to planning and developing services would also be of huge benefit. Obviously, there is considerable regional working (for example via the Society of Chief Librarians (SCL)), but, as public libraries are managed by individual local authorities, there is lacking the political will to streamline and deal with clear anomalies. For example, there are areas in the UK where libraries in neighbouring authorities are extremely close, yet other areas where there are very few library services at all – a regional approach could ensure that some of these issues are resolved.

Socially excluded communities do not stay within local authority boundaries, so regional approaches to working with them would bring enormous benefits, for example in sharing staff and stock, planning targeted outreach, and so on.

Local

Local leadership is vital. Whilst there is a strong case for establishing robust monitoring and evaluation at a national level, we think that the role of the public library has to be determined with local communities in order to meet their needs.

Table 7.1   Best practice examples and research into developing a needs-based library service

Aspect of developing a needs-based library service	Best practice and research
Strategy and vision	Working Together Project
Structures and systems	The right 'man' for the job
Organisational culture	Capturing the impact of libraries

Whatever governance model is in operation, it is vital that local people feel real ownership of their local services, and that 'library leaders' hear and listen to what they say.

Within this framework, we also identify the following as key issues:

- working in partnership with the local community, other local agencies, the Third Sector, commercial organisations, etc.;
- ensuring that, to keep social justice work at the core, there is sustained, mixed funding;
- co-production of services;
- co-location of our services with other relevant providers;
- providing different kinds of service to meet local needs …
- … delivered by different kinds of library staff;
- breaking the sad image that many people have of libraries – and their staff!
- the urgent need to move away from thinking 'library-centrically' and looking at how we can work with other agencies to help them hit their targets;
- exploring how we can stop being so risk-averse (successful work with communities in the way we have described does take risks).

Developing Needs-Based Library Services

This section combines a range of ideas and activities from the UK and abroad and brings together the best existing practices and research (Table 7.1).

Working Together Project

Our first case study is the Working Together Project in Canada (Working Together Project no date, *c.*2008), introduced by Kenneth Williment, Community Development Manager, Halifax Public Libraries:

> The four-year, four-city Working Together Project sent Community Development Librarians into diverse neighbourhoods across the country. Supported through funding agreements with Human Resources and Social Development Canada,

the Vancouver, Regina, Toronto, and Halifax public libraries worked in diverse urban neighbourhoods and with diverse communities – communities we traditionally consider socially excluded. Such communities included people new to Canada, such as immigrants and refugees, people of aboriginal descent, people living in poverty, people recovering from or living with mental illness, people recently released from federal institutions, and young people at risk.

Over this period, the Project's community-based librarians talked and engaged with literally thousands of socially excluded community members from diverse communities in the four large urban centres across Canada. The librarians working with the community took a community-practitioner-based approach. This approach moved community-based librarian work beyond discussions amongst librarian staff on how best to meet community needs, to discussions based upon the *lived experiences* of socially excluded community members and the librarians who engage with them as equal members of the community. Some librarians have previously worked with targeted socially excluded groups; however, the purpose of this project was not to review other works – rather, it was crucial to have community members' library experiences drive the Project, *not* library-based beliefs held by librarians nor internally generated professional literature.

It became clear that librarians' traditional approach to library services did not adequately address the needs of socially excluded community members. It also became clear that it is essential to begin a discussion around the use of traditional library service planning *versus* a community-led service planning model as the most effective way to make library services relevant to socially excluded community members …

Public library staff across Canada believe public libraries are inclusive institutions created equally for everyone in the community. Why would librarians believe otherwise? From day one, librarians frequently hear from co-workers, traditional library users, and teachers, about the inclusive nature of public libraries. When Community Development Librarians with the Working Together Project started talking with other librarians about social inclusion and exclusion, we heard many examples of library inclusiveness. For instance, we heard about free library collections which allow people to readily access and borrow materials, that anyone can walk through the front door of the public library, and we heard how libraries are already providing library services to socially excluded community members. (Williment 2009, 1–2)

It was suggested that:

people tend not to use library services because they are unaware of what libraries have to offer them. Librarians usually draw two conclusions from these examples: 1) It is a personal choice when people do not use library services; and 2) Libraries just need to do a better job marketing what they have to offer to the community. The belief that the public library is an inclusive institution is so ardently incorporated into the identity of public librarianship that questioning the social inclusiveness of libraries rarely occurs.

So is it just that simple? Are libraries the inclusive institutions they are claimed to be, or is something else going on?

To answer this question, Community Development Librarians started to engage in conversations with socially excluded community members who use libraries and those who are non-library users (Muzzerall et al. 2005). We quickly discovered that they did not affirm the same messages of inclusiveness that we were hearing from library staff. Instead, [these non-users] began to identify issues related to how they were excluded and the impact this had on their ability to utilize library services (Campbell 2005). Community members identified barriers in their personal lives and barriers generated by libraries, which made the library an intimidating place to enter and use.

Clearly defining and identifying social exclusion in communities can be a difficult task due to the wide range of social factors that cause people to be excluded from active social life in their community. Some of these factors include a person's race, gender, sexual orientation, or social class. The multidimensional causes of exclusion can be compounded by individual life circumstances such as low paying jobs, health issues, low levels of education, poor housing conditions, poverty, language difficulties, and cultural barriers. Since socially excluded people continually face these issues, many struggle on a daily basis to meet their immediate needs, making it difficult for them to participate in the social, political, economic, and cultural life of their community.

In conversations with individuals, Community Development Librarians immediately began to hear about obstacles individuals experienced when they tried to access library services. The most immediate barrier to library use was the impact of library fines. The impact of fines should not be underestimated. As one community member stated during a focus group:

'I didn't use the library for five years, because I thought I had fines. I finally got up the courage to go back to the library and found out that I didn't have any fines during the whole time.'

The perception of having a fine was enough to keep her away from the library. (Williment 2009, 2–3)

The Community Development Librarians:

also began to hear about barriers that traditional library users or librarians may not have been aware of, because they have never experienced them. This includes a number of issues – such as the use of library jargon … confusion regarding the arrangement of collections, a feeling of being judged and evaluated by the staff, and viewing library staff as 'trying to educate' them. (Williment 2009, 3)

Many non-traditional library users revealed that:

Table 7.2   Traditional library planning model

	Community assessment and needs identification		Service planning and delivery		Evaluation
	Community assessment	Needs identification	Service planning	Delivery	
Traditional planning	Staff review Demographic data Library use statistics Comment cards Community survey results	Staff identify service gaps or under-served communities	Staff review literature Staff consult with other staff and service providers Staff develop service response	Staff deliver service: *develop the collection,* *hold the* *programme,* *design* *facilities*	Staff review various inputs: *Feedback forms* *Programme attendance* *Collection use* *Library card enrolment* *[And] other statistics*

they do not feel comfortable in public libraries, and they do not feel that libraries play an important role in meeting their daily needs; therefore, they stay away from public libraries. Yet, the function of public libraries is to play a significant role in meeting the information needs of *all* community members. (Williment 2009, 3)

Citing work carried out in the UK (Pateman 1999; Muddiman et al. 2000c; Pateman 2003; Wilson and Birdi 2008), Ken Williment goes on to argue that:

Libraries and library staff are typically representative of middle class values and worldviews ... which unintentionally or purposely become integrated into library service planning and delivery. On the other hand, librarians are rarely, if ever, asked to theorize or conceptualize the traditional service planning model [see Table 7.2]: How libraries assess and identify community needs, then plan, deliver, and evaluate the generated services. Instead, librarians are traditionally taught how to plan and create individualized services ...

The implementation of the traditional library service planning model has become second nature to the way public library staff develop services for community. This internally-generated, linear process provides library staff with an efficient and comfortable method for generating library services for communities ...

For traditional library users, the traditional service planning model generally meets their needs. Traditional users, typically middle class individuals raised with many of the same values and other social experiences as librarians (Pateman 1999), are either aware of and familiar with library services, or feel comfortable asking for assistance. In addition, librarians know the needs of traditional library users who regularly enter their workplace and engage in conversations with staff; at times librarians consult traditional users during the service planning process. Based on these shared experiences, librarians respond in-house (through their direct engagement with members of this traditional community) to meet *all* library users' needs. But, does a service model which works fairly well with traditional users also address the needs of socially-excluded library users and non-users? If not, how can libraries respond? (Williment 2009, 3–4)

Internally created approaches to library service planning, targeting traditional library users, currently exist in Canadian public libraries; however, this approach does not work well when developing services for socially excluded community members. Why not? Because assessing, identifying, planning, delivering, and evaluating services within the confines of the library, without directly involving socially excluded community members in *each step* of the process fails to include the distinct and diverse voices of people outside the library's mainstream customer base. Only by stepping outside the traditional service planning model, and engaging socially excluded community members in the community, can librarians know if they are meeting their needs.

In order to begin this conversation with people outside the library's mainstream customer base, librarians need to understand that [they] are not experts on the needs of all community members. (Williment 2009, 4)

In addition:

librarians should not view themselves as spokespersons for community members with whom they work. Instead, librarians are primarily experts in organizing and finding information.

Traditional techniques for service development do not allow library staff to understand the library service needs or desires that excluded community members have. Methodologically, they do not provide librarians with the information necessary to access or gauge the needs of socially excluded people. Community assessments, with the use of tools such as demographic data, library use statistics, comment cards, and community surveys, do not provide library staff with reliable and valid feedback regarding the needs of socially excluded community members. Demographic statistics provide a rudimentary contextual snapshot of the social conditions in which people live; they do not explain the intricacies and influences social conditions have on library use. Surveys, a method of assessment libraries traditionally use, consist of pre-determined closed-ended questions. This method is indeterminate, since people do not offer responses other than the ones presented in front of them (Krosnick 1999). Comment cards are only completed by library users with the literacy skills and confidence to fill them out; and library use statistics are only applicable to community members who use library services. Traditional assessment tools do not work, because they do not access the needs of those who are not using the library – socially excluded community members.

Following the traditional needs assessment, library staff *internally* determine the needs of the community. For example, it may be determined that members of the public are having difficulty searching the library catalogue. In response, using the traditional service model, librarians would plan a service to address the issue. This process usually includes reviewing literature and talking with other professionals within a library system and possibly with staff at other libraries, regarding how they have addressed the issue. Staff then develop a response to the issue, with little or no public consultation or collaboration.

When library staff complete the traditional service development process, they engage the community, either in the branch with a program or in the community with outreach activities. (Williment 2009, 4–5)

During outreach, the community is informed about a particular service that has been developed, and members of the community are invited to attend library programmes. This model of community engagement is limited, since the entire process is based upon the librarian's perception of community need without collaboratively engaging the community to determine and address *their* needs.

After an outreach programme or internal program is delivered, [librarians] usually evaluate it based on statistical measures. For instance, [they] may count the number of people who attended or collect written feedback. These evaluation procedures do not take into account the impact, or lack of impact, the program has had on the community (Wavell et al. 2002). It is very easy for library staff to report that the program has been a success. For instance, [they] may report, after holding a community-based outreach program during which ... the catalogue [was reviewed], that it was successful because ... 22 community members attend[ed] and, by the end of the session, seven of them registered for library cards, and many others commented that they knew how to place an item on hold. On the surface, this sounds pretty impressive. However, what was the actual impact on the community? Have [librarians effectively] parachuted into the community, delivered a program and then left, feeling that [they] have 'helped' people? Have [they] been able to work with community members to understand their needs and then deliver a program or service that meets those needs? How could this traditional process be structured differently or improved? (Williment 2009, 5–6)

This recognition led Ken Williment and his colleagues to shape a new model:

Based on the long-term work in diverse and socially excluded communities, both inside and outside the library, the Working Together Project developed a new

Table 7.3   Community-led planning model

	Community assessment and needs identification		Service planning and delivery		Evaluation
	Community assessment	**Needs identification**	**Service planning**	**Delivery**	
Community-led planning	Staff review all of the traditional measures Staff spend time in community developing relationships with community members Staff hear from community about what is important to them	Staff discuss with community members and hear from the community what their priorities are	Service ideas are the community's ideas Community is engaged in the planning of the service Staff act as partners and facilitators rather than as creators and teachers	Community members and staff work together to deliver the service: *Community partners involved in selecting collection materials* *Community partners active in hosting the programme* *Community partners working collaboratively with the library to develop policy recommendations*	Staff review various inputs: *All of the traditional measures and* *Community and staff discuss:* *How did the process work?* *Did the service, policy, etc. actually address the need?* *What could have been done differently?*

community-based service model: The Community-Led Service Planning Model (Working Together Project 2008) [see Table 7.3]. Community-led service planning builds upon the traditional library service model and provides a *new* method, which brings library staff together with community members, to identify and meet community needs. Socially-excluded community members are involved in each step of the community-led service development process, from needs assessment to evaluation. This non-prescriptive model is flexible and can be applied in all library settings and to all program and service development. The Community-Led Service Planning Model is effective with both socially excluded community members and traditional library users. (Williment 2009, 6)

As we have shown elsewhere in this book:

By entering community spaces, outside the confines of the library, librarians can connect with members of the public who do not feel comfortable entering libraries. In order to make these connections, it is important to identify locations where socially excluded community members feel comfortable meeting. This includes a wide range of contact points: local service providers, shopping centres, parks, and other community identified meeting places. The locations are dependent upon the specific community in which the librarian is working. An asset map is an excellent instrument that can help library staff identify and conceptualize the potential connections the library could develop within a specific community, while also recognizing current community capacity and gaps …

   The development of relationships with individual socially excluded community members is the basis of the Community-Led Service Planning Model. Relationship-building is an essential first step, and it must continue throughout the entire service planning process, from initial community assessment through evaluation. To establish relationships, it is necessary to meet socially-excluded community members who do not come to the library. This can be accomplished with various techniques, such as going door-to-door, attending community events, word-of-mouth, or through third party facilitation (partnerships). It is necessary for librarians to establish relationships with individual community members, while relationships with traditional community contacts, such as service providers, are made to help facilitate access to community members. For example, the Community Development Librarian working in Vancouver met with the administrators of LOVE (Leave Out ViolencE) several times to discuss the library's need to talk directly with the teens coming to LOVE's drop-in sessions. It was important for LOVE's administrators to understand and feel comfortable with the goals of the librarian, which were to get to know the teens at LOVE and hear what they might want from the public library, before inviting her to meet with the teens.

   Relationship-building occurs by developing trust and mutual respect. When library staff enter a community and engage socially excluded people, it is important to understand the historical context of distrust some community members feel towards representatives of public institutions. This distrust is often due to prior negative experiences with organisations such as social services, the police, and/or educational institutions. Nevertheless, this distrust and power imbalance can be overcome by approaching individuals respectfully as equal members of the community and by actively engaging and listening to them. This approach creates a comfortable atmosphere for conversations. These conversations are the basis of relationships and the way community members can self-identify their needs. Community Development Librarians found that once relationships were established, they quickly heard community members identify and discuss their individual and community-based needs.

   Each of the four Working Together sites used various relationship-building techniques, including variations of hanging-out, attending or facilitating group discussions, and attending meetings and events in the community. For example, the Community Development Librarian in Toronto spent regular hours at a food bank, meeting and talking with people who used that service but might not use the library. The librarian issued library cards and arranged for community professionals to come to the food bank to assist people with financial, legal, and health issues. The relationships the librarian developed linked people to the library by demonstrating the library's commitment to meeting the needs of all community members.

Community members generate service ideas when sustained relations are in place. In order for this to occur, library staff need to reposition their role in the community from an expert to a facilitator. By becoming active listeners instead of disseminators of information, librarians take information from the community and place what they are hearing within the context of library services. Each community is unique and will identify need(s) for services based on its unique circumstances. For instance, Halifax's Community Development Librarian heard that a large proportion of food at a local food bank was spoiling because community members did not know how to prepare some of the food; in Regina, the community identified literacy as a major issue that they wanted to address with the library. Library staff continuously engaged the community in order to discover how the library could work with them to address their particular needs.

Once community members have identified a potential service area, they should engage and collaborate with library staff to plan a response. In one Working Together site, community members identified a need for introductory computer skills. Rather than deliver a standard pre-scripted library program, the Community Development Librarian worked with members of this community to find out what topics they were interested in exploring on the computer and what were their specific computer needs. The ensuing programme was a hybrid of community input and library facilitation that was adapted and changed as the program progressed, ensuring that the student's needs were met. By creating a collaborative working relationship between library staff and individual community members, not only is the service created together, it is also collaboratively delivered. This process allows all voices to be heard and all skills utilized when developing a library-based program or service. Moreover, it provides an opportunity for community members to develop new skills, to increase community knowledge and capacity, and to enhance community-based sustainability.

The final step to community-led service planning is evaluation. Community-led evaluation can incorporate traditional evaluation methods, while allowing the community to discuss their understanding and experience of the process. This qualitative approach lets everyone who took part in the process have a say in what worked, what did not work, and whether their needs, as they defined them, were addressed in a way that was significant to them. As well, through dialogue with the participants, community-led evaluation provides a context for understanding how community members feel success should be measured and how feedback should be interpreted.

Evaluation is a continual, ongoing process throughout the community-led service planning process. Targeted communities continuously evaluated service development during each stage of the service planning process, truly allowing for a community-driven process to work. (Williment 2009, 7–8)

Ken Williment concludes by asking: 'How can we make public libraries the socially-inclusive institutions we want them to be?':

> The Community-Led Service Planning Model provides libraries with a sustainable approach to working with underserved communities. This approach, working with individuals who tend to be non-users and socially excluded community members, increased the relevance and quality of library services. The many successes generated by the Working Together Project ... using the Community-Led Service Planning Model, demonstrates that libraries can successfully implement this model to increase and enhance [their] inclusiveness, and to [achieve] social goals, ideals, and potential. (Williment 2009, 9)

We would recommend that library services adopt the Community-Led Service Planning Model.

The Right 'Man' for the Job?

Our second case study draws on the research carried out by Kerry Wilson and Briony Birdi (2008) on the role of empathy in community librarianship. This research has indicated that the greatest weakness and the biggest challenge facing library services which want to tackle social exclusion is how to change the role of the librarian. Most public library staff in the UK are not able to design and deliver services for excluded groups. They require new skills and a different type of education and training. When a library service is transformed from a passive, traditional, provider-driven service to a proactive, needs-based, community-driven service, it is essential to provide a significant level of staff training, support and workforce development. Staff must be enabled to develop the skills they need to work in new ways.

Within the library service there is a huge need for the development of interpersonal skills and 'people skills'. There are a number of approaches to this:

- awareness training – what social exclusion is and how it can be tackled;
- cultural awareness training;
- training which helps staff to work with specific groups – courses on reaching out to looked-after children and Travellers, for example;
- operational training – how to draw up a community profile, how to identify community needs, how to manage successful partnerships, how to make

funding bids, consultation, marketing;
- leadership and management training – which reflect social responsibility issues;
- joint working – this involves short-term project working and longer term integrated service planning, delivery and monitoring with other services, agencies and organisations. In the process of working with other professionals, it is possible for library staff to learn new skills (for further discussion of training, please see Vincent 2009b).

In each case, staff training and development must be linked to job descriptions, competencies, service objectives and appraisal. With these frameworks in place, it is clear what is expected of existing staff with regard to skills and competencies. It is also clear what to look for when new staff are recruited. The primary skill set no longer revolves around technical library skills; staff must also have other skills which enable them to identify, prioritise and meet community needs via community development work, partnership working and funding bids. There has to be a mind shift from being task-focused to being community-focused. By having a community-focused mindset, staff will be more aware of what is going on around them, enabling them to be proactive in dealing with service users and anticipating their needs. A community-focused mindset encourages a 'can do' attitude which means that everyone within the library service appreciates the need to take responsibility for service delivery and the way in which the community perceives the library.

Staff attitudes and perceptions also play a vital role in the effectiveness of public libraries' contribution to social inclusion policy and objectives. Questions to be considered include whether or not the ethnicity and social and cultural background of staff can be a key driver in maintaining a positive attitude towards community librarianship. It is necessary to test the theory that an inclusive organisation facilitates an inclusive public library service, and that the ability to empathise through personal experience motivates the proactive and successful community librarian.

This will require an assessment of the relationships between staff's own ethnicity, social, cultural and professional background and their capacity to make an effective, empathic contribution to social inclusion objectives. This assessment should be based on the following data:

- staff demographics in terms of ethnicity, age, gender, social background, educational attainment, professional status, length of time in service;
- awareness of national social inclusion policy;
- perceptions of the community role for the public library;
- perceptions of socially excluded groups in the locality;
- perceptions of the extent to which these groups are being included;
- awareness of the ways in which exclusion is being addressed;
- attitudes towards professional roles and responsibilities in addressing

exclusion;

- the extent of staff participation (including willingness to become involved) in social inclusion policy implementation;
- the effects of internal politics, including communication, training and professional values upon attitudes towards social inclusion policy;
- the perceived impact of national government social inclusion policy and agenda on current practice;
- which excluded groups staff feel that the library service particularly targets and how;
- which groups staff feel that the library service excludes and how;
- future plans for social inclusion at a local level.

Wilson and Birdi have demonstrated that there is a significant empathy gap in public libraries between the homogenous nature of the staff and the increasingly diverse make-up of communities. Most library staff are female, older, white and with good educational backgrounds (indicating a middle-class bias). This compromises their ability to empathise with men and boys, younger people, ethnic minorities and working-class people. All of these groups are under-represented when their proportion of the general population is compared to their percentage of library users. The dominant staff member prefers to meet the needs of the dominant library user.

When tested, some staff can categorise 'worthy' and 'unworthy' library users, which is resonant of the Victorian attitude towards the 'deserving' and 'undeserving' poor. Within this typology, the homebound are deserving but the homeless are not. The least deserving of all are those communities on the fringes of society – asylum-seekers, refugees, migrant workers and Travellers. Research by Stonewall (Valentine and McDonald 2004) shows that these groups face high levels of public prejudice, driven by the media and the law.

Wilson and Birdi also found that many library staff were not aware of social exclusion policy in the context of public libraries, and the staff blamed this on management's failure to communicate with them. Another reason could be that staff do not want to engage with this agenda and so they claim no knowledge of it. Some library workers have expressed open hostility to social exclusion which they describe as 'political correctness'.

Staff training and development can go some way to enable staff to deal with social exclusion issues, but it cannot completely close the empathy gap, and neither can working with other agencies, partners and volunteers. At the end of the day, many white, older, middle-class staff cannot fully understand what it is like to be black, young, male or working class. Until there are diverse workforces which reflect the diversity of their communities, it will not be possible to develop fully inclusive and needs-based library services. We support Wilson and Birdi's recommendations:

- redefining public library roles and services – library authorities should 'relate their objectives more explicitly to … social policy relating to inclusion, equality and access. A one-size-fits-all categorization of services and initiatives ... is potentially damaging to service effectiveness and outcomes' (Wilson and Birdi 2008, 107).

- External partners and service networks – knowledge of these should be shared via a website or social networking type site, whereby individual public library services and practitioners would link to partners and associated service providers in the same way that Facebook and MySpace users link to friends. 'The resource would demonstrate the interconnectedness of public service providers, and enable users to connect with new potential partners and networks' (Wilson and Birdi 2008, 108).
- Staff recruitment and selection – recruitment teams 'should consider staff from other service sectors when seeking to fill posts with a strong social inclusion remit' (Wilson and Birdi 2008, 109). Job descriptions and person specifications 'should include an assessment of candidates' awareness and understanding of social inclusion policy and objectives' (Wilson and Birdi 2008, 109).
- Internal communication and staff support systems – frontline staff need to feel 'more empowered concerning the development and delivery of services for socially excluded groups, which requires a more inclusive approach to service planning' (Wilson and Birdi 2008, 109).
- Staff training and development – the priority is 'to address the apparent gap amongst staff in knowledge and understanding of social inclusion policy and political drivers. Staff at all levels ... should be fully informed of relevant external and political influences, and given the opportunity to question and discuss them further, and thus fully engage with the reasons for particular service developments and initiatives' (Wilson and Birdi 2008, 110).

The skills required to work in socially inclusive services are defined as 'advanced customer care' skills and include the following:

- Communication skills;
- Listening skills;
- Influencing relationships;
- Reflective practice;
- Improved confidence and assertiveness;
- Negotiation skills;
- Dealing with conflict. (Wilson and Birdi 2008, 110)

We also agree with Kerry Wilson and Briony Birdi's conclusion that 'the future recruitment of the right "man" for the job will be intrinsic to the effectiveness of public libraries' contribution to the social inclusion agenda, and should be an absolute priority for the future of community librarianship' (Wilson and Birdi 2008, 111).

Capturing the Impact of Libraries

Our third case study is the latest in many attempts to capture the impact of libraries. In November 2008, DCMS commissioned BOP Consulting to undertake a short study which identified existing data and research on capturing the impact of library services (BOP Consulting 2009). This work was used to support the DCMS Library Service Modernisation Review (ongoing).

The overall aim was 'to provide evidence of the type of data and research that is effective at capturing the impact of libraries on their local communities' (BOP Consulting 2009, 5). Of particular interest was how 'the intrinsic benefits delivered through libraries (e.g. enjoyment, participation, learning) [could] contribute to extrinsic benefits or "social goods" (e.g. improved well being and greater civic participation). There are essentially two mechanisms by which this happens: the wider effects of learning – both formal and informal; and social capital formation – establishing networks and relationships, and/or facilitating links to resources' (BOP Consulting 2009, 1).

Libraries can provide these social goods because of 'the centrality of literacy and learning to libraries' mission – which has been significantly enhanced over the last decade' (BOP Consulting 2009, 20).

According to BOP, the literature suggests that libraries are trusted institutions – 'users and non-users identify public libraries as inclusive, non-market, non-threatening, non-judgemental spaces. They can engage "hard to reach groups" with their own services, and provide access to these groups for other public services' (BOP Consulting 2009, 1). We would argue that this is a contested statement because our own research (Muddiman et al. 2000a, 2000b and 2000c) and practical experience suggest that some libraries can be perceived as exclusive, market-orientated, threatening and judgemental. We can also evidence how so-called 'hard-to-reach groups' have not been systematically engaged by public libraries.

The BOP literature review indicated 'that public libraries in England are involved in the delivery of a wide ranging menu of services, activities and resources' (BOP Consulting 2009, 1).

This very diversity of provision can make it difficult to demonstrate and communicate the impact of public libraries. In many of the so-called 'new' areas of library activity – such as 'early years support, adult basic skills provision, health support, information and guidance – libraries are not, and never will be, the lead delivery agency. This means that the interactions that people have with libraries in these areas will generally be less intensive' (BOP Consulting 2009, 1) and have a lower impact, than the direct service providers such as schools and health centres. It is therefore difficult to claim direct cause-and-effect relationships between library services and wider outcomes, but it is possible to evidence 'how libraries can "make a contribution towards"/"have a bearing on", a range of socio-economic priorities' (BOP Consulting 2009, 2).

BOP have used a logic chain to demonstrate the impact of libraries:

At the centre of the model is how public libraries contribute to the development of 'intermediate' or short term outcomes, that are known (through research evidence) to contribute to longer term outcomes, such as economic growth, longer life expectancy and enhanced local democracy and legitimacy.

The evidence base is relatively strong with regard to long term outcomes. This is due to the centrality of literacy and learning to the current public library offer, and the level of research resources devoted to investigating the wider socio-economic effects of these skills and capacities internationally from outside the libraries sector (e.g. education research, health and economics).

In terms of short term or intermediate outcomes, libraries contribution is strongest with regard to cognitive and non-cognitive skills development, health and well being and social capital formation. The ability to evidence this contribution does, however, vary according to different sub-groups of the population. Early priorities for 'quick wins' in demonstrating libraries' impact to government stakeholders lie in the broad learning agenda and for children and young people, particularly early years activities.

The main challenge for evidencing libraries impact is that, despite the relatively modest nature of what stakeholders are looking for libraries to demonstrate (that their activities make a measurable contribution to a range of intermediate outcomes, and that their services can reach particular target groups), the current evidence base still remains insufficient in a number of ways. Many of the weaknesses in the evidence base are generic, and have been identified in previous literature reviews, namely a:

- predominance of one-off evaluations of time-limited programmes and pilot schemes over research on core services;
- lack of baselines against which to measure change;
- lack of in-depth qualitative research that analyses the specific nature of the interactions that take place in libraries.

The policy areas in which libraries' impact is weak are business support and economic development more generally, with the important exception of adult basic skills, and environmental sustainability, where the sector is nowhere at present. (BOP Consulting 2009, 2)

Given this significant weakness in the evidence base BOP have made a number of very useful recommendations regarding ways in which the impact of libraries can be better captured and demonstrated:

Across all areas public libraries need to improve the comprehensiveness and consistency of basic management information on services and users, to aid:

- performance management and improvement,

- demonstrate libraries contribution to short term policy goals [such as Every Child Matters outcomes], principally at local level …,
- establish the base data for more complex impact analyses such as cost effectiveness [and social return on investment] approaches.

Without having credible baselines it is not possible to tell a compelling story about the 'new' public library, and how the library service can contribute to a range of stakeholders' agendas. (BOP Consulting 2009, 2–3)

BOP then go on to recommend:

- Children and young people, learning – Baselines of activity are particularly urgent with regard to learning activities, and for children and young people. Children have been the focus of much recent investment and activity in the sector and take up from the public has been strong, in the context of falling usage for other elements of library services and resources. (BOP Consulting 2009, 3)

While it is very important to evidence the impact of libraries on children and young people, the sector is not assisted in this by a National Indicator (NI9) which only measures the number of people aged over 16 who have used a public library in the last 12 months. NI9 fails to capture the work which many public libraries carry out with children and young people. One perverse outcome of NI9 could be that public libraries focus their resources and services away from those aged under 16 so that they can improve their NI9 assessment.

- *Stronger communities:* Although central and local government have accepted that participation in libraries on its own counts towards the development of more cohesive communities, there is very little comprehensive data on the degree to which people, particularly young people, are involved in the co-design and delivery of library services. This has become a strong agenda right across government [(for example Communities and Local Government 2009)], is key to understanding more about what the public expects of a modern library service and, in relation to young people, is a major sector commitment. (BOP Consulting 2009, 3)
- *Well being and health:* This is [another very high profile] agenda that libraries should be able to demonstrate a significant contribution towards, as it is a very close fit with the particular qualities of libraries as institutions and the activities and resources that they provide. However, at present the evidence is too piecemeal and insufficiently articulated in the emerging language of the field.

One very crude attempt was made to link libraries to health outcomes by using the amount of health related stock on the shelves of a library as a proxy measure. Libraries also 'need to understand more about the effectiveness of their, now widespread, health support and information activities in helping users to "co-produce" their own health' (BOP Consulting 2009, 3).

- Baselines of library activity need to be national. Although library services are organised locally, policy in all the areas in which libraries have a contribution to make is set nationally to be delivered locally according to (generally) statutory guidance. This means that being identified first as a national partner is key to playing a subsequent role locally.
- Wherever possible, baselines should … include demographic information. In many cases, a major element of the contribution that libraries [can] make is [their ability to] engage groups that other service providers find hard to reach. (BOP Consulting 2009)

However, having this ability and actually using it are two very different things, and, in our view, the majority of libraries do not systematically engage with so-called hard-to-reach groups. The Equality Act 2010 has introduced a new public sector duty to consider reducing socio-economic inequalities. There is also a potential contradiction 'in seeking to gain more comprehensive and detailed data on hard to reach users' (BOP Consulting 2009, 3) because this could undermine the main reason that they are attracted to the library in the first place – that few questions are asked. This means careful consideration must be given to exactly how baseline data can be improved.

- A biennial Census of Library Users – 'this would be a relatively light touch way, from the public's perspective, of significantly improving on what already exists … Of course, a Census would not be cheap. There again, at approximately £1bn per annum, neither is the public library service in England – and yet there appears to be chronically few resources devoted to researching and evaluating its impact'. (BOP Consulting 2009, 59)

Annual Library Plans and Public Library Standards, which both helped to raise the profile of libraries and made a case for resources, have been replaced by NI9, which is a very crude performance measure and does not appear as a key indicator in many Local Area Agreements.

Comprehensive Performance Assessment (CPA) has been replaced by Comprehensive Area Assessment (CAA), which is linked to Local Area Agreements, Local Public Service Agreements and Sustainable Community Strategies. Unlike CPA, the CAA does not feature a Culture Block (libraries, museums etc.), and so it could be argued that public libraries are now less well positioned to demonstrate the impact which they make to corporate agendas.

So, how are libraries going to demonstrate their value at a time of economic recession and changing political priorities? We believe that a needs-based approach to service delivery is the best way to future-proof library services and make them fit for purpose and able to tackle the challenges of modern British society. In addition, we think public libraries could benefit from revisiting the recommendations of Open to all? (Muddiman et al. 2000a) – included as the Appendix (see pp. 165–172) – this still gives a sturdy framework for the development of a relevant and socially just public library service, and could well form the backbone of a manifesto for change.

Appendix
The Recommendations from *Open to All?*

7.1   National Policy

(i)   At a national policy level, there needs to be a co-ordinated approach to the development of public library services to socially excluded people, to involve the Library Association, DCMS, Social Exclusion Unit, Re: source and other relevant agencies.

(ii)   To be effective, national policies should utilise broad definitions of social exclusion which:
   –   encompass social, economic and political exclusion;
   –   recognise the roots of exclusion in class, race and patriarchy;
   –   recognise the role that public services such as libraries can play in addressing inequality and discrimination, and in redistributing power and resources.

(iii) As part of this development of policy and practice, funding needs to be provided for further research into all aspects of social exclusion.

(iv)   Government should also introduce a NOF-style fund to support innovative responses to social exclusion.

7.2   Public Library Authority Policy

(i)   At local level, public library authorities should produce and implement long-term strategies for tackling social exclusion to involve targeting priority needs; secure and sustainable funding; advocacy and innovation; monitoring and evaluation.

(ii)   Social exclusion policies should be considered alongside existing policies such as equal opportunities and anti-poverty strategies.

(iii) Public library approaches to tackling social exclusion will require intervention, the targeting of resources, and positive action to fulfil individual needs.

(iv)   Public libraries should urgently start to target their resources towards socially excluded communities, and there needs to be further study of the ways in which public libraries should deal with service provision in areas with which all their community may not agree.

(v)   Local strategies are needed to redress the historical and current under-use of libraries by working class and other disadvantaged groups.

(vi) Public libraries should actively endeavour to make their vision, mission, outlook, work practices and rules aligned with the majority world perspective of their diverse communities and less Euro-centric. This search for relevance should explore the dynamic role that libraries can play in the people's struggles for social justice and economic liberation.

(vii) All public library authorities need to produce and utilise equalities policies which include all socially excluded groups. Such policies should include a clear statement challenging prejudice and discrimination, and services should not permit discrimination by users or by staff.

(viii) Existing tools, such as Roach and Morrison, Macpherson (Stephen Lawrence Inquiry, 1999) CRE Guidelines (Commission for Racial Equality, 1995) and Libraries for All (Department for Culture, Media and Sport, 1999) should be used to inform action plans and strategies for tackling social exclusion.

7.3   The Library Profession

(i) There needs to be an urgent review of the role of Library Association Branches, Groups and Organisations in Liaison to ensure that the needs of socially excluded people are taken on board at the highest level. We would recommend a structure similar to that of the American Library Association, with Round Tables and other means of access for socially excluded people and the library workers who provide services for them. Examples would include a Black Library Workers Group.

(ii) The Library Association should establish a Council Committee on Social Exclusion.

(iii) The Library Association should also sponsor research into the need for awards to recognise positive images in materials reflecting the lives of socially excluded people.

(iv) The Library Association should continue to support the work of the Social Exclusion Action Planning Network, for example by indexing successful projects and regular training support.

7.4   Consultation

(i) Public libraries need to develop methods for real and continuing consultation with socially excluded communities, groups and individuals, as well as means for implementing the relevant recommendations of this.

(ii) Social exclusion strategies and services should be developed with the active engagement of socially excluded people who should be involved in the planning, implementation and monitoring of services.

(iii) PLAs should ask socially excluded people when they would like libraries to be open and offer imaginative and creative opening hour patterns which meet these needs.

7.5 Needs Assessment and Research

(i) At local level all groups and individuals that are socially excluded or at risk of exclusion should be identified through community profiles and other methodologies such as needs analysis.

(ii) More research is needed into the perceptions of libraries by non-users and how barriers to access can be removed.

(iii) At national level, detailed and specific research into the information and library related needs of excluded groups and communities should be funded as a priority.

(iv) Detailed statistical monitoring of levels of library use by disadvantaged and working class users needs to be undertaken.

(v) A research programme should be funded to assist PLAs in developing guidelines for the provision of minimum services for community need e.g. community language provision; adult literacy provision; LGBT provision.

7.6 Library Image and Identity

(i) The image and identity of libraries need to be changed so that they do not appear as municipal, bureaucratic, unwelcoming and passive state institutions. This can be achieved according to local circumstances, by measures such as:
   – renaming libraries (e.g. Community Resource Centres, Idea Stores)
   – rebranding the traditional library name so that the new image is one of a proactive, friendly, relevant and easily accessible environment.

(ii) Library practices and processes need to be challenged to ensure that they do not create barriers to usage. Joining procedures should not be over-bureaucratic and mechanisms should be created to overcome problems with bureaucracy for groups such as homeless people.

(iii) The physical appearance of libraries needs to be audited to check that they are not forbidding from the outside and that the internal layout is easy to understand. Better signing, more self-help public access terminals and the removal of enquiry desks can all help overcome barriers to use experienced by some excluded people.

(iv) The geographical location of libraries should be a prime factor in resource allocation. Priority should be given to those libraries serving communities in greatest need. This may result in the need to consider the existing location of libraries. Relocation and colocation (with community centres, schools, pubs, shops, leisure centres and other places used by the socially excluded) can both improve the impact of libraries in tackling social exclusion.

(v) Where appropriate, PLAs also need to work with neighbouring authorities to deliver services to socially excluded communities, such as refugees and Travellers, who may be transient or who may span local authority boundaries, or where a service can be more effectively provided by the pooling of resources.

7.7 Outreach, Community Development and Partnerships

(i) Social exclusion strategies need to encompass:
   – proactive community librarianship based on outreach, advocacy and intervention
   – community development through grass roots, community-based approaches
   – partnerships with those in the public, voluntary and private sectors.

(ii) Public libraries need to ensure that they are offering relevant services where they are best used by socially excluded people. Locations should not be limited to library buildings, but include 'outreach' locations and services of all kinds.

(iii) Public libraries should support community-based initiatives, groups and organisations through outreach staff, materials and other resources.

(iv) Public libraries should develop community information services, in partnership with other providers such as Citizens Advice Bureaux, which help socially excluded people deal with their daily problems, including health, education, housing, family and legal matters.

(v) Learning centres, literacy centres and other lifelong learning activities should be developed by public libraries on a much wider scale than at present. Often, joint provision with education services, the not-for-profit sector, and local community groups will offer real advantages in terms of pooling of skills and funding and community involvement.

7.8 Information and Communication Technologies and Social Exclusion

(i) PLAs should be required to draw up ICT plans which include a strategy outlining how the needs of socially excluded communities are to be prioritised. ICT should be used as a means to tackle social exclusion – rather than as an end in itself.

(ii) ICT provision should be free at the point of access.

(iii) ICT initiatives should be targeted more closely at excluded groups and communities in a proactive way. Appropriate levels of skilled staffing and support should be offered to users.

(iv) Libraries should enthusiastically commit funding and support to neighbourhood ICT initiatives in line with the recommendations above, and those in the PAT 15 report Closing the Digital Divide.

7.9   Materials Provision

(i) Public libraries need to urgently develop materials selection policies to cover the requirements of socially excluded people. Existing library stock selection policies – and the stock on the shelves – need to be critically examined to ensure that they are relevant to the community which they serve.

(ii) Public libraries should systematically acquire underground and alternative material in all forms (including orature) which are created by, and are of interest to, those excluded from public library system.

(iii) Public libraries need to continue to raise with materials suppliers (writers, illustrators, publishers, booksellers, library suppliers) the range of materials available for socially excluded people and gaps in that provision.

7.10   Staffing, Recruitment, Training and Education

(i) Public libraries need to reassess their recruitment and selection policies (including reassessing the requirement for qualifications in librarianship) in order to attract more staff into the workforce from socially excluded backgrounds.

(ii) Public libraries should urgently analyse the training needs of their staff, to ensure that they have the necessary knowledge and skills to provide the best services for socially excluded people. Training programmes to be developed for all services linking equal opportunities, anti-racism, anti-sexism, cultural and social exclusion awareness.

(iii) Public libraries should adopt positive action programmes (for example via Quality Leader programmes) so that the library workforce incorporates socially excluded people more equitably than at present. All library authorities should aim to develop recruitment and selection statements outlining how this will be achieved.

(iv) Public libraries should challenge staff and organisational attitudes, behaviour, values and culture through staff development and training and a competency-based approach to staff recruitment and appraisal.

(v) Library authorities should change their staffing structures to bring them in line with their social exclusion strategies. This will require new job titles, job descriptions, person profiles and competencies which recognise the importance of outreach and proactive ways of working. A specifically designated team, with appropriate resources, should lead on service delivery to the socially excluded.

(vi) The DCMS should fund secondments of public library staff for learning experience and sharing of knowledge in the social exclusion sphere.

(vii) Schools of Information and Library Studies (SILS) should review their recruitment base to ensure that people from 'non-traditional' backgrounds are brought into library work.

(viii) SILS need to urgently reassess their course content in conjunction with public libraries. Courses should incorporate core modules which cover social exclusion issues, such as the causes of social exclusion, information poverty and equal opportunities.

7.11   Mainstreaming and Resourcing for Social Exclusion

(i) Social exclusion should be mainstreamed across all areas of library activity and management.

(ii) Demand-led resourcing is generally not equitable for socially excluded groups and communities. PLAs may have to redistribute or redirect resources to meet the needs of the socially excluded.

(iii) Guidelines should be developed to help authorities move to a needs-based service. This should include information for authorities on management and organisational structures that work for communities.

(iv) All services should introduce local service targets as part of detailed library planning and monitoring.

(v) With funded projects, the issue of sustainability needs to be addressed at Government level. A post-project tapering formula to help authorities mainstream successful initiatives should be considered.

7.12   Standards and Monitoring of Services

(i) National service standards should be established for public libraries activities related to social exclusion. Such standards should be both quantitative and qualitative, and should be incorporated in the DCMS standards currently being drawn up.

(ii)   Performance indicators and targets should be set to measure the success of library authorities in their attempts to tackle social exclusion. These should include a requirement to specify amounts spent on disadvantaged groups and deprived communities. All authorities should be encouraged to reach the upper quartile of best practice.

(iii)   Annual Library Plans should also be a key tool which helps DCMS monitor library authority policy and practice regarding social exclusion.

(iv)   An Oflib, or similar mechanism, should be established to monitor the performance of public libraries in meeting national standards, including those for social exclusion. Inspections of public libraries should be made as part of the Best Value process, and DCMS should intervene in authorities which are not making efforts to tackle social exclusion. In general, however, the body should be supportive in aiding library authorities to refocus their services to prioritise needs of the socially excluded. (Muddiman et al. 2000a, 60–6)

Bibliography

Adams, A.M. (1973), 'How to "open" a public library', *Library Association Record* 75:8, 152–4.

Alexander, Z. (1982), *Library Services and Afro-Caribbean Communities* (London: Association of Assistant Librarians).

Alibhai-Brown, Y. (2007), 'The view from India: horror at these barbarians', *Independent*, 22 January 2007, 31.

All-Party Parliamentary Group on Libraries, Literacy and Information Management (2009), *Report of the Inquiry into the Governance and Leadership of the Public Library Service in England* (London: APPG). www.cilip.org.uk/sitecollectiondocuments/PDFs/policyadvocacy/appgfinalreport.pdf (accessed December 2009).

Amgueddfa Cymru/National Museum Wales (2009) 'Equality and diversity policy', www.museumwales.ac.uk/en/46/ (accessed 22 July 2009).

Arad Consulting (2009), *Evaluation of the National Year of Reading in Wales 2008: Final Report* (Aberystwyth: Welsh Books Council).

Arnot, C. (2009), 'No such thing as a classless society', *Guardian*, 'Society Guardian', 7 October 2009, 2.

Aslib (1995), *Review of the Public Library Service in England and Wales for the Department of National Heritage* (London: Aslib).

Atkinson, R. (2000), 'Combating social exclusion in Europe: the new urban policy challenge', *Urban Studies* 37:5–6, 1037–55.

Bartlett, D. (2001), *An Evaluation of the Quality Leaders Pilot Project: a Pilot of Stage 2 of the Quality Leaders Project with London Borough of Merton and Birmingham City Council* (London: University of North London, Management Research Centre). www.seapn.org.uk/content_files/files/qlp2.pdf (accessed December 2009).

Barugh, J. and Woodhouse, R.G. (1987), *Public Libraries and Organisations Serving the Unemployed* (London: British Library) (British Library research papers, 0269-9257).

Becker, E. and Boreham, R. (2009), *Understanding the Risks of Social Exclusion Across the Life Course: Older Age* (London: Social Exclusion Task Force). www.cabinetoffice.gov.uk/media/226110/older-age.pdf (accessed 21 July 2009).

Beveridge, W. (1942), 'Social insurance and allied services', Cmd 6404 (London: HMSO).

Big Lottery Fund (2009), 'First Lotto library opens after £80 million investment', www2.biglotteryfund.org.uk/pr_030409_em_cl_first_lotto_library_opens_ after_80?regioncode=-uk&status=theProg&title=First%20Lotto%20library %20opens%20after%20£80%20million%20investment (accessed December 2009).

Big Lottery Fund (no date, *c.*2007), 'Community Libraries - summary of the programme', www2.biglotteryfund.org.uk/prog_community_libraries (accessed December 2009).

Birmingham City Council (2007), *Birchfield Library Community Consultation Project* (Birmingham: Birmingham City Council). www.bl.uk/aboutus/ acrossuk/workpub/laser/birchfield.pdf (accessed December 2009).

Birrell, D. (2009), *The Impact of Devolution on Social Policy* (Bristol: The Policy Press).

Black, A. (1996), *A New History of the English Public Library: Social and Intellectual Contexts 1850–1914* (Leicester: Leicester University Press).

Black, A. and Muddiman, D. (1997), *Understanding Community Librarianship: the Public Library in Post-modern Britain* (Aldershot: Avebury).

Blake, G., Diamond, J., Foot, J., Gidley, B., Mayo, M., Shukra, K. and Yarnit, M. (2008), *Community Engagement and Community Cohesion* (York: Joseph Rowntree Foundation). www.jrf.org.uk/sites/files/jrf/2227-governance-community-engagement.pdf (accessed December 2009).

Blears, H. (2009), 'Introduction', in Communities and Local Government (ed.) *Communities in Control: Real People, Real Power*, pp. iii–iv (Norwich: The Stationery Office). www.communities.gov.uk/documents/communities/ pdf/886045.pdf (accessed 21 July 2009).

Book Marketing Ltd (2004), *Serving Families Well: a Research Project for 'Framework for the Future: Action Plan 2003–2006'* (London: Early Years Library Network/MLA/Book Marketing Ltd).

Booth, C. (1889), *Labour and Lives of the People. Volume 1: East London* (London: Williams and Norgate).

BOP Consulting (2009), *Capturing the Impact of Libraries: Final Report* (London: DCMS). www.culture.gov.uk/images/publications/Capturing_the_impact_of_ libraries.pdf (accessed 21 July 2009).

Bottero, W. (2009), 'Class in the 21st century', in K.P. Sveinsson (ed.) *Who Cares About the White Working Class?*, pp. 7–15 (London: The Runnymede Trust). www.runnymedetrust.org/uploads/publications/pdfs/ WhoCaresAboutTheWhiteWorkingClass-2009.pdf (accessed October 2009).

Bowman, J.H. (ed.) (2006), *British Librarianship and Information Work 1991– 2000* (Aldershot: Ashgate).

Bowman, J.H. (ed.) (2007), *British Librarianship and Information Work 2001– 2005* (Aldershot: Ashgate).

Boyd, C. (2009), '"Social Justice" (Socialism) is what warmists yearn for … not global cooling', *Island Turtle*, http://islandturtle.blogspot.com/2009/12/social-justice-socialism-is-what.html (accessed December 2009).

Branston Community College (no date, *c.*2008), 'Community library', www. branstoncc.lincs.sch.uk/pages/community.htm (accessed December 2009).

Brewer, M., Muriel, A. and Wren-Lewis, L. (2009a), *Accounting for Changes in Inequality since 1968: Decomposition Analyses for Great Britain* (London: Institute of Fiscal Studies). www.equalities.gov.uk/pdf/Accounting%20for%2 0changes%20in%20inequality.pdf (accessed December 2009).

Brewer, M., Muriel, A. and Wren-Lewis, L. (2009b), 'More unequal – but why?', www.ifs.org.uk/publications/4713 (accessed December 2009).

Brown, A. (2009a), 'Including the excluded' [Powerpoint presentation]. Umbrella 2009 (Hatfield). www.cilip.org.uk/NR/rdonlyres/41FCEA9A-DB18-42DB-9D25-8C00852FFA6E/0/BradfordCILIPLibschangelivesaward2008. ppt#256,1, (accessed 27 September 2009).

Brown, E.F. (1971), *Library Service to the Disadvantaged* (Metuchen, NJ: Scarecrow Press).

Brown, G. (2009b) 'Foreword', in Communities and Local Government (ed.) *Communities in Control: Real People, Real Power*, pp. i–ii (Norwich: The Stationery Office). www.communities.gov.uk/documents/communities/ pdf/886045.pdf (accessed 21 July 2009).

Brown, L. (2009c), 'All-Party Parliamentary Group on Libraries, Literacy and Information Management', Letter to: Local Authority Chief Executives, 25 March 2009.

Buckley Owen, T. and Motion, A. (2009), 'A priming-place that lifts you off to speculate', *Library+Information Gazette* 5–18 June 2009, 5. http://edition. pagesuite-professional.co.uk/Launch.aspx?referral=other&pnum=&refresh= g08X19TzdD14&EID=7925c76c-9b6c-495a-b76e-1e5f8de51366&skip=true (accessed 21 July 2009).

Burnett, J. (2004), 'Community, cohesion and the state', *Race and Class* 45:3 (March 2004), 1–18.

Burns Owen Partnership (2005), *New Directions in Social Policy: Developing the Evidence Base for Museums, Libraries and Archives in England* (London: MLA). http://research.mla.gov.uk/evidence/documents/ndsp_developing_evidence_ doc_6649.pdf (accessed December 2009).

Cahn, E.S. (2007), 'Introducing the core economy and co-production', www. socialinclusion.org.uk/publications/Introcoreeco.pdf (accessed December 2009).

Campbell, B. (2005), '"In" vs "With" the community: using a community approach to public library services', *Feliciter* 51: 271–3.

Carpenter, H. (2010), *Leading Questions: Learning from the Reading and Libraries Challenge Fund* (London: Paul Hamlyn Foundation).

Cashman, H. (2009), *Streetcorner Universities and Urban Living-rooms: the Contribution of Public Libraries to the Prison Service*. www.seapn.org. uk/content_files/files/contribution_of_public_librariesoct09.doc (accessed December 2009).

Centre for Social Justice (2008), *Couldn't Care Less: a Policy Report from the Children in Care Working Group* (London: The Centre for Social Justice) (Breakthrough Britain). www.centreforsocialjustice.org.uk/client/downloads/C

ouldn't%20Care%20Less%20Report%20WEB%20VERSION.PDF (accessed 22 July 2009).

Centre for Social Justice (2009), www.centreforsocialjustice.org.uk/default. asp?pageRef=44 (accessed February 2009).

CILIP (2009a), 'Libraries Change Lives Award 2009 finalists', www.cilip.org. uk/PublicSites/cScape.CILIP.GenericTemplates/Information.aspx?NRMODE =Published&NRNODEGUID=%7b8F7F6BE0-5501-4E09-8CEA-2F728255 1529%7d&NRORIGINALURL=%2faboutcilip%2fmedalsandawards%2fLib rariesChangeLives%2flclafinalist09%2ehtm&NRCACHEHINT=Guest#one (accessed 23 September 2009).

CILIP (2009b), 'Libraries Change Lives Award finalists 2006', www.cilip.org.uk/ aboutcilip/medalsandawards/LibrariesChangeLives/lclafinalists06.htm?wbc_ purpose=Basic&WBCMODE=PresentationUnpublished#sight (accessed 23 September 2009).

CILIP (2009c), 'The CILIP Libraries Change Lives award', www.cilip.org.uk/ aboutcilip/medalsandawards/LibrariesChangeLives (accessed 23 September 2009).

CILIP (2009d), 'Libraries Change Lives finalists 2004', www.cilip.org.uk/ aboutcilip/medalsandawards/LibrariesChangeLives/lclafin04.htm?wbc_purp ose=Basic&WBCMODE=PresentationUnpublished (accessed 23 September 2009).

CILIP (2009e), 'Libraries Change Lives finalists 2005', www.cilip.org.uk/NR/ exeres/A45385F0-A6E8-4F4C-80AD-9E426144362E.htm?wbc_purpose=Ba sic&WBCMODE=PresentationUnpublished (accessed 23 September 2009)

CILIP (2009f), *What Makes a Good Library Service? Guidelines on Public Library Provision in England for Portfolio Holders in Local Councils* (London: CILIP). www.cilip.org.uk/get-involved/advocacy/public-libraries/Documents/What_ makes_a_good_library_service_CILIP_guidelines.pdf (accessed December 2009).

CILIP (2009g), 'Libraries Change Lives Award winner and finalists 2007', www. cilip.org.uk/aboutcilip/medalsandawards/LibrariesChangeLives/finalists07. htm?wbc_purpose=Basic&WBCMODE=PresentationUnpublished#welcome (accessed 23 September 2009).

CILIP (2009h), 'Community services group', www.cilip.org.uk/ specialinterestgroups/bysubject/communityservices/ (accessed March 2009).

CILIP (2009i), 'Libraries Change Lives Award winner and finalists 2008', www.cilip.org.uk/aboutcilip/medalsandawards/LibrariesChangeLives/ lclfinalists2008.htm?wbc_purpose=Basic&WBCMODE=PresentationUnpubl ished#bradford (accessed 23 September 2009).

CILIP (2009j), 'Libraries Change Lives finalists 2003', www.cilip.org.uk/ aboutcilip/medalsandawards/LibrariesChangeLives/lclafin03.htm?wbc_purp ose=Basic&WBCMODE=PresentationUnpublished (accessed 23 September 2009).

CILIP (2009k), 'Campaigning toolkit', www.cilip.org.uk/get-involved/ campaigning-toolkit/Pages/default.aspx (accessed December 2009).

CILIP Community Services Group (2009), 'Libraries Change Lives Award winners and finalists', www.cilip.org.uk/aboutcilip/medalsandawards/ LibrariesChangeLives/lclawins.htm (accessed 17 June 2009).

CIPFA Social Research (2009), 'Libraries', www.cipfasocialresearch.net/libraries (accessed December 2009).

Clock, M. (2009), 'Redefining social justice', *WORLDmagblog*, http://online. worldmag.com/2009/11/12/redefining-social-justice (accessed December 2009).

Clough, E. and Quarmby, J. (1978), *A Public Library Service for Ethnic Minorities in Great Britain* (London: Library Association).

Coates, T. (2004), *Who's in Charge? Responsibility for the Public Library Service* (London: Libri Trust).

Coleman, P. (1981), *Whose Problem? The Public Library and the Disadvantaged* (Newcastle under Lyme: Association of Assistant Librarians).

Collis, R. and Boden, L. (eds) (1997), *The Library Association Public Libraries Group Guidelines for Prison Libraries*. 2nd edn (London: Library Association).

Commission on Integration and Cohesion (2007), *Our Shared Future* (London: Commission on Integration and Cohesion). http://collections.europarchive. org/tna/20080726153624/http://www.integrationandcohesion.org.uk/~/media/ assets/www.integrationandcohesion.org.uk/our_shared_future%20pdf.ashx (accessed 22 July 2009).

Commission on Social Justice (1994), *Social Justice: Strategies for National Renewal* (London: Vintage Books).

Common, J. (1938), *Freedom of the Streets* (London: Secker).

Communities First/Cymunedau yn Gyntaf (c.2009), 'What is Communities First?', www.communities-first.org/eng/home/what_is_communities_first (accessed 21 July 2009).

Communities and Local Government (c.2005), 'New deal for communities', www. neighbourhood.gov.uk/page.asp?id=617 (accessed February 2009).

Communities and Local Government (2007), *The New Performance Framework for Local Authorities and Local Authority Partnerships: Single Set of National Indicators* (London: Department for Communities and Local Government). www.communities.gov.uk/documents/localgovernment/pdf/505713.pdf (accessed 23 July 2009).

Communities and Local Government (2009), *Communities in Control: Real People, Real Power*. Cm 7427 (Norwich: The Stationery Office). www.communities. gov.uk/documents/communities/pdf/886045.pdf (accessed 21 July 2009).

Communities Scotland (2007), 'Community engagement how to guide: what is community engagement?', www.communitiesscotland.gov.uk/stellent/groups/ public/documents/webpages/scrcs_006876.hcsp#TopOfPage (accessed 23 July 2009).

Corrigan, P. (1999), *Don't Count Me Out: a Brief History of Social Exclusion in London* (London: London Voluntary Service Council).

Corrigan, P. and Gillespie, V. (1978), *Class Struggle, Social Literacy and Idle Time* (Brighton: John L. Noyce).

Crowland Cares (2009), 'Care and support in your community: so who are we?', http://community.lincolnshire.gov.uk/crowlandcares/index.asp?catId=23193 (accessed December 2009).

Curry, A. (1997), *The Limits of Tolerance: Censorship and Intellectual Freedom in Public Libraries* (Lanham, MD: Scarecrow Press).

Cusworth, L., Bradshaw, J., Coles, B., Keung, A. and Chzhen, Y. (2009), *Understanding the Risks of Social Exclusion Across the Life Course: Youth and Young Adulthood – a Research Report for the Social Exclusion Task Force, Cabinet Office* (London: Social Exclusion Task Force). www.cabinetoffice. gov.uk/media/226116/youth.pdf (accessed 21 July 2009).

Daily Express (2009), 16 November 2009.

Davies, S. (2008), *Taking Stock: the Future of Our Public Library Service* (London: UNISON). www.unison.org.uk/acrobat/17301.pdf (accessed 21 July 2009).

DCMS (1999a), *Libraries for All: Social Inclusion in Public Libraries – Policy Guidance for Local Authorities in England* (London: DCMS).

DCMS (1999b), *Appraisal of Annual Library Plans 1998* (London: DCMS).

DCMS (2000), *Appraisal of Annual Library Plans 1999 – Progress and Issues Report* (London: DCMS).

DCMS (2001), *Libraries, Museums, Galleries and Archives for All: Co-operating Across the Sectors to Tackle Social Exclusion* (London: DCMS). www.culture. gov.uk/PDF/libraries_archives_for_all.pdf (accessed 3 August 2009).

DCMS (2003), *Framework for the Future: Libraries, Learning and Information in the Next Decade* (London: Department for Culture, Media and Sport). www.culture.gov.uk/reference_library/publications/4505.aspx (accessed July 2009).

DCMS (2008a), *Public Library Service Standards*. 3rd edition (London: DCMS). www.culture.gov.uk/images/publications/PulbicLibraryServicesApril08.pdf (accessed December 2009).

DCMS (2008b), 'Library service modernisation review', www.culture.gov.uk/ what_we_do/libraries/5583.aspx (accessed March 2009).

DCMS (2009a), *National Indicators 9, 10 and 11: Baselines for Local Authorities* (London: DCMS). www.dcms.gov.uk/images/research/NI_9-10-11_Baseline_ data_-_Revised_July_2009.xls (accessed December 2009).

DCMS (2009b), *Empower, Inform, Enrich – the Modernisation Review of Public Libraries: a Consultation Document* (London: DCMS). www.culture.gov.uk/ images/consultations/LibrariesReview_consultation.pdf (accessed December 2009).

Demos (2003), *Towards a Strategy for Workforce Development: a Research and Discussion Report Prepared for Resource* (London: Demos). www.

demos.co.uk/files/Towards_a_Strategy_for_Workforce_Development. pdf?1249904159 (accessed December 2009).

Denham, J. (2001) 'Foreword', in *Community Cohesion: a Report of the Independent Review Team Chaired by Ted Cantle,* p. 1. (London: Home Office). http://image.guardian.co.uk/sys-files/Guardian/documents/2001/12/11/ communitycohesionreport.pdf (accessed 22 July 2009).

Department for Environment, Food and Rural Affairs (2009), *Sustainable Development Indicators in Your Pocket 2009: an Update of the UK Government Strategy Indicators* (London: Defra). www.defra.gov.uk/sustainable/ government/progress/documents/SDIYP2009_a9.pdf (accessed December 2009).

Department for Schools, Children and Families (2009), *Children Assessed to be in Need by Children's Social Services, England 6 Months Ending 31 March 2009* (London: DCSF). www.dcsf.gov.uk/rsgateway/DB/STR/d000892/SR_Text_ Final.pdf (accessed December 2009).

Department for Schools, Children and Families/HM Treasury (2007), *Aiming High for Young People: a Ten Year Strategy for Positive Activities* (London: HM Treasury/DCSF). http://publications.dcsf.gov.uk/eOrderingDownload/PU214. pdf (accessed December 2009).

Department for Work and Pensions (*c.*2006), 'Publications: Introduction', www. dwp.gov.uk/publications/policy-publications/opportunity-for-all/indicators/ (accessed 22 July 2009).

Department for Work and Pensions (2007), *Opportunity for All: Indicators Update 2007* (London: Department for Work and Pensions). www.dwp.gov.uk/docs/ opportunityforall2007.pdf (accessed 22 July 2009).

Department for Work and Pensions (2008), *Working Together: UK National Action Plan on Social Inclusion* (London: Department for Work and Pensions). www. dwp.gov.uk/docs/uknationalactionplan.pdf (accessed 22 July 2009).

Department for Work and Pensions (2009a), 'European Year for Combating Poverty and Social Exclusion 2010', www.dwp.gov.uk/european-year-2010/ (accessed December 2009).

Department for Work and Pensions (2009b), *European Year for Combating Poverty and Social Exclusion: UK National Programme* (London: Department for Work and Pensions). www.dwp.gov.uk/docs/ey2010-uk-national-programme. doc (accessed 21 September 2009).

Department of Education and Science (1978), *The Libraries' Choice* (London: HMSO) (Library Information Series no.10).

Dixon, B. (1977a), *Catching them Young 1: Sex, Race and Class in Children's Fiction* (London: Pluto Press).

Dixon, B. (1977b), *Catching them Young 2: Political Ideas in Children's Fiction* (London: Pluto Press).

Dolan, J. (2007), *A Blueprint for Excellence: Public Libraries 2008–2011* (London: MLA). www.mlalondon.org.uk/uploads/documents/blueprint_v2_11233.pdf (accessed April 2009).

Domiciliary Services Group and London Housebound Services Group (1991), *The Library Association Guidelines for Library Services to People who are Housebound* (London: Library Association).

Durrani, S. (2000), 'Struggle against racial exclusion in public libraries: a fight for the rights of the people (Working Paper 13)', in D. Muddiman, S. Durrani, M. Dutch, R. Linley, J. Pateman and J. Vincent (eds) *Open to All? The Public Library and Social Exclusion. Volume 3: Working Papers*, pp. 254–349 (London: Resource).

Durrani, S. and Joyce, P. (2000), *Race Equality: Breaking the Stalemate in Library Services* (London: University of North London). www.seapn.org.uk/content_files/files/qlp4.pdf (accessed 27 October 2009).

Durrani, S. and Smallwood, E. (2009), *Skills for a Globalised World: Relevant Skills for Public Library Staff* (London: London Metropolitan University, Department of Applied Social Sciences). www.seapn.org.uk/content_files/files/sgwp_information_on_the_skills_for_a_globalised_world_____project.pdf (accessed December 2009).

Embervision (2006), '[Home]', www.embervision.cc/default.aspx?pageID=1&page=Home. (accessed December 2009).

Evans, M.K. (1998), 'Foreword', in P. Roach and M. Morrison (eds) *Public Libraries, Ethnic Diversity and Citizenship*, pp. 1–2 (Warwick: University of Warwick Centre for Research in Ethnic Relations and Centre for Educational Development, Appraisal and Research).

Fahmy, E., Levitas, R., Gordon, D. and Patsios, D. (2009), *Understanding the Risks of Social Exclusion Across the Life Course: Working Age Adults Without Dependent Children – a Research Report for the Social Exclusion Task Force, Cabinet Office* (London: Social Exclusion Task Force). www.cabinetoffice.gov.uk/media/226113/working-age-children.pdf (accessed 21 July 2009).

Fitzpatrick, S. (1999), 'Poverty and social inclusion in Glasgow [discussion paper for the Glasgow Alliance Social Inclusion Inquiry]'. Glasgow Alliance Social Inclusion Inquiry.

Fleming, A.E.D. (1971), 'Some comparisons between American and British city libraries', *Library Association Record* 73:2, 31–3.

Forrest, R. and Kearns, A. (1999), *Joined-up Places? Social Cohesion and Neighbourhood Regeneration* (York: YPS for the Joseph Rowntree Foundation).

Fraser, D. (2003), *The Evolution of the British Welfare State: a History of Social Policy since the Industrial Revolution.* 3rd edn (Basingstoke: Palgrave Macmillan).

Fyfe, A. (2009), *Tackling Multiple Deprivation in Communities: Considering the Evidence* (Edinburgh: Scottish Government Social Research).

Gannon, Z. and Lawson, N. (2008), *Co-production: the Modernisation of Public Services by Staff and Users* (London: Compass). http://clients.squareeye.com/uploads/compass/documents/CO-PRODUCTION.pdf (accessed December 2009).

Garner, S., Cowles, J., Lung, B. and Stott, M. (2009), *Sources of Resentment, and Perceptions of Ethnic Minorities Among Poor White People in England: Report Compiled for the National Community Forum* (London: DCLG). www. communities.gov.uk/documents/communities/pdf/1113921.pdf (accessed October 2009).

Gavron, K. (2009), 'Foreword', in K.P. Sveinsson (ed.) *Who Cares About the White Working Class?*, p. 2 (London: The Runnymede Trust). www.runnymedetrust. org/uploads/publications/pdfs/WhoCaresAboutTheWhiteWorkingClass-2009. pdf (accessed October 2009).

Geddes, M. (1999), *Strategies for Social Inclusion* (London: Local Government Information Unit) (Local Authorities and Social Exclusion (LASE) Research Paper 1).

Gillborn, D. (2009), 'Education: The numbers game and the construction of white racial victimhood', in K.P. Sveinsson (ed.) *Who Cares About the White Working Class?*, pp. 15–22 (London: The Runnymede Trust). www.runnymedetrust.org/ uploads/publications/pdfs/WhoCaresAboutTheWhiteWorkingClass-2009.pdf (accessed October 2009).

Glennerster, H. (2004), 'Poverty policy from 1900 to the 1970s', in H. Glennerster, J. Hills, D. Piachaud and J. Webb (eds) *One Hundred Years of Poverty and Policy*, pp. 63–91 (York: Joseph Rowntree Foundation). www.jrf.org.uk/sites/ files/jrf/1859352227.pdf (accessed 23 June 2009).

Glennerster, H., Hills, J., Piachaud, D. and Webb, J. (2004) 'Poverty and progress for the next generation?', in H. Glennerster, J. Hills, D. Piachaud and J. Webb (eds) *One Hundred Years of Poverty and Policy*, pp. 163–70 (York: Joseph Rowntree Foundation). www.jrf.org.uk/sites/files/jrf/1859352227.pdf (accessed 23 June 2009).

Global Greens (2001), *Charter of the Global Greens, Canberra, 2001* (Canberra: Global Greens). www.global.greens.org.au/Charter2001.pdf (accessed 28 October 2009).

Governance and Social Development Resource Centre (2006), 'Social exclusion', www.gsdrc.org/go/topic-guides/social-exclusion/definitions-and-different-understandings-of-social-exclusion (accessed January 2010).

Government Equalities Office (2009), *A Fairer Future: the Equality Bill and Other Action to Make Equality a Reality* (London: Government Equalities Office). www.equalities.gov.uk/pdf/NEWGEO_FairerFuture_may09_acc.pdf (accessed October 2009).

Great Britain (1986), *Local Government Act 1986* (London: HMSO).

Great Britain (1988), *Local Government Act 1988: Elizabeth II. 1988. Chapter 9* (London: HMSO).

Great Britain (2007), *Local Government and Public Involvement in Health Act 2007. Chapter 28.* (London: The Stationery Office). www.opsi.gov.uk/acts/acts2007/ pdf/ukpga_20070028_en.pdf (accessed December 2009).

Great Britain, Board of Education, Public Libraries Committee (1927), *Report on Public Libraries in England and Wales* (London: HMSO).

Great Britain, Welsh Office (1999), *Building an Inclusive Wales: Tackling the Social Exclusion Agenda* (Cardiff: Welsh Office).

Green, A. (1990), *Education and State Formation: the Rise of Education Systems in England, France and the USA* (London: Macmillan Press).

Greenwood, T. (1891), *Public Libraries: a History of the Movement and a Manual for the Organisation and Management of Rate-supported Libraries.* 4th edn (London: Cassell).

Griffiths, V., Blishen, S. and Vincent, J. (2007), *Paul Hamlyn Foundation Reading and Libraries Challenge Fund: Right to Read 2001 - 2005: Summary of the Current Outcomes* (London: Paul Hamlyn Foundation). www.seapn.org.uk/content_files/files/right_to_read_2001_2005_summary_of_outcomes_1.doc (accessed 23 September 2009).

Grimwood-Jones, D. (2003), *Mapping Social Inclusion in Publicly-funded Libraries in Wales: a Final Report Submitted to LISC (Wales).* (Cardiff: Welsh Assembly Government). http://wales.gov.uk/depc/publications/cultureandsport/mal/mappinginclusion/mappinge.pdf?lang=en (accessed 23 June 2009).

Guardian (2009), 'Social mobility: ambition is everything', *Guardian*, 22 July 2009, www.guardian.co.uk/commentisfree/2009/jul/22/all-party-social-mobility-report (accessed October 2009).

guardian.co.uk (2009), 'guardianjobs', 14 October 2009, http://jobs.guardian.co.uk/ (accessed October 2009).

Gundara, J. (1981), *Indian Women in Britain: a Study of Information Needs* (London: Polytechnic of North London, School of Librarianship) (Occasional Publication no. 2).

Harman, H. (2009), 'Foreword', in Government Equalities Office (ed.) *A Fairer Future: the Equality Bill and Other Action to Make Equality a Reality*, p. 1 (London: Government Equalities Office). www.equalities.gov.uk/pdf/NEWGEO_FairerFuture_may09_acc.pdf (accessed October 2009).

Hetherington, P. (2009), 'Who will give more power to town halls?', *Guardian*, 10 June 2009, www.guardian.co.uk/society/joepublic/2009/jun/10/local-government-david-cameron (accessed November 2009).

Hewitt, M. (2006), 'Extending the public library 1850–1930', in A. Black and P. Hoare (eds) *The Cambridge History of Libraries in Britain and Ireland. Volume III: 1850–2000*, pp. 72–81 (Cambridge: Cambridge University Press).

Hill, J. (ed.) (1971), *Books for Children: the Homelands of Immigrants* (London: Institute of Race Relations).

Hill, J. (1973), *Children are People* (London: Hamish Hamilton).

Hill, O. (1883), *Homes of the London Poor* (London: Macmillan).

Hill, S. (2009), '"The white working class" aren't racists', *Guardian*, 15 October 2009, www.guardian.co.uk/commentisfree/2009/oct/15/white-working-class-denham (accessed October 2009).

Hills, J., Brewer, M., Jenkins, S., Lister, R., Lupton, R., Machin, S., Mills, C., Modood, T., Rees, T. and Riddell, S. (2010a), *An Anatomy of Economic Inequality in the UK: Report of the National Equality Panel* (London:

Government Equalities Office/Centre for Analysis of Social Exclusion). www.equalities.gov.uk/pdf/NEP%20Report%20bookmarked.pdf (accessed February 2010).

Hills, J., Brewer, M., Jenkins, S., Lister, R., Lupton, R., Machin, S., Mills, C., Modood, T., Rees, T. and Riddell, S. (2010b), *An Anatomy of Economic Inequality in the UK: Summary* (London: Government Equalities Office/ Centre for Analysis of Social Exclusion). www.equalities.gov.uk/pdf/ NEP%20Summary.pdf (accessed February 2010).

Hills, J., Sefton, T. and Stewart, K. (eds) (2009a), *Towards a More Equal Society? Poverty, Inequality and Policy Since 1997* (Bristol: The Policy Press).

Hills, J., Sefton, T. and Stewart, K. (2009b), 'Conclusions: climbing every mountain or retreating from the foothills?', in J. Hills, T. Sefton and K. Stewart (eds) *Towards a More Equal Society? Poverty, Inequality and Policy since 1997*, pp. 341–59 (Bristol: The Policy Press).

Hodge, M. (2009), 'Review of public libraries: ministerial perspective', Public Library Authorities Conference (Bristol), 8 October 2009, www.culture.gov.uk/ reference_library/minister_speeches/6372.aspx (accessed December 2009).

Home Office (2001a), *Building Cohesive Communities: a Report of the Ministerial Group on Public Order and Community Cohesion* (London: Home Office). www.communities.gov.uk/documents/communities/pdf/ buildingcohesivecommunities.pdf (accessed July 2009).

Home Office (2001b), *Community Cohesion: a Report of the Independent Review Team Chaired by Ted Cantle* (London: Home Office). http://image.guardian. co.uk/sys-files/Guardian/documents/2001/12/11/communitycohesionreport. pdf (accessed 22 July 2009).

Hopkins, L. (ed.) (2000), *Library Services for Visually Impaired People: a Manual of Best Practice* (London: Resource).

House of Commons (2009a), *Equality Bill (HC Bill 85 I & II)* (London: The Stationery Office).

House of Commons (2009b), *Hansard: Written Answers 28 April 2009.* 491, 66 (London: Hansard). http://services.parliament.uk/hansard/Commons/ ByDate/20090428/writtenanswers/part007.html (accessed October 2009).

Hylton, T. (2004), *New Directions in Social Policy: Cultural Diversity for Museums, Libraries and Archives* (London: MLA). www.mla.gov.uk/what/ publications/~/media/Files/pdf/2004/ndsp_cultural_diversity.ashx (accessed December 2009).

IDeA (2008), 'Community Cohesion policy: background and definition', www. idea.gov.uk/idk/core/page.do?pageId=8799519 (accessed 22 July 2009).

IDeA (2009a) 'Useful definitions', www.idea.gov.uk/idk/core/page. do?pageId=10773112 (accessed 23 July 2009).

IDeA (2009b), 'Community empowerment – the basics', www.idea.gov.uk/idk/ core/page.do?pageId=9569550 (accessed 23 July 2009).

IDeA (2009c), 'The Equalities Bill', www.idea.gov.uk/idk/core/page. do?pageId=8890195 (accessed 23 July 2009).

IDeA (2009d), 'About comprehensive area assessment (CAA)', www.idea.gov. uk/idk/core/page.do?pageId=8811993 (accessed March 2009).

Institute of Community Cohesion (2009a), 'The nature of community cohesion: how the concept of community cohesion has developed', www.cohesioninstitute.org. uk/Resources/Toolkits/Health/TheNatureOfCommunityCohesion (accessed December 2009).

Institute of Community Cohesion (2009b), 'Faith, interfaith and cohesion: the education dimension – a toolkit for practitioners: overview', www. cohesioninstitute.org.uk/Resources/Toolkits/Faith (accessed 22 July 2009).

Joint Committee of the Library Association and British Institute of Adult Education (1923), *The Public Libraries and Adult Education: Being an Interim Memorandum on Co-operation Between Public Libraries and Bodies Concerned with Adult Education* (London: Cole).

Jolliffe, H. (1962), *Public Library Extension Activities* (London: Library Association).

Joseph Rowntree Foundation (2008a), 'Community engagement and community cohesion [description of publication]', www.jrf.org.uk/publications/ community-engagement-and-community-cohesion (accessed December 2009).

Joseph Rowntree Foundation (2008b), *Community Engagement and Community Cohesion* (York: Joseph Rowntree Foundation) (Findings). www.jrf.org.uk/ sites/files/jrf/2240.pdf (accessed December 2008).

Kelly, T. (1977), *A History of Public Libraries in Great Britain 1845–1975* (London: Library Association).

Kelly, T. and Kelly, E. (1977), *Books for the People: An Illustrated History of the British Public Library* (London: Andre Deutsch).

Kerley, L. (no date, *c.*2004), *A Diversity Toolkit* (Winchester: South East Museum Library and Archive Council).

Krosnick, J. (1999), 'Survey research', *Annual Review of Psychology* 50: 537–67.

Lambert, C.M. (1969), 'Library provision for the Indian and Pakistani communities in Britain', *Journal of Librarianship and Information Science* 1: 41–61.

Laser Foundation (2007), *Public Libraries – What Next? Final Report on the Work of the Laser Foundation* (London: Laser Foundation). www.bl.uk/aboutus/ acrossuk/workpub/laser/artwork.pdf (accessed December 2009).

Leadbetter, C. (2003), *Overdue: How to Create a Modern Public Library Service* (London: Demos) (Laser Foundation Report). www.demos.co.uk/files/overdue. pdf?1240939425 (accessed December 2009).

Leicester City Libraries (2000), *Achieving Inclusion ... Review Report 2000* (Leicester: Leicester City Council, Arts and Leisure).

Leicester City Libraries (2003), *Position Statement 2003* (Leicester: Leicester City Council: Leicester City Libraries).

Levitas, R., Pantazis, C., Fahmy, E., Gordon, D., Lloyd, E. and Patsios, D. (2007a), *The Multi-dimensional Analysis of Social Exclusion* (London: Cabinet Office.

Social Exclusion Task Force). www.cabinetoffice.gov.uk/media/cabinetoffice/
social_exclusion_task_force/assets/research/multidimensional.pdf (accessed
18 July 2009).

Levitas, R., Pantazis, C., Fahmy, E., Gordon, D., Lloyd, E. and Patsios, D. (2007b),
The Multi-dimensional Analysis of Social Exclusion – Appendix 7 (London:
Cabinet Office. Social Exclusion Task Force). www.cabinetoffice.gov.uk/
media/cabinetoffice/social_exclusion_task_force/assets/research/chapters/
appendix7.xls (accessed 18 July 2009).

Leyland, E.A. (1938), *The Wider Public Library* (London: Grafton and Co.).

Lincolnshire County Council Culture and Adult Education (2008), *New Arrivals
Project* (Lincoln: Lincolnshire County Council). www.seapn.org.uk/content_
files/files/new_arrivals_work_for_rem.doc (accessed December 2009).

Linley, R. (2004), *New Directions in Social Policy: Communities and Inclusion
Policy for Museums, Libraries and Archives* (London: MLA).

Local Government Association (2002), *Partnership in Action: a Brief Guide to the
Shared Priorities for Public Services Agreed Between Central Government and
the LGA, and How You Can Help Implement Them* (London: Local Government
Association). www.lga.gov.uk/lga/aio/21880 (accessed December 2009).

London Councils (*c.*2009), 'Community engagement – what is it and why is it
important?', www.londoncouncils.gov.uk/crimeandpublicprotection/publications/
engagingcommunities/whyisitimportant.htm (accessed 23 July 2009).

London Voluntary Service Council (1998), *Barriers: Social and Economic
Exclusion in London* (London: LVSC).

Lovett, W. (1967), *Life and Struggles of William Lovett* (London: MacGibbon &
Kee).

Luckham, B. (1971), *The Library in Society* (London: Library Association).

Mablethorpe and Sutton Town Council (no date, *c.*2009), 'Library and Community
Services Centre', www.mablethorpe.info/town/library.htm (accessed December
2009).

Machell, J. (1996), *Library and Information Services for Visually Impaired
People: National Guidelines – Prepared for Share the Vision and the Library
Association by Jean Machell* (London: Library Association).

MacIntyre, D. (1993), 'Major pulls party back to basics: Prime Minister emphasises
need for unity and says any infighting must be kept behind closed doors'
Independent, 9 October 1993, 4. www.independent.co.uk/news/major-pulls-
party-back-to-basics-prime-minister-emphasises-need-for-unity-and-says-
any-infighting-must-be-kept-behind-closed-doors-1509581.html (accessed
April 2009).

Mandelson, P. (1997), *Labour's Next Steps: Tackling Social Exclusion* (London:
Fabian Society).

Mayhew, H. (1851), *London Labour and the London Poor: a Cyclopedia of the
Conditions and Earnings of Those that Will Work, Those that Cannot Work,
and Those that Will Not Work*, 4 vols. (London: Woodfall).

McColvin, L. (1937), *Libraries and the Public* (London: Allen and Unwin).

McColvin, L.R. (1927), *Library Extension Work and Publicity* (London: Grafton & Co).

McColvin, L.R. (1942), *The Public Library System of Great Britain: a Report on its Present Condition with Proposals for Post-war Reorganization* (London: Library Association).

McMenemy, D. (2009), *The Public Library* (London: Facet Publishing).

Mearns, A. and Preston, W.C. (1883), *The Bitter Cry of Outcast London* (London: James Clarke & Co.).

Milburn, A. (2009), 'Foreword', in Panel on Fair Access to the Professions (ed.) *Unleashing Aspiration: the Final Report of the Panel on Fair Access to the Professions*, pp. 5–9 (London: Panel on Fair Access to the Professions, The Cabinet Office). www.cabinetoffice.gov.uk/media/227102/fair-access.pdf (accessed October 2009).

Miller, C. and King, E. (1999), *Managing for Social Cohesion* (London: Office for Public Management). www.pmfoundation.org.uk/resources/papers/practice/managing_for_social_cohesion_WEB.pdf (accessed 22 July 2009).

Miller, D. (2005), 'What is social justice?', in N. Pearce and W. Paxton (eds) *Social Justice: Building a Fairer Britain*, pp. 3–20 (London: Politico's Publishing).

Miller, J. (1992), *More has Meant Women: the Feminisation of Schooling* (London: Tufnell Park Press).

Morrison, M. and Roach, P. (1998), *Public Libraries and Ethnic Diversity: a Baseline for Good Practice* (Warwick: University of Warwick Centre for Research in Ethnic Relations) (British Library Research and Innovation Report 113).

Mowlam, M. (2000), 'Foreword', in D. Muddiman, S. Durrani, M. Dutch, R. Linley, J. Pateman and J. Vincent (eds) *Open to All? The Public Library and Social Exclusion. Volume 1: Overview and Conclusions* (London: Resource) (Library and Information Commission Research Report 84). www.seapn.org.uk/content_files/files/ota_volume_1_final_version_sept_211.doc (accessed 21 September 2009).

Muddiman, D. (1999a), 'Public libraries and social exclusion: the historical legacy (Working Paper 2)', in D. Muddiman, S. Durrani, M. Dutch, R. Linley, J. Pateman and J. Vincent (eds) *Open to All? The Public Library and Social Exclusion. Volume 3: Working Papers*, pp. 16–25 (London: Resource) (Library and Information Commission Research Report 86).

Muddiman, D. (1999b), 'Images of exclusion: user and community perceptions of the public library', in D. Muddiman, S. Durrani, M. Dutch, R. Linley, J. Pateman and J. Vincent (eds) *Open to All? The Public Library and Social Exclusion. Volume 3: Working Papers*, pp. 179–88. (London: Resource) (Library and Information Commission Research Report 86).

Muddiman, D. (2006), 'Public library outreach and extension 1930–2000', in A. Black and P. Hoare (eds) *The Cambridge History of Libraries in Britain and Ireland. Volume III: 1850–2000*, pp. 82–91 (Cambridge: Cambridge University Press).

Muddiman, D., Durrani, S., Dutch, M., Linley, R., Pateman, J. and Vincent, J. (2000a), *Open to All? The Public Library and Social Exclusion. Volume 1: Overview and Conclusions* (London: Resource) (Library and Information Commission Research Report 84). www.seapn.org.uk/content_files/files/ota_volume_1_final_version_sept_211.doc (accessed 10 July 2009).

Muddiman, D., Durrani, S., Dutch, M., Linley, R., Pateman, J. and Vincent, J. (2000b), *Open to All? The Public Library and Social Exclusion. Volume 2: Survey, Case Studies and Methods* (London: Resource) (Library and Information Commission Research Report 84).

Muddiman, D., Durrani, S., Dutch, M., Linley, R., Pateman, J. and Vincent, J. (2000c), *Open to All? The Public Library and Social Exclusion. Volume 3: Working Papers* (London: Resource) (Library and Information Commission Research Report 86).

Museums, Libraries and Archives Council (2003), *Framework for the Future Action Plan* (London: MLA).

Museums, Libraries and Archives Council (2004a), *Learning for Change: Workforce Development Strategy* (London: MLA).

Museums, Libraries and Archives Council (2004b), *'Access for All' Toolkit: Enabling Inclusion for Museums, Libraries and Archives* (London: MLA).

Museums, Libraries and Archives Council (2007), 'MLA social justice and inclusion topical workshop, 5 July 2007', www.seapn.org.uk/content_files/files/social_justice_and_inclusion_paper300707.doc (accessed February 2009).

Museums, Libraries and Archives Council (2008a), 'Driving best practice', www.mla.gov.uk/what/raising_standards/best_practice (accessed December 2009).

Museums, Libraries and Archives Council (2008b), 'Find out about disability', www.mla.gov.uk/what/support/toolkits/libraries_disability/find_out_about_disability (accessed December 2009).

Museums, Libraries and Archives Council (2008c), *Participation in Libraries and Museums at the Local Level: Summary Findings from Active People Data* (London: MLA). http://research.mla.gov.uk/evidence/documents/MLA%20Research%20Briefing%206%20-%20Active%20People%2018_12_08.pdf (accessed December 2009).

Museums, Libraries and Archives Council (2008d), *Framework for the Future: MLA Action Plan for Public Libraries – 'Towards 2013'* (London: Museums, Libraries and Archives Council). www.mla.gov.uk/what/strategies/~/media/Files/pdf/2008/library_action_plan (accessed February 2009).

Museums, Libraries and Archives Council (2009), *MLA Workforce Development Statement* (London: MLA). www.mla.gov.uk/what/raising_standards/~/media/Files/pdf/2009/MLA_Workforce_Position_Statement_2009 (accessed December 2009).

Muzzerall, D., McLeod, P.-L., Pacheco, S. and Sharkey, K. (2005), 'Community Development Librarians: starting out', *Feliciter* 51: 265–7.

MVA (1998), *Community Consultation on Library Services: Report on Focus Groups. Prepared for London Borough of Merton* (London: MVA).

'N' (1927), 'Short notices', *Library Association Record* 5 (New Series), 135.

National Council on Archives (2001), *Taking Part: an Audit of Social Inclusion Work in Archives* (Sheffield: The National Council on Archives). www. ncaonline.org.uk/materials/takingpart.pdf (accessed 21 September 2009).

Ngyou, J. (2009), *Museums, Libraries and Archives – Supporting New Communities and Responding to Migration Trends* (London: MLA). www. mla.gov.uk/what/policy_development/communities/~/media/Files/pdf/2009/ New_Communities_Position_Piece (accessed 28 September 2009).

NHS (2009), 'LINks', www.nhs.uk/NHSEngland/links/Pages/links-make-it-happen.aspx (accessed December 2009).

Northern Ireland Assembly. Research and Library Services (2001), *New Targeting Social Need (New TSN)* (Stormont, Belfast: Northern Ireland Assembly) (Research Paper 04/01). www.niassembly.gov.uk/io/research/0401.pdf (accessed 23 June 2009).

Northern Ireland Assembly. Research and Library Services (2008), *People and Place: a Strategy for Neighbourhood Renewal* (Stormont, Belfast: Northern Ireland Assembly) (Briefing Note 124/08). www.niassembly.gov.uk/io/ research/2008/12408.pdf (accessed 22 July 2009).

Number10.gov.uk (2007), 'Gordon Brown outlines his security strategy', www. number10.gov.uk/Page12678 (accessed 22 July 2009).

Office of Arts and Libraries (1988), *Financing our Public Library Service: Four Subjects for Debate* (London: HMSO).

Office of the Deputy Prime Minister (2002), *Young Runaways: a Report by the Social Exclusion Unit* (London: Social Exclusion Unit). www.cabinetoffice. gov.uk/media/cabinetoffice/social_exclusion_task_force/assets/publications_ 1997_to_2006/young_runaways.pdf (accessed April 2009).

Office of the Deputy Prime Minister (2003), *A Better Education for Children in Care: Social Exclusion Unit Report* (London: Social Exclusion Unit). www. cabinetoffice.gov.uk/media/cabinetoffice/social_exclusion_task_force/assets/ publications_1997_to_2006/abefcic_full%20report_1.pdf (accessed February 2009).

Office of the Deputy Prime Minister (2004), *Mental Health and Social Exclusion: Social Exclusion Unit Report* (London: Office of the Deputy Prime Minister). www.cabinetoffice.gov.uk/media/cabinetoffice/social_exclusion_task_force/ assets/publications_1997_to_2006/mh.pdf (accessed February 2009).

Office of the First Minister and Deputy First Minister (2006), *Lifetime Opportunities: Government's Anti-poverty and Social Inclusion Strategy for Northern Ireland* (Belfast: OFMDFM). www.ofmdfmni.gov.uk/antipovertyandsocialinclusion. pdf (accessed 22 July 2009).

Oroyemi, P., Damioli, G., Barnes, M. and Crosier, T. (2009), *Understanding the Risks of Social Exclusion Across the Life Course: Families with Children – a Research Report for the Social Exclusion Task Force, Cabinet Office* (London:

Social Exclusion Task Force). www.cabinetoffice.gov.uk/media/226107/ families-children.pdf (accessed 21 July 2009).

Orr, D. (2009), 'Diversity and equality are not the same thing', *Guardian*, 22 October 2009, www.guardian.co.uk/commentisfree/2009/oct/22/diversity-equality-deborah-orr (accessed 27 October 2009).

Orton, A. (2009), *What Works in Enabling Cross-community Interactions? Perspectives on Good Policy and Practice* (London: DCLG). www. communities.gov.uk/documents/communities/pdf/1165960.pdf (accessed 28 September 2009).

Outside Story (2009), 'Welcome to Outside Story …', www.outsidestory.org.uk/ (accessed December 2009).

Panel on Fair Access to the Professions (2009), *Unleashing Aspiration: the Final Report of the Panel on Fair Access to the Professions* (London: The Panel on Fair Access to the Professions). www.cabinetoffice.gov.uk/media/227102/fair-access.pdf (accessed 21 July 2009).

Pateman, J. (1996), 'Public libraries: let's get back to basics', *Library Campaigner* 54: 7–8.

Pateman, J. (1999), 'Public libraries and social class', in D. Muddiman, S. Durrani, M. Dutch, R. Linley, J. Pateman and J. Vincent (eds) *Open to All? The Public Library and Social Exclusion. Volume 3: Working Papers*, pp. 26–42 (London: Resource) (Library and Information Commission Research Report 86).

Pateman, J. (2003), *Developing a Needs Based Library Service* (Leicester: NIACE) (Lifelines in Adult Learning, no.13).

Paul Hamlyn Foundation (*c.*2007), 'Reading and Libraries Challenge Fund – about the Fund', www.phf.org.uk/page.asp?id=104 (accessed 23 September 2009).

Percy-Smith, J. (ed.) (2000a), *Policy Responses to Social Exclusion: Towards Inclusion?* (Buckingham: Open University Press).

Percy-Smith, J. (2000b), 'Introduction: the contours of social exclusion', in J. Percy-Smith (ed.) *Policy Responses to Social Exclusion: Towards Inclusion?* (Buckingham: Open University Press).

Pitcher, J. and Eastwood-Krah, M. (2008), *Extended Evaluation of Quality Leaders Project (Youth) Initiative: Interim Report* (London: QLP). www.seapn.org.uk/ content_files/files/qlp_y_extended_evaluation_nov08.pdf (accessed December 2009).

Policy Action Team 10 (*c.*1999), *Policy Action Team 10: a Report to the Social Exclusion Unit* (London: DCMS). www.cabinetoffice.gov.uk/media/ cabinetoffice/social_exclusion_task_force/assets/publications_1997_to_2006/ pat_report_10.pdf (accessed February 2009).

Policy Action Team 15 (2000), *Closing the Digital Divide: Information and Communication Technologies in Deprived Areas – an Executive Summary of the Report by Policy Action Team 15 and CD-ROM of Full Report* (London: Department for Trade and Industry). www.cabinetoffice.gov.uk/media/ cabinetoffice/social_exclusion_task_force/assets/publications_1997_to_2006/ pat_report_15.pdf (accessed February 2009).

Prisoners' Education Trust (2009) 'Finding the reading champions in prison', http://pet.netefficiency.co.uk/index.php?id=316 (accessed 23 September 2009).

Putnam, R.D. (2000), *Bowling Alone: the Collapse and Revival of American Community* (London: Simon & Schuster).

Rankin, C., Brock, A. and Matthews, J. (2009), 'Why can't every year be a National Year of Reading? An evaluation of the NYR in Yorkshire', *Library and Information Research* 33:104, 11–25, www.lirg.org.uk/lir/ojs/index.php/lir (accessed 29 October 2009).

Reay, D. (2009), 'Making sense of white working class educational underachievement', in K.P. Sveinsson (ed.) *Who Cares About the White Working Class?*, pp. 22–8 (London: The Runnymede Trust). www.runnymedetrust.org/uploads/publications/pdfs/WhoCaresAboutTheWhiteWorkingClass-2009.pdf (accessed October 2009).

Resource (2003), *Cross-domain Training for Social Inclusion: Report on Lessons from Phase One* (London: Resource).

Ridge, T. (2009), *Living with Poverty: a Review of the Literature on Children's and Families' Experiences of Poverty* (London: DWP) (Research Report no 594). http://research.dwp.gov.uk/asd/asd5/rports2009-2010/rrep594.pdf (accessed 28 September 2009).

Roach, P. and Morrison, M. (1998), *Public Libraries, Ethnic Diversity and Citizenship* (Warwick: University of Warwick Centre for Research in Ethnic Relations and Centre for Educational Development, Appraisal and Research) (British Library Research and Innovation Report 76).

Robert Gordon University (no date), 'An introduction to social policy: British social policy, 1601–1948', www2.rgu.ac.uk/publicpolicy/introduction/ukgovt.htm (accessed March 2009).

Roberts, A. (2009), 'Labour targets "white poor"', *Morning Star*, 2 August 2009, www.morningstaronline.co.uk/index.php/news/content/view/full/78795 (accessed October 2009).

Room, G. (1993), *Anti-Poverty Action-research in Europe* (Bristol: Policy Press).

Rowntree, B.S. (1901), *Poverty: a Study of Town Life* (London: Macmillan).

Salford City Council (2009), 'Welcome to Pendleton Gateway', www.salford.gov.uk/pendletongateway.htm (accessed December 2009).

Sandell, R. (1998), 'Museums as agents of social inclusion', *Museum Management and Curatorship* 17:4, 401–18.

Sanglin-Grant, S. (2003), *Divided by the Same Language? Equal Opportunities and Diversity Translated* (London: Runnymede Trust) (Runnymede Trust Briefing Paper). www.runnymedetrust.org/uploads/publications/pdfs/DividedByLanguage.pdf (accessed December 2009).

Scottish Executive (1999), *Social Justice ... a Scotland Where Everyone Matters* (Edinburgh: Scottish Executive). www.scotland.gov.uk/Resource/Doc/158142/0042789.pdf (accessed February 2009).

Scottish Executive (2000), 'Social justice annual report Scotland 2000', www.scotland.gov.uk/library3/social/som-00.asp (accessed 23 June 2009).

Scottish Executive (2001), *Social Justice ... a Scotland Where Everyone Matters: Annual Report 2001* (Edinburgh: Scottish Executive). www.scotland.gov.uk/Resource/Doc/925/0051662.pdf (accessed 23 June 2009).

Scottish Government (2006), 'History of the social justice strategy and the milestone data', www.scotland.gov.uk/Topics/People/Social-Inclusion/17415/milestones (accessed 23 June 2009).

Scottish Government (2008a), *Achieving Our Potential: a Framework to Tackle Poverty and Income Inequality in Scotland* (Edinburgh: The Scottish Government). www.scotland.gov.uk/Resource/Doc/246055/0069426.pdf (accessed 23 June 2009).

Scottish Government (2008b), 'Closing the opportunity gap – anti poverty framework', www.scotland.gov.uk/Topics/People/Social-Inclusion/poverty/17415-1 (accessed 23 June 2009).

Scottish Government and COSLA (2009), *Equal Communities in a Fairer Scotland: a Joint Statement* (Edinburgh: The Scottish Government). www.scotland.gov.uk/Resource/Doc/1031/0088727.pdf (accessed January 2010).

Scottish Office (1999), *Social Inclusion: Opening the Door to a Better Scotland* (Edinburgh: The Scottish Office). www.scotland.gov.uk/library/documents-w7/sima-00.htm (accessed 23 June 2009).

Sefton, T., Hills, J. and Sutherland, H. (2009), 'Poverty, inequality and redistribution', in J. Hills, T. Sefton and K. Stewart (eds) *Towards a More Equal Society? Poverty, Inequality and Policy since 1997*, pp. 21–45 (Bristol: The Policy Press).

Simsova, S. (1982), *Library Needs of the Vietnamese in Britain* (London: Polytechnic of North London, School of Librarianship and Information Studies) (Research report 10).

Simsova, S. and Chin, W.T. (1982), *Library Needs of Chinese in London* (London: Polytechnic of North London, School of Librarianship and Information Studies) (British Library Research and Development Reports no. 5718 / Research report – Polytechnic of North London. School of Librarianship and Information Studies no. 9).

SLAINTE: Information and Libraries Scotland (*c*.2009), 'Falkirk: home sound', www.slainte.org.uk/inclusivesvcs/casestudies.htm (accessed December 2009).

Sloan, M. and Vincent, J. (2009), *Library Services for Older People – Good Practice Guide* (Nadderwater, Exeter: The Network). www.seapn.org.uk/content_files/files/library_services___good_practice_guide_1336795.pdf (accessed December 2009).

Smith, A. (1785), *An Inquiry into the Nature and Causes of the Wealth of Nations*, 2 vols, 4th edn (with additions) (Dublin: W Colles).

Social Exclusion Task Force (2006), *Reaching Out: an Action Plan on Social Exclusion* (London: Cabinet Office).

Social Exclusion Task Force (2009), 'Context for social exclusion work', www.
cabinetoffice.gov.uk/social_exclusion_task_force/context.aspx   (accessed
February 2009).

Social Exclusion Unit (1998), *Bringing Britain Together: a National Strategy for
Neighbourhood Renewal. Cm 4045* (London: The Stationery Office).

Social Exclusion Unit (1999), *Bridging the Gap: New Opportunities for 16-18
Year Olds Not in Education, Employment or Training. Cm 4405* (London:
The Stationery Office). www.cabinetoffice.gov.uk/media/cabinetoffice/social_
exclusion_task_force/assets/publications_1997_to_2006/bridging_gap.pdf
(accessed February 2009).

Social Exclusion Unit (2001), *Preventing Social Exclusion: a Report by the Social
Exclusion Unit* (London: Cabinet Office). www.housing.infoxchange.net.au/
library/ahin/housing_policy/items/00054-upload-00001.pdf (accessed April
2009).

Social Exclusion Unit (2004), *Breaking the Cycle: Taking Stock of Progress and
Priorities for the Future – a Report by the Social Exclusion Unit* (London:
Office of the Deputy Prime Minister). www.cabinetoffice.gov.uk/media/
cabinetoffice/social_exclusion_task_force/assets/publications_1997_to_2006/
breaking_report.pdf (accessed February 2009).

Social Exclusion Unit (2005), *Transitions: Young Adults with Complex Needs
– a Social Exclusion Unit Final Report* (London: Office of the Deputy Prime
Minister).

Social Inclusion Executive Advisory Group to CILIP (2002), *Making a Difference –
Innovation and Diversity: the Report of the Social Inclusion Executive Advisory
Group to CILIP* (London: CILIP). www.cilip.org.uk/NR/rdonlyres/6315E6DA-
785D-4A08-9FCD-33C07A57CAA1/0/sereport2.pdf (accessed 21 September
2009).

Society of Chief Librarians (2009), 'Libraries inspire', www.goscl.com/libraries-
inspire/ (accessed December 2009).

Southend Borough Libraries. Community and Diversity Team (2008), *"Chatty
Readers" – a Skills for Life Success Story* (Southend: Southend Borough
Libraries).   www.seapn.org.uk/content_files/files/chatty_readers_report_oct_
2008_.doc (accessed 23 September 2009).

Southend Borough Libraries. Community and Diversity Team (2009), *Welcome
to Southend Libraries: Working in Partnership with the Polish Community*
(Southend: Southend Borough Libraries). www.seapn.org.uk/content_files/files/
southend_polish_partnership_report_jan09.doc (accessed December 2009).

Stephens, L., Ryan-Collins, J. and Boyle, D. (2008), *Co-production: a Manifesto for
Growing the Core Economy* (London: New Economics Foundation). http://doc.
abhatoo.net.ma/doc/IMG/pdf/Co-production__A_Manifesto_for_growing_the_
core_economy.pdf (accessed December 2009).

Stewart, K. (2009), '"A scar on the soul of Britain": child poverty and disadvantage
under New Labour', in J. Hills, T. Sefton and K. Stewart (eds) *Towards a More*

Equal Society? Poverty, Inequality and Policy Since 1997, pp. 47–69 (Bristol: The Policy Press).

Stones, R. (1988), '13 other years: The Other Award 1975–1987', *Books for Keeps* 53:November, 22.

Stones, R. (1994), 'I din do nuttin … to Gregory Cool', *Books for Keeps* 88: September, 5.

Sutton Trust (2009), 'News', www.suttontrust.com/news.asp (accessed 21 July 2009).

Sveinsson, K.P. (ed.) (2009a), *Who Cares About the White Working Class?* (London: The Runnymede Trust). www.runnymedetrust.org/uploads/publications/pdfs/ WhoCaresAboutTheWhiteWorkingClass-2009.pdf (accessed October 2009).

Sveinsson, K.P. (2009b), 'Introduction – the white working class and multiculturalism: is there space for a progressive agenda?', in K.P. Sveinsson (ed.) *Who Cares About the White Working Class?*, pp. 3–6 (London: The Runnymede Trust). www.runnymedetrust.org/uploads/publications/pdfs/ WhoCaresAboutTheWhiteWorkingClass-2009.pdf (accessed October 2009).

Swaffield, L. (2008), 'Users and staff together can revive public life', *Library + Information Update* October, 14.

Sydney, E. (1938), 'The public library and adult education', in H.V. Usill (ed.) *Year Book of Education 1938* (London: Evans Bros.).

Taylor, B. and Pask, R. (2008), *Community Libraries Programme Evaluation: an Overview of the Baseline for Community Engagement in Libraries* (London: MLA). www.mla.gov.uk/what/publications/~/media/Files/pdf/2008/ community_libraries_evaluation_Updated.ashx (accessed 28 September 2009).

The Network (2008), www.seapn.org.uk/default.asp?page_id=2 (accessed March 2009).

The Network (2009a), 'Skills for a globalised world project', www.seapn.org.uk/ editorial.asp?page_id=69 (accessed December 2009).

The Network (2009b), 'Empower, inform, enrich – the modernisation review of public libraries: a consultation'. Response from The Network – tackling social exclusion (Nadderwater, Exeter: The Network). www.seapn.org.uk/content_ files/files/dcms_review_network_response.doc. (accessed February 2010).

The Network (c.2007), 'What is the Quality Leaders project?', www.seapn.org.uk/ qlp/ (accessed 27 October 2009).

The Reading Agency (2005), *Partners for Change – Project Summary, October 2005* (Winchester: The Reading Agency). http://hbr.nya.org.uk/files/ Summary%20PfC_0.doc (accessed 23 September 2009).

Thomson, A. (2009), *Reading: the Future* (London: Reading for Life). www. readingforlife.org.uk/fileadmin/rfl/user/21522_NYR_Guide_AW_v3.pdf (accessed April 2009).

Totterdell, B. and Bird, J. (1976), *The Effective Library: Report of the Hillingdon Project on Library Effectiveness* (London: Library Association).

UK Parliament (2007), 'Section 138: involvement of local representatives', in *Local Government and Public Involvement in Health Act 2007, Elizabeth II Chapter*

28, p. 14 (Norwich: The Stationery Office). www.opsi.gov.uk/acts/acts2007/ ukpga_20070028_en_14 (accessed 23 July 2009).

UNISON (2009), *Shaping the Future: UNISON's Vision for Public Services* (London: UNISON). www.unison.org.uk/file/B4004.pdf (accessed December 2009).

University of Bristol (2009), '2.6 million adults experience social exclusion', bristol.ac.uk/news/2009/6768.html (accessed January 2010).

Usherwood, B. (2007), *Equity and Excellence in the Public Library: Why Ignorance is Not Our Heritage* (Aldershot: Ashgate).

Valentine, G. and McDonald, I. (2004), *Understanding Prejudice: Attitudes Towards Minorities* (London: Stonewall). www.stonewall.org.uk/documents/pdf_cover_ _content.pdf (accessed February 2010).

Vincent, J. (1986a), 'The heart of the matter', *Assistant Librarian* 79:5, May, 63–4.

Vincent, J. (1986b), 'Censorship and selection in public libraries', in J. Dixon (ed.) *Fiction in Libraries*, pp. 127–34 (London: Library Association).

Vincent, J. (1993), 'A broken heart?', *Assistant Librarian* 86:7, July, 98–9.

Vincent, J. (1999), 'Public libraries, children and young people and social exclusion', in D. Muddiman, S. Durrani, M. Dutch, R. Linley, J. Pateman and J. Vincent (eds) *Open to All? The Public Library and Social Exclusion. Volume 3: Working Papers*, pp. 144–78 (London: Resource).

Vincent, J. (2000), 'Political correctness', in D. Muddiman, S. Durrani, M. Dutch, R. Linley, J. Pateman and J. Vincent (eds) *Open to All? The Public Library and Social Exclusion. Volume 3: Working Papers*, pp. 350–61 (London: Resource).

Vincent, J. (2004), *Access to Books and Reading Projects for Young People in Public Care: The Librarians' Training Kit – Final Report* (Nadderwater, Exeter: The Network). www.seapn.org.uk/content_files/files/phf_final_report. pdf (accessed December 2009).

Vincent, J. (2008), 'Do we have values for what we do?', *Public Library Journal* Summer, 24–6. www.cilip.org.uk/NR/rdonlyres/7DDDDF3A-6AE3-46CF-9AA1-7B2CB6CF376F/0/plj232vincent.pdf (accessed 29 October 2009).

Vincent, J. (2009a), *The Role of Reading, Literacy, Libraries, Museums, Archives and Cultural Heritage: Response by 'The Network – Tackling Social Exclusion ...'* (Nadderwater, Exeter: The Network). www.seapn.org.uk/content_files/ files/c4eo_response.doc (accessed December 2009).

Vincent, J. (2009b), 'Inclusion: training to tackle social exclusion', in A. Brine (ed.) *Handbook of Library Training Practice and Development, Volume 3*, pp. 123–46 (Farnham: Ashgate).

Vincent, J. (2009c), 'Public library provision for Black and minority ethnic communities – where are we in 2009?', *Journal of Librarianship and Information Science* 41:3, 137–47.

Vincent, J. (2009d), 'Social justice and community cohesion – what are they exactly and how do we respond?'. Umbrella (Hatfield), www.cilip.org. uk/NR/rdonlyres/4AE9FAF9-9566-4D54-91DE-426DE2BFAB4C/0/ SocialjusticeandcommunitycohesionUmbrellapaperfullversion.doc (accessed 28 September 2009).

Wales Audit Office (2009), *Communities First: Report Presented by the Auditor General to the National Assembly on 9 July 2009* (Cardiff: Wales Audit Office). www.wao.gov.uk/assets/englishdocuments/Communities_First_eng.pdf (accessed 23 September 2009).

Wallis, M., Moore, N. and Marshall, A. (2002), *Reading our Future: Evaluation of the DCMS/Wolfson Public Libraries Challenge Fund 2000–2001* (London: Resource). www.cmis.brighton.ac.uk/research/siru/reading_our_future.pdf (accessed 27 October 2009).

Wavell, C., Baxter, G., Johnson, I. and Williams, D. (2002), *Impact Evaluation of Museums, Archives and Libraries: Available Evidence Project* (Aberdeen: Robert Gordon University). www.rgu.ac.uk/files/imreport.pdf (accessed February 2010).

Weisen, M. (2004), *New Directions in Social Policy: Health Policy for Museums, Libraries and Archives* (London: MLA). www.mla.gov.uk/what/publications/~/media/Files/pdf/2004/ndsp_health.ashx (accessed December 2009).

Welcome To Your Library (2009), www.welcometoyourlibrary.org.uk/ (accessed March 2009).

Wellum, J. (1981), *Black Children in the Library: a Brief Survey of the Library Needs of Pupils Attending the West Indian Supplementary Education Schemes in London* (London: School of Librarianship, Polytechnic of North London) (Research report no. 8).

Welsh Assembly Government (2001), *Plan for Wales 2001* (Cardiff: Welsh Assembly Government).

Welsh Assembly Government (2003), *Wales: a Better Country – the Strategic Agenda of the Welsh Assembly Government* (Cardiff: Welsh Assembly Government). http://wales.gov.uk/docrepos/40382/dhss/strategies/walesabettercountry_-e.pdf?lang=en (accessed 23 June 2009).

Welsh Assembly Government (2007), *One Wales: a Progressive Agenda for the Government of Wales – an Agreement Between the Labour and Plaid Cymru Groups in the National Assembly 27th June 2007* (Cardiff: Welsh Assembly Government). http://wales.gov.uk/strategy/strategies/onewales/onewalese.pdf?lang=en (accessed 21 July 2009).

Welsh Assembly Government (2009a), 'Local partnerships key to developing community cohesion', http://wales.gov.uk/news/latest/091203commcohesion/;jsessionid=snv9LXvP1ZTVh8xlL2VyhGlwv5wHy915hZVBLqJT4hpncSXykk22!1963699030?lang=en (accessed January 2010).

Welsh Assembly Government (2009b), *Getting on Together: a Community Cohesion Strategy for Wales* (Cardiff: Welsh Assembly Government). http://wales.gov.uk/docs/dsjlg/publications/commsafety/091130ccstraten.pdf (accessed January 2010).

Welsh Assembly Government (*c.*2009), 'Social justice and local government', http://wales.gov.uk/about/departments/dsjlg/;jsessionid=ByQ9KlCcJNqsfZ8XqJZQGq30MTM5YsBfSZf5QR1Q1261drCGLMJn!514291769?lang=en (accessed 21 July 2009).

Welsh Assembly Government (no date), 'Social justice', http://wales.gov.uk/topics/socialjustice/?lang=en (accessed February 2009).

Welsh Books Council (2008), 'National Year of Reading Wales', www.yearofreadingwales.org.uk/home (accessed December 2009).

Wetherell, M. (ed.) (2009), *Identity in the 21st Century: New Trends in Changing Times* (Basingstoke: Palgrave Macmillan).

Wikipedia (2009), 'Global Green Charter', http://en.wikipedia.org/wiki/Global_Greens_Charter (accessed 28 October 2009).

Wilcox, D. (1994), *The Guide to Effective Participation* (Brighton: Partnership Books).

Wilkinson, R. and Marmot, M. (eds) (2003), *Social Determinants of Health: the Solid Facts*. 2nd edn (Copenhagen: World Health Organisation). www.euro.who.int/DOCUMENT/E81384.PDF (accessed 28 September 2009).

Wilkinson, R. and Pickett, K. (2009), *The Spirit Level: Why More Equal Societies Almost Always Do Better* (London: Penguin/Allen Lane).

Williment, K.W. (2009), 'It takes a community to create a library', *Partnership: the Canadian Journal of Library and Information Practice and Research* 4:1, www.criticalimprov.com/index.php/perj/article/view/545/1477 (accessed February 2010).

Wilson, K. and Birdi, B. (2008), *The Right 'Man' for the Job? The Role of Empathy in Community Librarianship* (Sheffield: Department of Information Studies, University of Sheffield). www.shef.ac.uk/content/1/c6/07/85/14/AHRC%202006-8%20final%20report%2004.08.pdf (accessed March 2009).

Winckler, V. (ed.) (2009), *Equality Issues in Wales: a Research Review* (Manchester: Equality and Human Rights Commission). http://edit.equalityhumanrights.com/en/publicationsandresources/Documents/Equalities/Equality%20issues%20in%20Wales%20-%20a%20research%20review.pdf (accessed 23 September 2009).

Wintour, P. (2006), 'New taskforce to focus on alleviation of social exclusion', *Guardian*, 13 June 2006, www.guardian.co.uk/politics/2006/jun/13/uk.socialexclusion (accessed April 2009).

Working Together Project (no date, *c.*2008), 'Working Together', www.librariesincommunities.ca/?page_id=8 (accessed February 2010).

Working Together Project (2008), *Community-led Libraries Toolkit* (Vancouver: Working Together Project). www.librariesincommunities.ca/resources/Community-Led_Libraries_Toolkit.pdf (accessed February 2010).

Index